湖北省博物館
HUBEI PROVINCIAL MUSEUM

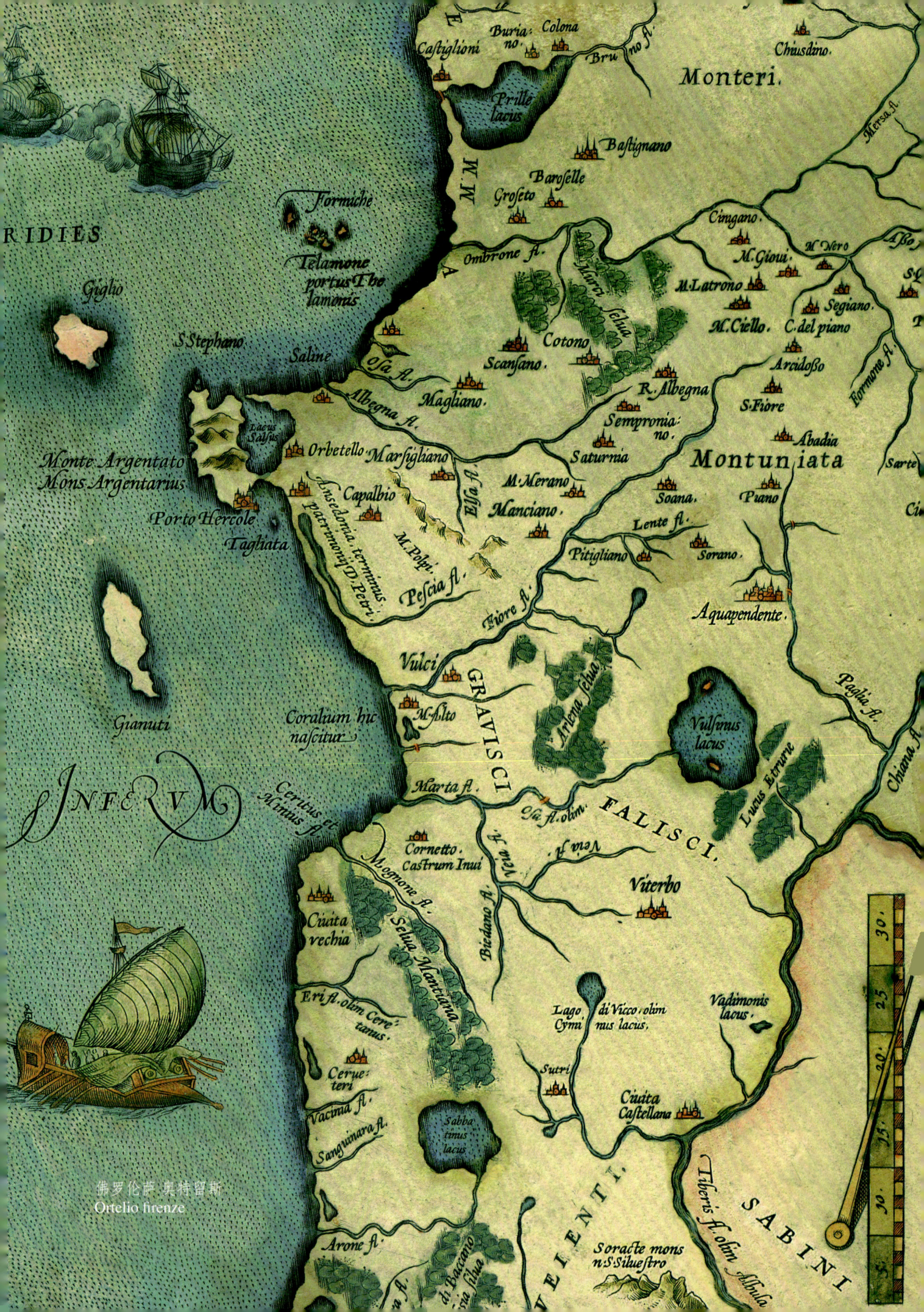

RIDIES

Monteri.

Buria no
Colona
Castiglioni
Bru no fl.
Chiusdino.

Prilie lacus

Bastignano
Barofelle
Grofeto

Cingano
M. Nero
A. Bo
Ombrone fl.
M. Gioui
M. Latrono
Segiano
Mauri selua
M. Ciello
C. del piano
Cotono
Scanfano
Arcidoſſo
Fiormone fl.
R. Albegna
S. Fiore

Formiche

Telamone portus The Iamonis

Saline
Talã fl.
Albegna fl.
Magliano
Sempronia no.
Abadia
Giglio
Saturnia
Montuniata
Sarte

S. Stephano
Orbetello
Marsigliano
Soana.
Piano
Cie

Lacus Salſus
Capalbio
M. Merano
Lente fl.
Monte Argentato
Manciano
Mons Argentarius
Ameſedonia terminus Patrimonij D. Petri.
M. Polpi.
Pitigliano
Sorano
Porto Hercole
Pescia fl.
Tagliata

Aquapendente

Gianuti

Vulci
Fiore fl.
Vulſinus lacus
Coralium hic naſcitur
M. Alto
GRAVISCI
Paglia fl.

INFERVM
Ceruus et Minius fl.
Marta fl.
Artenia ſelua
Lucus Etruriæ
Chiana fl.

FALISCI.
Marta fl. olim
Veia fl.
Vei a fl.
Cornetto. Castrum Inui
Viterbo
Mognone fl.
Biedano fl.
Ciuita vechia
Selua Mantiana
Vadimonis lacus.
Eri fl. olim Cere tanus.
Lago di Vicco. olim mis lacus.
Cerue teri
Vacina fl.
Sutri
Sanguinara fl.
Sabba tinus lacus
Ciuita Castellana
VELENTI.
Tiberis fl. olim Albula.
SABINI
佛罗伦萨 奥特留斯
Ortelio hrenze
Arone fl.
di Baccano Sia ſelua
Soracte mons n S. Siluestro

曙光時代
意大利的伊特鲁里亚文明

THE ETRUSCANS
The Dawn of Ancient Italy

湖北省博物馆 编
Edited by Hubei Provincial Museum

文物出版社
Cultural Relics Press

展览主办 Sponsored by	湖北省博物馆 Hubei Provincial Museum 馆长　方勤 Fang Qin　Director
	浙江省博物馆 Zhejiang Provincial Museum 馆长　陈浩 Chen Hao　Director
	广东省博物馆 Guangdong Provincial Museum 馆长　魏峻 Wei Jun　Director
	秦始皇帝陵博物院 Emperor Qinshihuang's Mausoleum Site Museum 院长　曹玮 Cao Wei　Director
展出时间 Exhibition Date	湖北　2013年9月27日至2014年1月10日 Hubei　September 27th, 2013 to January 10th, 2014 浙江 2014年1月21日至2014年4月 20 日 Zhejiang　January 21th, 2014 to April 20th, 2014 广东 2014年4月30日至2014年 8月 24 日 Guangdong　April 30 th, 2013 to August 24th, 2014 陕西 2014年 9月 5日至2014年 12月 7日 Shaanxi　September 5st, 2014 to December 7th, 2014
组织 Organization	湖北省博物馆 Hubei Provincial Museum 希吉龙（意大利，特拉维索） Sigillum
总裁 Director	阿德里亚诺·马达罗 Adriano Màdaro
行政管理 Office	阿德里亚诺·马达罗　弗朗西斯卡·马达罗　陆辛 Arianna Màdaro, Francesca Màdaro and Lu Xin
科研项目 Scientific Project	朱塞平娜·卡洛塔·钱菲诺尼博士 国家考古博物馆（佛罗伦萨）馆长 Dr. Giuseppina Carlotta Cianferoni Director, National Museum of Archeology, Florence
参与协作 Collaboration	罗萨尔巴·赛特索尔蒂 Rosalba Settesoldi
总协调 General Coordination	王纪潮　马提欧·克罗塞拉　伊丽莎白·西塔里 Wang Jichao, Matteo Crosera and Elisabetta Setari
展品出借方 Lenders To Exhibition	佛罗伦萨国家考古博物馆 Soprintendenza per i Beni Archeologici della Toscana National 托斯卡纳大区考古遗产监管局 Museum of Archeology, Florence 锡耶纳考古博物馆 Museum of Archeology, Siena
展品图录翻译 Catalogue Translations	意译英：基伦·贝利　亚历山大·马力诺 Kieren Bailey and Alexa Marino（Italian to English） 英译中：中国对外翻译出版公司 China Translation & Publishing Corporation (English to Chinese)

美术设计 Graphic Design	阿皮尔卡，帕多瓦 Applika and Padova
摄影 Photography	卡罗·波纳滋 麦克·伯图拉图 丹尼尔·万斯 托斯卡纳考古遗产监管局 Carlo Bonazza, Mirco Bortolato and Daniel Virtuoso Archivio Soprintendenza per i Beni Archeologici della Toscana
插图设计 Illustrations	宝拉·蒙特拉斯泰利 Paola Monterastelli
博物馆项目 MUSEUM PROJECT	AL 14工作室，米兰 STUDIO AL14, Milano 乔凡娜·科伦坡 马可·萨拉 Giovanna Colombo and Marco Sala 及卢卡·丁内里，西蒙尼·马尔凯蒂，费德里科·如菲诺体，格洛丽亚·扎纳尔多 with Luca Dinelli, Simone Marchetti, Federico Ruffinotti and Gloria Zanardo
美术设计 Graphic Design	奥多设计工作室 Ottodesign.it 曼努埃拉·科伦坡 克劳迪娅·塞索 托马斯·加顿 玛蒂娜·斯宾纳西 Manuela Colombo, Claudia Ceso, Tommaso Gornati and Martina Spinaci
文物保护 CONSERVATION	佛朗哥·塞奇 Franco Cecchi 托斯卡纳考古遗产监管局 Soprintendenza peri Beni Archeologici della Toscana
保管 REGISTRAR	塞巴斯蒂亚诺·索尔多 玛利亚娜·奇雅奇 Sebastiano Soldi and Miriana Ciacci
监管 SOVRINTENDENTE	安德鲁·佩思纳博士 dott. Andrea Pessina
主管 DIRECTOR	朱塞平娜·卡洛塔·钱菲诺尼博士 dott.ssa Giuseppina Carlotta Cianferoni
图录编辑 Catalogue editor	湖北省博物馆 Hubei Provincial Museum
图录主编 Guest Curators	方勤 陈浩 魏峻 曹玮 Fang Qin, Chen Hao, Wei Jun and Cao Wei
副主编 Deputy editor	万全文 雍泰岳 肖海明 郭向东 Wan Quanwen, Yong Taiyue, Xiao Haiming and Guo Xiangdong
执行编辑 Managing Editor	王纪潮 Wang Jichao
展览协调 Coordinators	湖北：姚嫄 余文扬 伍莹 曾攀 张翔 程陶 曾凌燕 冯冠洲 王圆圆 李蔚 Hubei, Yao Yuan, Yu Wenyang, Wu Ying, Zeng Pan, Zhang Xiang, Cheng Tao, Zeng Lingyan, Feng Guanzhou, Wang Yuanyuan and Li Wei 浙江：王炬 李卫平 曾莹 周鸿远 朱文晶 乐俏俏 Zhejiang: Wang Ju, Li Weiping, Zeng Ying, Zhou Hongyuan, Zhu Wenjing and Le Qiaoqiao 广东：刘莉 骆伟雄 符凯 徐汉良 范耀强 戴福临 刘丹妮 胡锐韬 陈宇 黄苏哲 车智斌 欧艳 宋敏 谢秋晖 段小红 聂柯妍 黄青松 郭舒琳 兰维 张欢 王亚丽 王小迎 黄涛坚 陈伦贤 林荣声 Guangdong: Liu Li, Luo Weixiong, Fu Kai, Xu Hanliang, Fan Yaoqiang, Dai Fulin, Liu Danni, Hu Ruitao, Chen Yu, Huang Suzhe, Che Zhibin, Ou Yan, Song Min, Xie Qiuhui, Duan Xiaohong, Nie Keyan, Huang Qingsong, Guo Shulin, Lan Wei, Zhang Huan, Wang Yali, Wang Xiaoying, Huang Taojian, Chen Lunxian and Lin Rongsheng 陕西：彭文 王锐 张升 赵昆 马生涛 郑宁 shannxi: Peng Wen, Wang Rui, Zhang Sheng, Zhao Kun, Ma Shengtao and Zheng Ning

维罗图尼亚的皮特拉大墓内部，1882年发掘
Vetulonia Pietrera int

目 录
CONTENTS

切尔韦泰里古城的伊特鲁里亚人墓群
Etruscan tomb from the old city of Cerveteri

前　言
Foreword

伊特鲁里亚文明在公元前1000年到公元前100年间兴盛于意大利中西部亚诺河与台伯河之间。伊特鲁里亚文明的繁荣与此地丰饶的物产密切相关，肥沃的土地带来了丰产的农作物，曲折的海岸线和平原上的潟湖为人们出海捕鱼和交易提供了合适的停泊场所。更重要的是，这一地区蕴藏了大量的铜、铁、锡等矿藏，正是依靠这些矿藏，伊特鲁里亚人几乎控制了地中海地区的矿物冶炼业，并随之形成了一个影响整个地中海地区的贸易网。贸易的发达和文化的交融构成了伊特鲁里亚文明的基础。

伊特鲁里亚人的来源有本土、海上和北方移民三种，至今无定论。伊特鲁里亚的早期文明称"维兰诺万时期"。公元前8世纪希腊人被矿藏所吸引，逐渐来到意大利南部，海洋贸易开始兴盛。希腊人、腓尼基人带来的语言、文化和财富使得伊特鲁里亚文明迅速发展，贵族阶层成长起来，村庄逐渐发展为市镇。在公元前725至公元前600年的"东方化时期"，伊特鲁里亚城邦走向繁荣，城邦国家流行君主贵族统治，但它们只是一个松散的联盟。由于与东方的频繁交往，当地的艺术深受埃及、小亚细亚的影响。同时，希腊文化对于伊特鲁里亚的影响最为深远。希腊人将字母传入伊特鲁里亚，伊特鲁里亚人也接受了希腊的神话、习俗和社会风尚。在向南扩张的过程中，伊特鲁里亚影响了其他地区，公元前616年伊特鲁里亚人卢修斯·塔克文·布里斯库取得罗马王位，从此伊特鲁里亚人统治罗马约一个世纪之久。

公元前6世纪，伊特鲁里亚文明达到了顶峰，几乎横跨整个亚平宁山脉。但在接下来的时期，伊特鲁里亚人在与希腊人争夺地中海霸权的战争中多次失败，罗马人也在公元前509年放逐了伊特鲁里亚人国王，结束了王政时代。罗马在意大利的扩张意味着伊特鲁里亚文明的衰落。公元4世纪，伊特鲁里亚人屡次败于罗马的武力之下。公元前280年，伊特鲁里亚城邦成为罗马的盟邦，伊特鲁里亚风格艺术品逐渐消失，与罗马风格融合在一起，最终消失于罗马文明夺目的光辉之中。

伊特鲁里亚文明是多种文化交融的产物，其艺术品具有独特的风格。伊特鲁里亚金属制造加工技术享誉地中海世界，从日用器物到奢侈品无一不精，尤其是微颗粒加工的金器可谓精美绝伦。其陶器继承了希腊艺术风格，形成了所谓"伊特鲁里亚——科林斯"陶器。伊特鲁里亚文明对于罗马文明也有着深刻的影响，罗马人正是通过伊特鲁里亚人学习到希腊文化，不仅罗马城是以伊特鲁里亚工艺构筑起来的，其神庙等大型建筑的修建也聘用伊特鲁里亚技师。伊特鲁里亚文明将罗马文明带入了"辉煌时代"。

随着伊特鲁里亚文明的消失，它的语言、文字、典籍逐渐失传，长期以来人们只有通过希腊、罗马人的记录才能够了解到这一古老文明的片段。直到文艺复兴时期，对于古典艺术的兴趣才使得学者们重新研究伊特鲁里亚文明。19世纪以来，现代考古学的发展进一步揭示了伊特鲁里亚的文明历程，对于其文字、艺术、风俗的研究日益深入。本次《曙光时代——意大利的伊特鲁里亚文明》以意大利托斯卡纳大区考古发掘文物为主，内容涉及伊特鲁里亚文明的政治、艺术、宗教信仰、日常生活各个方面，较全面地反映出伊特鲁里亚文明的面貌。了解世界同期文明，是考察本地文化应有的视角。随州叶家山西周早期墓地出土的成组编钟，表明公元前1000年前后，根植于湖北的曾国文化已经步入礼乐时代。公元前6世纪前后，正是楚国文化辉煌发达的高峰期。不断进行文明比较，培养观众的国际视野，是我馆展览的基本任务之一。

《曙光时代——意大利的伊特鲁里亚文明》是本馆2012年举办的《辉煌时代——罗马帝国文物》展的延续，我们希望通过这一系列展，使广大观众更深入地了解意大利的早期文明，进一步增进两国人民的相互了解。在此我向为展览付出努力的各界人士表示衷心感谢！

祝展览取得圆满成功！

湖北省博物馆馆长
湖北省文物考古研究所所长

The Etruscan civilization flourished from 1000 B.C.E. to 100 B.C.E. between two rivers, the Arno and the Tiber, in central-western Italy, and its prosperity was closely associated with the abundance of resources Etruria was endowed with. Fertile land brought in bumper crops. The long coastline and lagoons on the plain provided proper berthing spaces for people engaged in fishing and trading. More importantly, Etruria was rich in mineral deposits such as copper, iron, and tin. It was relying on those deposits that the Etruscans gained control over the metal melting industry almost across the Mediterranean region and established a trade network influencing the entire region. The booming trade and the fusion of cultures constituted the foundation of the Etruscan civilization.

The origin of the Etruscans has been believed to be in Italy, Asia or the north, and the issue is still being debated today. The beginning of the Etruscan civilization was the Villanovan period. In the eighth century B.C.E., more and more Greeks were attracted to southern Italy by the mineral deposits there, and maritime trade started to flourish. The languages, cultures, and wealth brought by Greeks and Phoenicians led to the fast growth of the Etruscan civilization, the emergence of the aristocracy, and the transformation of villages into towns. The Etruscan city-states prospered during the Orientalizing period (725 B.C.E.-600 B.C.E.). City-states were mostly ruled by the monarch or the aristocracy but they were just a loose alliance. Due to the frequent exchanges with the East, local art was deeply influenced by Egypt and Asia Minor, and the most profound influence came from the Greek culture. The Greeks brought the alphabet to Etruria and the Etruscans embraced the Greek myths and customs. Etruria also exerted impacts on other regions in its southward expansion. In 616 B.C.E., an Etruscan named Lucius Tarquinius Priscus became the king of Rome. From then on, Rome was ruled by the Etruscans for about a century.

In the sixth century B.C.E., the Etruscan civilization reached its peak, spanning almost the entire Apennines. In the following years, however, the Etruscans lost the war against the Greeks for hegemony in the Mediterranean. The Etruscan king of Rome was also exiled in 509 B.C.E., bringing an end to the era of the monarchy. The Roman expansion in Italy signaled the decline of the Etruscan civilization. In the fourth century B.C.E., the Etruscans were defeated by the Romans many times. In 280 B.C.E., Etruscan city-states forged alliance with Rome; the Etruscan style of artworks was gradually blended with the Roman style and eventually disappeared in the dazzling Roman civilization.

The Etruscan civilization was an outcome of the convergence of various cultures and its artworks had a unique style. It was well-known in the Mediterranean for its metal manufacturing and processing technologies, and the exquisite metal products ranged from household utensils to luxuries, particularly those made of metal micro-particles. The Etrusco-Corinthian pottery was developed based on the Greek style of art. The Roman civilization was also heavily influenced by the Etruscan civilization. It was from the Etruscans that the Romans learned about the Greek culture. In addition, Etruscan processes were used to build the city of Rome and Etruscan technicians were employed for the construction of large buildings such as temples. It was the Etruscans who led the Roman civilization to a "splendid time".

Gone with the Etruscan civilization were its language, writing, and books. For a long time, people could only learn about the fragments of this ancient civilization from the records kept by the Greeks and the Romans. Until the Renaissance, scholars driven by the interest in classical art started to re-examine the Etruscan civilization. Since the 19th century, modern archaeologists have unveiled more about the civilization's course of development and researched deeper into the writing, art, and customs of the Etruscans. This exhibition *"The Etruscans: The Dawn of Ancient Italy"*, featuring the findings of archaeological excavations in Tuscany, Italy, is intended to give people a full picture of the Etruscan civilization, including its politics, art, religion, and the Etruscans' everyday life. One indispensable part of the effort to examine a local culture is to know more about other civilizations of the world during the same period. The set-bells unearthed from the tombs of early Western Zhou Dynasty in Yejiashan, Suizhou indicate that the State of Zeng, located in today's Hubei Province, already entered into the era of ritual and music around 1000 B.C.E. The heyday of the State of Chu was right around the sixth century B.C.E. Comparing cultures and fostering visitors' international vision has always been one of the purposes of the exhibitions presented by Hubei Provincial Museum.

"The Etruscans: The Dawn of Ancient Italy" is a continuation of the exhibition *"A Splendid Time: The Heritage of Imperial Rome"* held in 2012. The exhibition series are expected to help the visitors better understand the early civilizations in Italy and promote the mutual understanding of the two peoples. I would like to thank friends of all sectors for the efforts you have made for this exhibition.

May the exhibition achieve a full success!

Fang Qin
Director, Hubei Provincial Museum
Director, Hubei Provincial Institute of Cultural Relics and Archaeology

　　伊特鲁里亚人是谁？他们的文化像历史上其他神秘而古老的文明一样，由于文字记载的缺失而隐退于历史的迷雾之中。公元前9世纪左右，伊特鲁里亚人开始定居于意大利中部，公元前5世纪左右，社会形成，城市兴起，出现了大型建筑和纪念性雕塑，并受到希腊爱奥尼亚和雅典样式影响，大规模青铜作坊也在这一时期产生。公元前4世纪伊特鲁里亚人被迫臣服于罗马统治，文化开始衰弱，直至被同化消失。一般认为，欧洲的文明主要来源于希腊与伊特鲁里亚，并且更直接地来源于伊特鲁里亚。在经历了近1000年的发展和繁荣之后，伊特鲁里亚文明最后消隐在历史迷雾的深处。伊特鲁里亚人作为一个种族也已经消失，留给我们的只有一些公路桥梁、城池的断壁残垣和大量的坟墓。

　　伊特鲁里亚人充满勃勃生机，懂得享受生活，崇尚美食、美酒和艺术，他们热爱自由和智慧，热情而浪漫，连坟墓中也洋溢着愉快的气氛。伊特鲁里亚人保留着对纯自然力的崇拜观念，把握了生命的真谛，摆脱了沉重理性的压迫，更多地保持了生命力和善良。他们懂得生命的灵敏律动和短暂而永恒的天真，透过时间的迷雾和人为的破坏，我们仍能看到天真。伊特鲁里亚人在他们平易的几个世纪中，如呼吸般自然平易地干着自己的事情，平易、自然。但文化上的富足和优雅却并不一定带来军事上的强盛，精致艺术和高雅的生活方式往往臣服于强悍的金戈铁马。伊特鲁里亚人的悲剧就在于俘获了罗马人的心，也招致了罗马人的贪欲。伊特鲁里亚人曾对罗马文化有过巨大的影响，罗马人的生活方式和习俗都来源于此，罗马人的文字和数字都可能来源于伊特鲁里亚人。

　　尽管希腊和拉丁文献中伊特鲁里亚人的相关资料寥若晨星，但近年来丰富的考古发现和深入研究已经廓清了公元前9世纪到公元前1世纪的伊特鲁里亚历史发展脉络。此次，我馆联合湖北省博物馆、广东省博物馆、秦始皇帝陵博物院引进意大利卡萨雷兹博物馆的《曙光时代——意大利的伊特鲁里亚文明》特展，希望透过展示伊特鲁里亚人留下的大量遗物，拨开历史的尘罩，让我们能够了解伊特鲁里亚人独特的文化、艺术、宗教信仰和民族特性。

浙江省博物馆馆长　陈浩

Who were the Etruscans? Due to the lack of written records, as many other ancient civilizations, the Etruscan culture is surrounded by mysteries. Around the 9th century B.C., Etruscans started to settle down in central Italy, and by the 5th century B.C., their society had taken shape. As cities sprang up and large constructions and commemorative sculptures appeared, large bronze workshops emerged, too under the influence of the Greek-Ionian and Athenian styles. In the 4th century B.C. when the Etruscans were forced to bow their heads to the Romans, their culture began to decline and was ultimately assimilated. It is generally believed that the European civilization today owes its origin mainly to the Greeks and the Etruscans, and more directly to the latter. After nearly a thousand years of development and prosperity, the Etruscan civilization faded away into profound historic mysteries. The Etruscans, as a race, have disappeared, leaving nothing but traces of roads, bridges, dilapidated cities and a number of tombs.

The Etruscans were full of vitality. They enjoyed life; loved great food, wine and arts; and valued freedom and wisdom. They were passionate and romantic; even their graves were permeated with joy. The Etruscans worshipped pure natural forces, grasped the truth of life, freed themselves from the burden of rational thinking, and maintained more vitality and goodwill. They understood the dynamic rhythm of life and the transient yet eternal charm of innocence which after thousands of years and human damages can still be seen and felt today. The Etruscans led a plain and simple life as natural as breath for centuries, unassumingly and unaffectedly. However, cultural richness and elegance did not promise strong military force; on the contrary, fine arts and an elegant lifestyle were always subdued by mighty warriors. The tragedy of the Etruscans was that they captured the hearts of the Romans and drew out the monster of greed. The Etruscans had huge impact on the Roman culture, giving them their lifestyle and customs, and probably their writing system and digits, too.

Although there were very limited information about the Etruscans in documents in both Greek and Latin, numerous archaeological findings and in-depth studies made in recent years have given us a clearer picture of what the Etruscans went through from the 9th to the 1st century B.C. Here, together with Hebei Museum, Guangdong Museum and Emperor Qinshihuang's Mausoleum Site Museum, we brought in the special exhibition of *The Etruscans: The Dawn of Ancient Italy* from Casa dei Carraresi Museum, Italy in the hope that the display of a large number of relics of the Etruscans will dissolve the historic mysteries and unveil to us the unique culture, arts, religions and ethnic characteristics of the Etruscans.

Chen Hao
Director of Zhejiang Provincial Museum

公元纪元到来之前一千年漫长的岁月中，黄河、长江流域孕育的两周和秦汉文化不断散发出璀璨的东方文明之光。而与此同时，位于遥远西方世界——亚平宁半岛中西部，同样诞生与发展出神秘而璀璨的伊特鲁里亚文明。创造这个文明的伊特鲁尼亚人在亚诺河与台伯河之间定居繁衍、发展农业、构筑村落、组建城邦，他们的风俗习惯、宗教仪式、建筑和文化艺术对古罗马文明产生了显著而又深远的影响，罗马数字和拉丁字母就是古罗马人在学习、继承伊特鲁尼亚文明成果的基础上产生并广为流传的。经过中意两国文物机构的共同努力，这样一个古老文明所创造的精彩物质文化如今来到东方，将向中国观众揭开她神秘的面纱，开启在博物馆中的东西文明的时空对话。

作为世界上最伟大的两个文明古国，中国和意大利之间的交往源远流长，早在东汉时期两地的居民已开始了直接的接触，成为东西方国家交流和往来的先导。广东作为中国的沿海大省，在长达两千年的历史上一直是"海上丝绸之路"的重要起点，扮演着中外贸易、文化交流的重要角色。近年来，广东和意大利在经济、文化、社会各领域的交流、合作快速发展，并于2011年签署了关于加强交流合作的备忘录，广东省博物馆也相继引进了《重返巴洛克——那不勒斯的黄金时代绘画展》等多个来自意大利的优质外展，获得了社会各界的广泛关注和良好反响。如今，《曙光时代——意大利的伊特鲁里亚文明》亮相广东省博物馆，相信必然能为广东观众带来近距离认识、了解西方文明的全新非凡体验。

藉此机会，我要向意大利托斯卡纳考古遗产监管局、卡萨德·卡萨雷兹博物馆、佛罗伦萨考古博物馆致以由衷的谢意，感谢他们为我们提供了珍贵的伊特鲁尼亚文物瑰宝！同时，我要向为本次展览统筹付出辛勤汗水的湖北省博物馆表达衷心的感谢！

预祝本次展览圆满成功！

广东省博物馆馆长 魏峻

During the 1,000 years before the Common Era, cultures nurtured in basins of the Yellow and Yangtze Rivers in the Western and Eastern Zhou Dynasties as well as Qin and Han Dynasties continuously emitted the brilliant light of Eastern civilization. Meanwhile, in the central west part of Apennine peninsula in the remote Western world, the mysterious and colorful Etruscan civilization also originated and developed. The Etruscans who created the civilization settled down between Arno and Tevere rivers, developed agriculture, and built villages and cities. Their customs, religious ceremonies, architecture and cultural art had exerted a prominent and profound influence on the ancient Roman civilization. For example, Roman numerals and Latin alphabet were created and widely promoted by ancient Roman people on the basis of studying and inheriting the results of the Etruscan civilization. Thanks to joint efforts of Chinese and Italian cultural heritage institutions, the brilliant physical culture created by such an old civilization comes to the East and will unveil its mystery to start a dialogue on museums between Eastern and Western civilizations.

As two greatest countries of ancient civilizations in the world, China and Italy have had a long history of mutual communication. As early as the Eastern Han Dynasty, people from both sides began direct contact and led the communication and exchanges between Eastern and Western countries. In the past 2,000 years, Guangdong, a major province in the coastal area of China, had always been an important starting point of the Maritime Silk Road and played a significant role in trade and cultural communication between China and foreign countries. In recent years, economic, cultural and social communication and cooperation between Guangdong and Italy developed rapidly. In 2011 they signed a memorandum on strengthening communication and cooperation between them. Guangdong Museum has introduced *The Golden Age of Neapolitan Art: Masterpieces from the Museum of Capodimonte in Naples* and many other quality exhibitions from Italy, which have attracted great attention and won wide acclaim in the society. Now show *The Etruscans: The Dawn of an Ancient Civilization* will be held in Guangdong Museum, and we firmly believe it will bring Guangdong audiences closer to the Western civilization and offer them a new and extraordinary chance to deepen their understanding.

I hereby would like to extend my sincere gratitude to Soprintendenza per i Beni Archeologici della Toscana, Casa dei Carraresi Museum, Treviso, and National Museum of Archeology, Florence, for their loan of some of the precious Etruscan treasures. My thanks also go to Hubei Provincial Museum for its hard work in coordinating this exhibition.

Wish the exhibition a great success!

Wei Jun
Director of Guangdong Museum

　　继2013年"辉煌时代——罗马帝国文物特展"之后，由湖北省博物馆、浙江省博物馆、广东省博物馆、秦始皇帝陵博物院四家接力举办的"曙光时代——意大利的伊特鲁里亚文明"展，今天在湖北省博物馆首站开幕了。这次由国内多家博物馆再度合作举办的文物特展，充分体现了博物馆人勇于探索、以国际视野和科学发展理念，实践建设文化强国、推动社会主义文化大繁荣、服务大众的共同目标和愿景。

　　伊特鲁里亚文明是公元前10世纪至公元前1世纪（相当于中国的西周中晚期至西汉时期）亚平宁半岛的古代文明，对古罗马以及后世西方文明的发生和发展产生了深远的影响。此次展览汇集了意大利佛罗伦萨考古博物馆等多家单位的藏品300余件，包含了种类繁多的生活用品、造型各异的金首饰和雕刻精美的石刻等，这些洋溢着浓烈的异国风情的文物，从不同的侧面凸显了伊特鲁里亚人从勃兴至完全归属古罗马帝国的千年沧桑。将这些文物置身于楚文化集中地湖北省博物馆，将使观众在欣赏神秘、诡谲的楚文化的同时，也能体味异域文化的不同风采！兼收并蓄且丰富多彩的人类文明，促进了人类社会在多种文化并存下的共同发展，让我们穿梭于东西方文化之间，一起领略与中华文明截然不同的异域文明！

　　作为一名考古工作者，我非常感谢意大利考古界的同行，本次展览的所有文物，是他们辛勤工作成果的体现。同时，我也代表秦始皇帝陵博物院，感谢湖北省博物馆、意大利卡萨雷兹博物馆为本次展览的成功举办所付出的辛劳，因为他们的努力，才使3000年前源于亚平宁半岛的西方文明呈现在东方观众的面前！

　　预祝本次展览在湖北省博物馆取得圆满成功！同时，期待2014年"曙光时代——意大利的伊特鲁里亚文明"展在秦文化的中心秦始皇帝陵博物院的展出，同样绽放绚丽多彩的时代曙光！

秦始皇帝陵博物院院长　　曹玮

Following A Splendid Time: The Heritage of Imperial Rome in 2013, Hubei Provincial Museum, Zhejiang Provincial Museum, Guangdong Museum, and Emperor Qinshihuang's Mausoleum Site Museum will, in succession, stage another grand exhibition, *The Etruscans: The Dawn of Ancient Italy*. Today, it is unveiled at Hubei Provincial Museum as the first session. As the second special exhibition staged with joint efforts of several domestic museums, it showcases our pioneering spirit, international outlook, and scientific understanding of development, and marks our shared goal and vision of contributing to the building of a culturally strong country, promoting the prosperity of the socialist culture, and serving the general public.

The Etruscan civilization lasted from the 10th to the 1st century B.C. (from mid- and late West Zhou Dynasty to West Han Dynasty in ancient China) in the Apennine peninsula and had a profound influence on ancient Rome and the Western civilization that followed. This exhibition will present over 300 items from the Museum of Archeology, Florence and several other museums in Italy, including various daily items, gold ornaments and delicate stone carvings. Bearing strong exotic features, these items will reveal to us the history of the Etruscans of nearly a thousand years from their emergence till the final assimilation into the Roman Empire. With this special exhibition on show, Hubei Provincial Museum will provide visitors with both an understanding of the mysterious Hubei culture and the experience of a charming exotic civilization. Human civilization, inclusive and diverse as it is, plays an important role in promoting shared development of the entire human race. Let's have an excellent tour across Eastern and Western cultures and enjoy the special splendor of a civilization totally different from our own.

As an archaeologist, I'm sincerely grateful to my Italian peers. Without their hard work, such a grand exhibition will not be possible. On behalf of Emperor Qinshihuang's Mausoleum Site Museum, my heartfelt thanks also go to Hubei Provincial Museum and Casa dei Carraresi for their generous contribution which helped present the fabulous Apennine civilization 3,000 years ago to visitors in the East today.

Wish *The Etruscans: The Dawn of Ancient Italy* a great success in Hubei Provincial Museum and look forward to staging it in Emperor Qinshihuang's Mausoleum Site Museum which is the center of the Qin culture.

Cao Wei
Director, Emperor Qinshihuang's Mausoleum Site Museum

将近10年来，意大利卡萨马卡基金会（Fondazione Cassamarca）在卡萨德·卡拉雷兹博物馆（Casa dei Carraresi）举办了一系列有关中华文明的重要展览，题为"丝绸之路与中国文明"的系列展由四部分构成，通过1500多件精美的展品展现了中国两千多年的文明史，受到意大利当地群众的极大好评。此前，意大利从未举办过类似展览。

现在，我们正在筹备一系列同样具有突破性意义的大展，通过与中国著名博物馆合作，向中国观众展现意大利文明。首个展览的主题为伊特鲁里亚文明。

卡萨马卡基金会和卡萨德·卡拉雷兹博物馆的共同目标在于，通过此次展览进一步促进中意两国之间的文化交流和友好关系。

卡萨马卡基金会主席　迪诺·德波利

For almost a decade the Fondazione Cassamarca, in its museum at the Casa dei Carraresi, hosted a series of major exhibitions dedicated to Chinese civilisation. More than 1500 magnificent exhibits reflecting over two thousand years of history were displayed in a series of four exhibitions entitled "The Silk Road and Chinese Civilisation". The exhibitions, the like of which had never been seen before, met with enormous success amongst the Italian public.

We are now engaged in an inverse, but equally groundbreaking, process: with the collaboration of the most important museums in China, it is our aim to present Italian civilization to the Chinese people, beginning with a major exhibition regarding the Etruscans.

The common intent of the Fondazione Cassamarca and Casa dei Carraresi is once again to reinforce the cultural relationships and friendship between our two countries.

Avv.On Dino De Poli

President, Fondazione Cassamarca

毫无疑问，伊特鲁里亚人在西欧历史上著名的各种文明中扮演着主人翁的角色。伊特鲁里亚人起源于地中海地区，并在那里发展壮大。在罗马帝国建立之前，他们是一个重要而独特的民族，即使是强大的罗马，也曾在很长一段时间内接受伊特鲁里亚人的统治。

伊特鲁里亚文明一度被团团迷雾笼罩，而后谜团又通过一些学术研究和考古发现渐渐揭开，不过伊特鲁里亚的魅力却从未消散。事实上，从艺术到手工艺、宗教和占卜，他们所创造的文明在生活各个方面都达到了极高的水平，此外，他们也具备了极强的能力来接受和发展来自希腊和近东历史边缘的启示和影响。

同时，伊特鲁里亚人充当了优雅的地中海文化和中欧各民族之间的中间人，他们的影响在凯尔特贵族和部落的习俗中都有体现。

现代人发现伊特鲁里亚文明的过程本身也同样引人入胜。18世纪的寻宝者和古董商，以及后来的考古学家和学者们，将伊特鲁里亚文明的点点滴滴拼凑串联，渐渐廓清了它的面貌。在伊特鲁里亚文明的巅峰期，它贯穿了意大利半岛的中部，从北部的亚诺河直到南部的台伯河，还曾向北扩张，到达帕达纳平原，向南也有扩张。

中国是一个文明高度发达的国家，留下了无数艺术瑰宝和珍贵的手工艺品，所以中国观众一定会迷上高雅精致的伊特鲁里亚文明。

由于展览组织者和湖北省博物馆、浙江省博物馆、广东省博物馆和秦始皇帝陵博物院的努力，《曙光时代——意大利的伊特鲁里亚文明》展将又一次让古老的文明彼此碰撞，在今天的文化间开启崭新的对话，为我们带来启迪。

托斯卡纳区考古美术遗产总监　安德里·白西纳博士

Without any doubt, the Etruscans played the role of protagonists among the various civilizations that marked the history of Western Europe. They represented one of the most important and peculiar peoples that originated and developed in the area of the Mediterranean Sea before the establishment of Rome's power that, however, was dominated too by the Etruscan rule for a long time.

Though a halo of mystery has surrounded this civilization for a certain period of time, despite several scholarly researches and archaeological findings that helped to dissolve it, Etruscans still keep their fascination. The civilization they developed, in fact, reached very high levels in every aspect of their life, from art to craftsmanship, to religion and divinatory practices as well as in their ability to accept and elaborate hints and influences derived from Greece and the Near East on the verge of History.

Etruscans, at the same time, acted as intermediaries between the refined Mediterranean cultures and the Central European populations as it appears evident in the habits of Celtic aristocracies and tribes.

The history of "modern" discovery of the Etruscan civilization is equally fascinating in itself, how treasure hunters and antique dealers in the XVIII century and archaeologues as well as scholars in the following years were able to put together the facts and events of this civilization that, at its apex, spread their presence within the central area of the Italian peninsula, from the rivers Arno, in the Northern part of the country, Southwards to the river Tevere, heading North in the Padana plain and in South Italy too.

It is evident that the Chinese audiences could not be but intrigued by such a refined and elaborated civilization, being China a place where civilization reached very high levels of civilization, producing art treasures and precious craftsmanship examples.

Thanks to the organisers of this exhibition and to the availability of the Hubei Provincial Museum, Zhejiang Provincial Museum, Guangdong Museum and Emperor Qinshihuang's Mausoleum Site Museum, the show *The Etruscans. The Dawn of an Ancient Civilization* will offer again the possibility of a lively and stimulating confrontation between ancient civilizations as well as a renewed dialogue between present cultures.

DOTT. ANDREA PESSINA

**Superintendent for the Archaeology Fine Arts
Heritage Tuscany Region**

《曙光时代——意大利的伊特鲁里亚文明》展览展示了文化沟通带来的中国和伊特鲁里亚两大文明的汇聚。文化将不同的民族联系在一起，推动他们互相学习，彼此发现和了解，共同建设一个充满信任与合作的未来。

能够为这样一项不同凡响的活动作出贡献，并通过出借部分最重要的代表展品举行展览，来切实推动文化的沟通与交流，佛罗伦萨国家考古博物馆感到非常荣幸。本次出借的展品包括：展现最出色的样板工艺手工艺作品、珠宝、日用工具、宗教用品和陪葬品。

这是一次难得一见的展览，它的成功举办得益于所有参与人员所付出的努力、热情、专业精神和各种资源。在此，我谨代表我个人，向帮助我们组织此次展览的所有人表示衷心的感谢。

同时，我希望举办这次展览的四个中国城市的观众从中受到启发，能够深入了解伊特鲁里亚文明史，伊特鲁里亚这个曾统治意大利中部长达几个世纪的民族，是骄傲的，而且至今仍带有几分神秘色彩。我也希望通过这种方式，将大家投入到这次展览中的热情传扬出去。这是我们首次有机会为加强远东和西方世界的对话搭建更坚固的桥梁，而这绝不会是最后一次机会。

朱赛平娜·卡洛塔·钱菲诺尼博士
佛罗伦萨国家考古博物馆馆长

The show *The Etruscans. The Dawn of an Ancient Civilization* celebrates the meeting between two major civilizations – the Chinese and the Etruscan one – thanks to the cultural connection. Thus culture bridges and promotes the reciprocal approach and discovery of different peoples who are building together a future made of trust and collaboration.

The Florence Archaeological Museum then is proud for being able and contributing to such an exceptional event and make it true through the loan of some of its most important masterpieces: works of art that witness examples of craftsmanship, jewellery, everyday tools, religious items and funerary ornaments.

This is a precious exhibition that has been made possible only through to the energy, enthusiasm, professionalism and resources of all the people who collaborated to this event. My personal and heartfelt thank goes to all those who helped us to make it true.

At the same time, I wish to express my personal wish that visitors to this exhibition in the four Chinese venues might be stimulated and go into depth in their approach of history of the Etruscan civilization – a proud and still someway mysterious population ruling for centuries over central Italy – and spread in this way the passion we all devoted to this project which is the first but surely not the last chance we have to build a stronger bridge to enrich the dialogue between the Far East and the Western worlds.

DOTT. GIUSEPPINA CARLOTTA CIANFERONI

Director
Florence Archaeological Museum

十年来，我一直在为举办一系列题为《丝绸之路与中华文明》的大型展览而努力工作。通过一系列波澜壮阔的考古展品和一批价值连城的清朝皇家收藏品，两千多年的中国历史徐徐展开，将一段由多个插曲组成的故事娓娓道来，并在意大利公众中获得了巨大成功。特拉维索的卡拉雷兹博物馆是一座距威尼斯仅一箭之遥的13世纪时期的建筑——与马可波罗同时代，就在它古老的高墙之内，四场具有历史意义的、让人难以忘怀的展览将古老的中华文明展现在了世界眼前。我有幸担任了这一系列展览的策展人，我从这一角色中深入学习了有关中国博物馆系统的知识，并熟悉了它们馆藏的非凡财富——包括远至公元前3世纪的西安秦始皇兵马俑，近至中国末代皇帝溥仪的个人物品，令人赞叹不已。此外，我还与中国数十家博物馆的馆长、主任、考古学家、专家学者建立了深厚的友谊。

现在，我却发现自己在这场文化"合作"中站到了对面的位置：我参与组织了一系列由中方举办的以"意大利文明"为主题的大型展览，旨在介绍我的祖国——拥有着同样灿烂非凡的古老历史的意大利数千年来为人类所做的贡献。中国的数家大型博物馆（武汉的湖北省博物馆，杭州的浙江省博物馆，广州的广东省博物馆和西安的秦始皇帝陵博物院），将首次举办以伊特鲁里亚文明为主题的展览。伊特鲁里亚人建立了意大利半岛上最古老的文明，并为后来的罗马文明奠定了基础，并为当时的罗马文明做出了部分贡献。

感谢意大利文化遗产部、托斯卡纳考古遗产监管局、佛罗伦萨国家考古博物馆，以及意大利中部伊特鲁里亚地区多家博物馆提供了宝贵且不可或缺的合作，以及丰富的考古遗址所提供的展品，我们才有机会举办这次具有重大文化和历史意义的展览，并进一步加强意中两国间已经坚固的联系。两国被一条史上罕见的古代文化纽带联系起来，这已经向对方展示了自己最深的敬意和关注。

这一传统将我们紧密相连，并构建了一条让两国人民真正理解对方的桥梁，能为这种传统做出微薄奉献，我们深感荣幸。伊特鲁里亚的历史与古代中华文明有着相似之处，这将给中国观众带来惊喜。正是由于对逝者的崇拜和来自神秘来生的吸引力，以及向后世传递对逝去文明的遗物的必要——依靠这些遗物，我们——包括中国人和意大利人，才有机会对我们文明的演变加以了解。通过对我们祖先的过去进行研究和表示充满敬意的认可，我们可以找到对现时代存在的问题的解答，甚至可以以此为据，想象未来世界的面貌。

阿德里亚诺·马达罗
中华文明大型展览策展人
卡拉雷兹博物馆馆长，特拉维索

For ten years I worked hard on a series of major exhibitions entitled "The Silk Road and Chinese Civilisation". More than two thousand years of Chinese history were presented through magnificent archaeological exhibits and priceless objects from the imperial collections of the Qing Dynasty, recounting an episodic story which met with enormous success amongst the Italian public. Within the ancient walls of the Casa dei Carraresi in Treviso, a thirteenth-century building from the time of Marco Polo, a stone's throw from Venice, Chinese civilisation was revealed to the world in four historic and memorable exhibitions. I acted as the curator for these exhibitions, and in this role I acquired a deep knowledge of the Chinese museum system and became familiar with the extraordinary wealth of their collections, from the third century BCE terracotta warriors and horses of Xian, to the personal effects of the Last Emperor, Pu Yi. Furthermore, I have become firm friends with directors, curators, archaeologists, experts and scholars in dozens and dozens of museums throughout the length and breadth of China.

I now find myself involved in a reverse cultural "operation": the organisation of a series of major exhibitions in China dedicated to "Italian Civilisation", to the contribution that my country has made to humanity over the millennia through it's equally glorious and extraordinary history. A number of the most important Chinese museums (Hubei Province Museum in Wuhan, Zhejiang Province Museum in Hangzhou, Guangdong Province Museum in Guangzhou and the Museum of Terracotta Warriors and Horses in Xian) will, in turn, host the first exhibition dedicated to the Etruscans, the people who established the most ancient civilisation of the Italian peninsula, and laid the foundations for the successive and partly contemporaneous Roman civilisation.

Thanks to the precious and essential collaboration of the Italian Ministry of Culture, the Superintendence for the Archaeological Heritage in Tuscany, the National Archaeological Museum in Florence, and the museums of the Etruscan area in central Italy with their wealth of archaeological sites which provided the exhibits, it has been possible to mount this exhibition of great cultural-scientific importance, which further strengthens the already strong ties between Italy and China. Two countries linked by an ancient cultural relationship rarely seen in history, which have always demonstrated the deepest respect and interest for each other.

We are proud to make our small contribution to the tradition that brings us together and represents the path leading to true understanding between peoples. The history of the Etruscan people will surprise the Chinese public for the similarities it bears to that of ancient Chinese civilisation. It is thanks to the cult of the dead, to the attraction of the mysteries of the afterlife, to the need to hand down to posterity some evidence of a past existence that we can learn, both in China and in Italy, about the evolution of our civilisations. For it is in the study and respectful recognition of our ancestors' past that we can find the answers to the existential questions of our time, and perhaps even begin to imagine what the future will hold.

Adriano Màdaro

Curator of the Great Exhibitions of the Chinese Civilization Casa dei Carraresi Museum, Treviso

伊特鲁里亚古城维图罗尼亚同名遗迹的图穆罗·德拉·皮特拉墓
Etruscan tomb, known with the name of Tumulo della Pietrera, from
the old Etruscan city of Vetulonia

专 文

ESSAYS

伊特鲁里亚——历史与社会

朱塞平娜·卡洛塔·钱菲诺尼

在希腊语中，伊特鲁里亚人被称为第勒尼伊人（*tyrrhenoi*）。罗马人则称他们为托斯其人（*Tusci*）或伊特鲁斯坎人（*Etrusci*）。而他们则似乎自称为罗散那人（*Rosanna*）。

在古意大利所有居民中，伊特鲁里亚是一种最能激发公众想象力的文明，而且这支文明仍将在公众心中维持一种神秘而富有吸引力的形象。但是，假如我们认真审视这种历史吸引力，并将其真实的存在与其他古代社会相比较，我们则很明显地发现，我们不能再将其称为"神秘的伊特鲁里亚人"。毕竟，伊特鲁里亚文明是前罗马时期意大利文明中最著名的一支文明。

严格意义上的伊特鲁里亚边界由两条河流确定，即阿诺河和台伯河。它包括现在的托斯卡纳，翁布里亚的一部分、以及罗马北部的拉丁姆的一部分，而台伯河的右岸则是伊特鲁里亚。伊特鲁里亚还扩张至南部的坎帕尼亚区以及北部的波河谷（伊特鲁里亚-帕纳达），在这两个区域可以发现他们的纪念碑和其他艺术和文化的反映。但是，当我们谈论起伊特鲁里亚艺术时，我们务必要注意，这个术语不包含民族含义，它只是指一种特定的艺术生产，这种艺术生产与意大利半岛上9世纪首次出现并于公元前1世纪被罗马人摧毁的一种文化相关。

记住这点很重要：伊特鲁里亚城邦之间非常独立，同时对统一化行动非常抵制，因此他们未能相互联合起来对付共同的敌人——罗马，罗马才得以将伊特鲁里亚城邦一一攻破。

最近几年的发现和研究已经明确地揭开了伊特鲁里亚文化的神秘外衣，尽管希腊和罗马文学来源中有关该文化的信息十分稀少，但考古研究表明这种文化十分丰富且十分微妙，这又一次为伊特鲁里亚人在公元前一千年赢得了自己的历史地位。

长期以来，考古学家们对于伊特鲁里亚人的起源一直存在着争议。古代的流行说法认为，伊特鲁里亚人来自亚洲，是佩拉斯吉人（*Pelasgi*）的后裔，其祖先为逃避一场可怕的饥荒，而在吕底亚王阿提司之子第勒尼（*Tyrrhenus*）的率领下来到了第勒尼安海岸。

这种说法曾长期流行，并一直持续到现代，但19世纪初出现了第二种假说。这种说法可被视为第一种说法的自然延续，认为伊特鲁里亚人是源自北方主要移民的祖先，根据这种说法，他们是跨越阿尔卑斯山来到意大利。

以上两种说法都基于同一个假说，即这个民族的祖先来自外部移民。但第三种理论并不从外部追溯伊特鲁里亚人的起源，相反，提出伊特鲁里亚人就来自意大利本土。这一本土说得到了古代历史学家的强烈支持，即哈利卡纳苏斯的狄俄尼索斯。

以上这些假设在今日看来，都已显得过时了。这应归功于20世纪意大利最杰出的考古学家之一，马西莫·帕罗提诺（Massimo Pallottino）先生。他指出，以上各种理论都有其自身无法克服的局限性。他认为，把民族起源做为研究的主要方向本身就是一个错误。研究一个民族的历史，应该关注其形成的过程，而非单纯的起源。任何一种文化的特征都是在多种因素的共同作用下形成的。从这一前提出发，探索文化形成的唯一途径便是调查研究其消化吸收各种民俗与文化因素相互作用影响而实现发展的可能性。

同伊特鲁里亚人的起源一样，其语言也一直是一个谜，但这并不都是事实。其实，伊特鲁里亚语言并不难读，因为其采用的字母是首批希腊殖民者带到意大利的，只是稍作调整而已。值得注意的是，其文字是从右到左书写的，而且在早期文字中没有断句。稍晚，开始用点或空格来分隔词组。

然而，在解读伊特鲁里亚语言时，仍存在许多问题。其中主要困难在于这种语言不同于至今仍在使用的希腊语，它早已消亡了两千余年。另外，可供研究的文字也很少，都是断片残简，破败不堪。而且大量的文字材料都十分简短而且重复，大都是关于丧葬的内容，往往是死者的姓名或铭文所载器物的名称。

波乔·布库墓地一座已发掘的伊特鲁里亚墓葬的石头入口
Entrance of an Etruscan tomb which was excavated in the stone within the necropolis of Poggio Buco

伊特鲁里亚文明的起源（公元前9世纪-公元前8世纪后期）

　　伊特鲁里亚文明的开始可追溯至公元前9世纪，与最早的维兰诺万文化现象同期，该文化得名于博洛尼亚附近的小镇维兰诺万（Villanovan），即首次发现具有该时期特征文化的遗址的地点。有关维兰诺万时期的考古文献几乎全部源自墓地。对"死亡之城"的建造，我们已掌握丰富的资料，但对生者的居住状况，我们却知之甚少。

　　造成这类信息匮乏的原因有许多，但最重要的原因可能是考古研究的史学方法论问题。过去，考古学家主要关注墓葬和圣殿的发掘，重视具有特定历史和艺术价值的物品，而忽略对聚落的研究，这种方法论对日常生活的各个方面毫无兴趣。此外，许多伊特鲁里亚聚落一直兴旺发达至罗马和中世纪时期；事实上，直至今天，许多地方仍有人居住。这就是为何伊特鲁里亚聚落的脆弱结构为何几乎被人们从记忆中完全抹去的原因。

　　维兰诺万聚落一般建筑在广阔且易于防守的高地上，并濒临河流或溪流，以方便获得水资源。村落由有限数量的椭圆形或矩形棚屋组成的小型自治群体构成。

　　从现存聚落的平面图可知，似乎这些棚屋的分布没有任何明显规律。棚屋之间相隔较远，说明农业用地或驯养牲畜的土地被居民进一步细分。只有房屋地基保存至今。棚屋的形状仅能依靠地基挖方、柱洞，以及多少保持几分原状的土壤上留下的层层居住遗迹来辨认。

　　对这些残余的遗迹分析表明，伊特鲁里亚房屋存在多种平面布局。文献记载了圆形、椭圆形、方形和矩形等多种平面布局，而且这些布局似乎没有时间顺序上的差异；所有形状的布局均可在同一时期出现，这种多样性同样反映在同时期的棚屋状骨灰瓮中。骨灰瓮主要用于公元前10世纪至8世纪，是对原史时期聚落进行重建的最重要文献。房屋建筑使用的材料包括藤条和树枝，上面覆盖着黏土。支撑茅草屋顶的则是一个形状类似龟甲的木质结构。

从伊特鲁里亚古城波普洛尼亚眺望第勒尼安海
View of the Tyrrheanian Sea from the old Etruscan City of Populonia

伊特鲁里亚古城维图罗尼亚闻
名遐迩的图穆罗·德拉·皮特拉墓
Etruscan tomb, known with the
name of Tumulo della Pietrera,
from the old Etruscan city of
Vetulonia

　　火葬是最普遍的丧葬仪式，大多数情况下，骨灰被放置在一种双锥状的黏土瓮中，盖上形似覆碗的盖子，或是青铜或黏土制作的头盔。有时骨灰瓮做成棚屋的造型，以象征性地再现死者在世时的住所。死者火葬时的物品则摆放在骨灰瓮内，而盛放家用物品的器皿则安放在骨灰瓮旁在岩石上凿出的小孔里，或是在上方覆盖石头。

　　维兰诺万文化的发展历经两个世纪，公元前7世纪上半叶发生的一件至关重要的事情标志着该文化的演变，即希腊在坎帕尼亚区殖民的开始，和皮塞库萨(伊萨奇)（Pithecusae (lschia)）的埃维亚（Chalchidian）中心和库迈（Cumae）殖民地的建立。

　　与希腊世界的接触带来了许多外国物品的进口，此外，由于控制了许多资源丰富的矿藏地区，如拉丁姆的托尔发山脉或"金属山脉"，和托斯卡纳的厄尔巴岛，伊特鲁里

坦斯帕达纳

威尼吉亚和伊斯特拉

Transpadana

Venetia et Istria

艾米利亚

Liguria

Aemilia

翁布里亚

利古里亚

Umbria

ETRURIA

伊特鲁里亚

Etruria

皮塞努姆

Picenum

Latium
et Campania

阿普利亚区和卡拉布里亚

拉丁姆和坎帕尼亚

Apulia et Calabria

萨伦蒂尼和艾尔皮尼

Salentini et Irpini

Sardinia

Lucania
et Brutti

撒丁岛

卢尔尼亚和布鲁提

西西里

Sicilia

意大利及伊特鲁尼亚地图
Map of Italy and Etruscan

亚城邦具有极大的经济潜力，被这点所吸引，许多工匠和商人纷纷开设商行。与另一大文明的联系加快了技术知识的发展，进而对农业和手工业生产产生影响。

新的作物品种和栽培方式——尤其是葡萄和橄榄的栽培被引进伊特鲁里亚，同时传入的还包括一些重要的技术革新，如陶轮。这些新的元素促进了维兰诺万社会结构的进一步转型，一个更为复杂的文明开始崛起，这点可从大量蓬勃发展的生产活动中看出。已经掌握娴熟技艺的青铜冶炼作坊和陶器作坊迅速利用这些来自希腊的有利条件，并将其与本地的形式和装饰技艺明智地结合起来。于是，城市的体系结构赋予了自身更多的活力，同时必然促进了土地私有的发展。

维兰诺万的墓葬较好地记录了这一转变，尤其是伊特鲁里亚沿海一些最重要的中心城市里的墓葬。维兰诺万社会的最早期，即公元前9世纪，陪伴死者下葬的家用物品体现出统一化的、"平均主义"的一面，反映了当时的社会没有出现较大分化，但维兰诺万后期，墓葬中家用物品的差异增大，说明了社会结构的演变和社会阶层的明确划分，一个由富有贵族组成的新阶级脱颖而出，成为下个世纪里辉煌发展的东方化时期的主人翁。

自最久远的史前时代开始，首领们就一直被描绘成为英武的勇士。即使在意大利中西部的伊特鲁里亚海岸，自铁器时代早期开始，据墓葬物品的记载，勇士的角色也是被人们颂扬的。卓越的男性通常被描绘为勇猛的战士，而他们的殉葬品则以武器和盔甲为主。于是，公元前8世纪出现在历史舞台的贵族阶级则主要以其财富和武士意识形态为特色。羊毛纺织是妇女标志性的工作，正如舞刀弄枪是男性追求的标记一样；如果说生育和教育子女是妇女们的宿命，那么纺织羊毛也是她们的一项重要标志。分配给男性和女性的古老角色的区别可从殉葬品中得到很好的证明，我们能找到具有其生活职责特征的器械和工具的遗迹。女性墓葬中最常见的物品便是代表纺织活动的纺轮和线轴；这些在初民社会时期的墓葬中较为常见。每个墓葬中通常有多个这类殉葬品，偶尔发现有50个或更多。纺轮有多种种类，包括球形、平顶圆锥形、双锥形、多面体形，甚至有

索瓦纳古城一座开放的墓葬
The monumental tomb from the old city of Sovana

从伊特鲁里亚科萨古城的海角
眺望第勒尼安海
View of the Tyrrhenian Sea
from the promontory of the old
Etruscan City of Cosa

一些带有雕刻和印花装饰图案的纺轮。线轴的种类较少，仅分为两种：凹面顶端和平面顶端，且极少饰有装饰图案。偶有文献记载有平顶金字塔形的织机纺坠。对于出现大量纺轮的墓葬，人们猜测它们可能不仅与纺线有关，还可能与织布活动有关。纺纱杆通常与纺锤相关联，但人们只在富人的墓葬中发现这种由青铜、骨头或玻璃等材质制作的物品。其他墓葬中可能有由木头制作的纺纱杆，但和纺锤一样，没有找到它们的痕迹。

领主文化（公元前8世纪—公元前6世纪前25年）

东方化时期，即公元前8世纪最后几十年至公元前6世纪前25年间的时期，可称为伊特鲁里亚历史上最具有标志性的时期。这段时期，伊特鲁里亚人在地中海的舞台上具有绝对统治权，并在与希腊、意大利半岛和东方各民族之间的活跃联系中占主导地位。这段时期最明显、最显著的一个现象便是奢侈品的普遍出现，这些奢侈品或者从近东地区和希腊进口，或者由本地工匠模仿东方风格制造。这些物品包括金银器、装饰富丽的银质器皿和青铜器皿、象牙雕刻的物品，彩釉陶瓶和精美的人物形象陶器。

他们与希腊殖民地的联系（公元前8世纪至公元前7世纪）将覆盖屋顶用的红陶瓦引进了意大利。这类红陶瓦的使用最早可追溯至公元前7世纪下半叶。随着时间的推移，原先简陋的房屋地基被石头所取代，墙壁则由未经烧制的黏土砖和栅栏状材料堆砌。长方形是最普遍的房屋结构，各房间分布在两侧。公元前6世纪，各个房间通常都朝向一个中心区域，这个中心或者是正厅，或者是露天的庭院。起初，最重要的私人住宅和公共建筑的屋顶最初装饰着屋脊雕塑、人物形象瓦檐饰和彩绘瓦。后来，屋顶上通常装饰着描绘主人宴会、打猎、家庭聚会及建立战功等生活场景的门楣雕饰。

公元前8世纪上半叶，伊特鲁里亚本土民族与希腊人和腓尼基人建立了联系，并开始学习希腊和腓尼基的装饰图案和艺术技巧，不久也开始接受他们的文化。文字记载、新的用餐方式，和一种英雄主义的丧葬思想都被引入伊特鲁里亚本土社会。总之，他们开始了一种新的贵族式生活方式，正是这种方式深刻地改变了他们社会的性质。

以餐桌礼仪为中心，他们构建了一个荷马史诗中描绘的世界。极富象征意义的食物——譬如肉和葡萄酒，均为特殊场合使用保存下来，并按照特定的仪式享用。普通大众只能偶尔吃到肉类。根据文学作品的记载（尤其是与希腊古风时期有关的记载），享用肉类的姿势和奉献祭品的姿势没有区别，而且都被认定为基本的社交方式。举办宴会的机会并不少见，相反，宴会是常有的事件，并遵照一个复杂的节日日程表进行。

这一历史时期，真正吃肉喝酒的宴会与社交酒会有着根本区别，社交酒会往往伴随着演讲和其他社交仪式。在我们看来，社交酒会是以饮酒为中心的节庆娱乐。在公元前8世纪至公元前7世纪，作为重要的社交与联系的时机，社交酒会这一习俗被认为是贵族生活一种最初的表现形式，与一种真正的、具有鲜明特征的贵族阶层的出现有关。这时，这一社会阶层开始变得可以辨认、定义和区分。

公元前8世纪末期，一系列引人注意的花瓶、杯或饮用杯、斟倒饮料的瓶罐、混合酒和水的容器，均记载了伊特鲁里亚普遍的饮酒风俗，甚至包括葬礼上的饮酒习俗。

葡萄酒和橄榄油，之前均从希腊引进，但很快在伊特鲁里亚本地生产，并被视为最贵重的产物。事实上，早在公元前6世纪，葡萄和橄榄的特殊文化就已经被引入伊特鲁里亚。

根据墓葬类型学和殉葬品推断，从社会经济学和文化的角度来看，这一阶段伊特鲁里亚社会的特征表现为社会阶层的明显分化，顶层阶级是一群被称为"领主"的精英群体，这是由一些占统治地位的家族集团的诞生所决定的。一方面，领主们将其权力建立在土地所有权上，因为他们拥有开发土地资源的机会，主要包括农业资源，也包括畜牧业、狩猎和渔业等资源。另一方面，这种特权使他们得以控制交通要道，并因此获得与较远区域进行商业交流的特权。后来，对矿藏资源的开采也为他们带来了额外的财富；那些发展得最快的中心城市都是与重要的矿藏保持紧密联系的城市，这并不是偶然。

墓葬是了解东方时期伊特鲁里亚精英阶层的主要信息来源。建造可供同一个家族的多位成员合葬的室墓为这一阶段的墓葬特征。起初，这些室墓都是各自独立的，与维兰诺万时期的常见墓穴一样，墓室呈盒状，由光滑平坦的石头堆砌而成，上方则是墓冢，有时还摆上一圈石子以划清界限。至公元前7世纪上半叶开始，墓室的规模开始扩大，墓冢也变得更加雄伟壮观；到了公元前7世纪下半叶，墓冢的规模可超过10米。在较为壮观的墓穴里，建有一条长门廊通往一个大的主墓室，墓室呈圆形或四边形，上方覆盖有圆顶或拱顶。

在盛产石灰华和石灰岩的伊特鲁里亚南部，墓穴通常在地下，因为这类石头较易开凿。但在伊特鲁里亚北部，大型坟墓全部建在地上。庞大的坟茔占据着较高的位置，规

索拉诺遗址的伊特鲁里亚墓葬
入口
Entrance of some Etruscan
tombs within the archaeological
site of Sorano

模宏大，气势雄伟，清楚地表明了该家族的财富和重要性。伊特鲁里亚墓室的内部结构则通常堪称建筑上的杰作，类型繁多，不仅体现了建造者的高超技艺，也体现了要求苛刻、优雅讲究的墓主的品味。

在伊特鲁里亚北部的一些中心城市，人们还发现了另一种类型的"领主"墓葬，即"环形"墓穴，这种墓穴或是各自独立，或是集体出现，墓室均垂直挖向地底，周围则放置着一圈石头。

不管是哪种情况，坟墓中丰富多样的殉葬品——通常包括许多奢侈品，象牙或骨头雕刻的物品、琥珀、金银制品、陶器，均表明了逝者的身份。

器皿——尤其是社交酒会器皿，则反映了伊特鲁里亚人的生产活动和娱乐活动；铁或青铜制作的武器则反映了他们的英雄主义理想；一些代表公民权利的象征，例如权杖和法西斯标记（*fasces lictariae*）；还有一些其他物品，如香膏盒、扇子或香炉，则与宗教仪式有关。

兵器与盔甲表现出更明显的装饰特征。伊特鲁里亚多个社群的墓葬中均发现有高耸的，带有顶饰的头盔、饰有浮雕图案的大圆盾、短剑，以及肉搏战使用的带青铜矛头的重矛。主要根据图像学证据推测，似乎是在公元前7世纪后期，希腊重甲步兵的盔甲开始为人知晓。及至公元前6世纪末期，伊特鲁里亚人开始模仿希腊重甲步兵的武器制造一些军事武器：譬如科林斯式头盔、双把盾、护胫甲、短剑，以及至少三种形式的长矛。希腊重甲步兵方阵踏着乐号的拍子行军，就像波普洛尼亚战车墓地的方阵，该兵马

从塔拉莫纳奇奥神庙的海角眺望
第勒尼安海
View of the Tyrrheanian Sea from
the promontory at Talamonaccio

俑可追溯至公元前7世纪第25年至50年，并可能证明了埋葬在该墓穴里的领主是一位军事领袖。

有些女性的殉葬品中可能包括一副马衔，而且到了公元前8世纪末期，马车甚至可以充当葬礼中的交通工具；这个时期，女性似乎只能乘坐两匹马拉的马车。女性墓葬中的马衔可能指代双马四轮马车，而男性墓葬中的马衔则可能指代战车或狩猎用的马车。毫无疑问，只有上层阶级中的女性——可能是某位武士领袖的配偶——的墓葬中才陪葬有马衔。

女性服饰通常比男性服饰华贵，并配有奢侈的成套首饰，表现出一些搭配组合的特点。装扮华贵的妇女本身是其家族集团的一笔财产，象征着家族集团的地位。其他女性则是与其他贵族集团进行交换的必要财产。这些可供交换的物品包括贵金属制品、琥珀，以及一些美丽的手镯或服饰上的装饰物。婚姻似乎是上层阶级中的社群和家族结盟的工具。

东方化时期的伊特鲁里亚贵族所取得的巨大财富的最重要标志，恐怕就是领主坟墓中陪葬的奢华富丽的黄金制品。这些物品堪称冶铁艺术的杰作，证明了伊特鲁里亚工匠所取得的高超技艺，青铜制品亦是如此：上面的浮雕工艺证明了伊特鲁里亚人是娴熟掌握这门艺术的大师。

事实上，冶铁历来被认为是伊特鲁里亚艺术成就的一个最重要表现，公元前5世纪的雅典诗人就高度颂扬了来自伊特鲁里亚的青铜器，而罗马的奥古斯都时代，伊

伊特鲁里亚城武尔奇附近的湖泊
Lake near the Etruscan city of Vulci

索瓦纳古城大墓入口
Entrance of a monumental tomb in the old city of Sovana

特鲁里亚仍被视为当地的一笔巨大财富。

　　区分伊特鲁里亚精英阶层的一个重要标志，便是该阶层对文字书写的掌握，墓碑上的铭文则是无可辩驳的证据，这些文字表示了与物品有关的事物，有时描绘一项宗教供奉的捐赠者或施舍者，有时则指代一项礼物的接受方。此外，他们不仅以文字书写为荣，而且还开始教授这门技能，器皿或其他物品上出现的字母表——例如马塞里亚那城的"象牙圈"出土的著名的象牙写字板，则间接证明了这一点。

城邦社会（公元前7世纪末期至公元前4世纪）

　　到了公元前7世纪末期，伊特鲁里亚主要群落的城邦结构已经多少定型：城墙已将较大的村落包围起来，公共建筑、神庙和私人住宅则坐落其中。与希腊一样，卫城也是伊特鲁里亚城邦政治生活的必要部分。卫城坐落在易于防守的高地，有着可靠的供水；另外，作为神庙所在地，卫城也为人民提供神圣保护。

　　公元前7世纪下半叶，建筑的性质开始发生改变：由木头、编制藤条和植物纤维等易腐烂的材料建造的乡村棚屋开始被垫高地基的房屋所取代，建造房屋的材料包括未经烘焙的黏土砖，以及用木头和涂有黏土层的藤条编制的牢固的网格状支撑结构，人字形屋顶则覆盖着红陶瓦。这类房屋也同样有着开阔的院子，一天的多数时间都在这里度过。

　　这段时期的财富分布更为普遍——下一个时期，财富则为少数贵族家族所掌握——促进了一个中间阶层的出现。这个阶层主要从事商业和手工业，并很快对伊特鲁里亚的经济和政治产生重大影响。大规模公墓的出现充分再现了这一社会转型。这时，领主阶层的大型陵寝已经被中产阶级的公墓所取代。这一时期的坟墓也体现出当时家庭住宅的建筑特征，同样也用于整个家族的合葬。

　　城邦时期的金属矿藏开发变得条理化，而经济活动的组织也更加系统化。自公元前7世纪末期至公元前6世纪末期，商贸活动由希腊——主要是小亚细亚海岸上的萨摩斯（Samos）、米勒斯（Miletos）和福西亚（Phocaea）等城市的商人控制（尽管他们只充当中间人）。他们带来珍贵的商品，以及一些消耗品，如香水、服饰，以及运输葡萄酒和油的安夫拉双耳瓶（amphorae）和日用陶瓷。公元前6世纪中叶之前，双耳瓶都在柯林斯和希腊东部制造，而公元前5世纪上半叶之前则在雅典生产。同时，来自其他地区的熟练工匠仍然依照传统在伊特鲁里亚居住并工作，并对手工业生产的各个部门——包括陶器、壁画和建筑用红陶砖的生产产生了深远影响。

　　出口贸易的主要目的地为法国南海岸，出口的商品包括葡萄酒、青铜器皿、精美的陶器和陶器，以及模仿科林斯样式制作的伊特鲁里亚陶器。这些商品甚至远销科西嘉岛、撒丁岛、迦太基和希腊的西西里群岛殖民地。对第勒尼安海域的经济控制也得到了巩固，这得益于与迦太基的紧密联系，以及对意大利其他人口密集区的扩张政策；通过殖民，伊特鲁里亚在意大利北部（伊特鲁里亚的帕达纳）的地位也更加稳固，而在南部，根据同时代文学作品的记载，罗马受到了丘西国王波塞内（Porsenna）的攻击。尽管这场对峙的结果并不明朗，但很可能这座城市被伊特鲁里亚人控制了一段时期；总之，很有必要记住罗马国王塔克文·布里斯库（Tarquinius Priscus）、塞尔维乌斯·图利乌斯（Servius

比萨
Pisa

Fiesole
菲耶索莱

沃尔泰拉
Volterra

阿雷佐
Arezzo

科多纳
Cortona

波普罗尼亚
Populonia

丘西
Chiusi

Perugia
佩鲁贾

维图罗尼亚
Vetulonia

罗塞尔
Roselle

奥维多
Orvieto

布尔塞拉
Bolsena

Talamone
塔拉莫纳奇

比森齐奥
Bisenzio

武尔奇
Vulci

塔尔奎尼亚
Tarquinia

切尔韦泰里
Cerveteri

Veio
维伊

Roma
罗马

伊特鲁里亚城邦地图
Map of Etruscan city

Tullius）和塔克文·苏佩布（Tarquinius Superbus）均有着伊特鲁里亚血统。

　　公元前5世纪初，伊特鲁里亚还是一个扩张性国家，但到了世纪末，它就已经迅速走向衰落。公元前6世纪下半叶，伊特鲁里亚的疆域已经扩展到罗马的边境，但仅仅一百余年（公元前396）后，罗马就占领了伊特鲁里亚的城邦维伊（Veii），并以摧枯拉朽之势横扫整个意大利。毫无疑问，伊特鲁里亚走向衰败的原因之一，便是因为迦太基和锡拉库扎的崛起而失去对第勒尼安海域商贸通道的控制。伊特鲁里亚舰队和锡拉库扎舰队之间的库迈之战（公元前474）起到了决定性作用；锡拉库扎取胜后，伊特鲁里亚人就不再充当第勒尼安海域商贸活动的中间者，其海军势力也一落千丈。这次战败迫使伊特鲁里亚关闭了其在第勒尼安海域的港口；而雅典人主导的希腊贸易则调整政策，开始锁定繁荣富饶的亚德里亚海市场，尤其是位于波河河口的港口城市斯皮那（Spina）。

第勒尼安海域控制权的丧失反过来对依赖海上贸易的伊特鲁里亚南部海岸城邦产生了影响，但是，对于出口目的地为其他区域或以农业经济为主的其他城邦而言，所承受的损失相对较小。尽管如此，也有些例外的城邦，譬如波普洛尼亚（Populonia）。公元前6世纪末，波普洛尼亚的冶铁工业变得十分发达，吸引了希腊人的注意；厄尔巴岛的采矿业也相当发达。

城邦的困境对从事商业活动和工艺生产等活动的伊特鲁里亚中产阶级也带来了冲击，他们的社会地位开始逐渐瓦解。权力完全转移到贵族阶级手中；在伊特鲁里亚的邻邦国家的帮助下，贵族阶级解决了一些内部问题，例如，在塔尔奎尼亚和罗马的先后帮助下，阿雷奥（Areuo）的奴隶暴动得到了镇压。

与此同时，其他阴云开始笼罩伊特鲁里亚上空。公元前430年，坎帕尼亚的库迈城邦，即上个世纪最强大的伊特鲁里亚城邦落入了本土民族的手中，随后又被来自亚平宁的萨姆尼人（Samnites）所占领。在北部，在此前已经占领伦巴底广大疆域的凯尔特部落的压制下，伊特鲁里亚帕达纳终于投降；后来，凯尔特人又以帕达纳为突破口，发起了一系列威胁到罗马的侵袭活动（公元前391年）。据考古文献记载，到了公元前4世纪初，高卢人就已经出现在这一区域。小型伊特鲁里亚群落开始消失，而较大的群落则开始表现出凯尔特（Celtic）特征。

希腊化时期和罗马时期（公元前334年至公元前1世纪）

伊特鲁里亚贵族阶级的统治权开始慢慢丧失，在历史学家看来，伊特鲁里亚未能正确面对罗马势力的崛起，这标志了伊特鲁里亚走向衰败的开始。罗马对伊特鲁里亚社会进行扩张所带来的影响变得越来越明显。

公元前396年，维伊成为首个被罗马人控制的伊特鲁里亚城邦。此后的一段时期，伊特鲁里亚与罗马维持着相对平静的关系，部分原因在于，他们要共同面对来自北方高卢人的威胁——高卢人甚至在公元前387年临时计划占领罗马。但不久之后，罗马的侵略性政治又开始显露无疑。伊特鲁里亚城邦曾努力抵御罗马的进攻，但徒然无功。最初，伊特鲁里亚城邦意图单独与罗马抗衡（公元前358-351年，罗马-塔尔奎尼亚之战），后来甚至与翁布里亚人、萨姆尼人甚至高卢人联盟抗敌，也都未成功。

公元前283至282年，罗马人攻破了伊特鲁里亚人的最后防线，并逐渐控制了所有的伊特鲁里亚聚落。最后陷落的城邦是切尔韦泰里（公元前273年），此后，伊特鲁里亚城邦慢慢开始与罗马缔结联盟条约。这些条约规定了双方的特定义务：罗马负责为当地统治阶级提供支持，包括政治上和道德上的支援；而伊特鲁里亚城邦则需要对罗马保持忠诚，并为罗马的军事行动提供支援。例如，正如我们所知道的那样，伊特鲁里亚曾为小西庇阿（Scipio）远征迦太基时提供了装备和粮草。这些供应清单被李维（罗马历史学家）保留下来，并成为了了解公元前3世纪伊特鲁里亚各城邦经济状况的重要来源。据清单记载，切尔韦泰里提供谷物和各种粮食，塔尔奎尼亚提供制作船帆的亚麻布，阿雷佐供应武器、工具和谷物，佩鲁贾、丘西和罗塞尔提供谷物和造船用的木料，波普洛尼亚提供铁，沃尔泰拉则提供谷物和鱼。

伊特鲁里亚南部的战败使贵族地主们失去了不少土地，致使数个最重要的伊特鲁里亚群落的衰败，并造成了艺术生产的逐渐衰落。只有塔尔奎尼亚制作石棺的作坊逃脱了这一厄运，这个部门的高端艺术生产也得以存活。此外，经济的萧条使得中产阶级普遍陷入贫困，参与商贸活动或手工艺生产的中产阶级尤为如此。这些人不得不开始寻找其他谋生方式，而大多数情况下，他们成为了职业军人。早在公元前4世纪，迦太基军队里就出现了大量的伊特鲁里亚雇佣兵。

经济衰落对中产阶级造成冲击的进一步影响，便是许多伊特鲁里亚人开始移民到偏远地区以寻找更好的未来。例如，在突尼斯发现的伊特鲁里亚晚期墓碑（cippi），以及在萨格勒布发现的《亚麻书》均证明这波移民潮的存在。这本亚麻书是如何从意大利抵达埃及并成为木乃伊裹布的，我们至今仍然无法知晓。

伊特鲁里亚北方内地的境地迥然不同。这里的城邦普遍享受着安宁的幸福，在它们的领土上，制造业机构大量涌现，农业生产也十分繁荣。占主导地位的则是由拥有中小型产业的自由工人和半自由工人组成的阶级。这种生产活动允许更多的人口——一个新的社会阶层——接触到种类更丰富的艺术品和物质文化。于是，希腊化时期的艺术和手

伊特鲁里亚之地的托斯卡纳景色
General view of Tuscany landscape, the land of Etruscans

工艺生产表现出越来越明显的工业化特征，并促使了一种标准化手工作坊生产的形成：陶器、供奉用的红陶，甚至青铜都开始成批生产。最典型的大规模生产要数沃尔泰拉、丘西和佩鲁贾手工作坊制作的骨灰瓮，以及在塔尔奎尼亚和托斯卡纳仍有生产的石棺。

就陶器制作而言，我们可以看到陶器上描绘的主题开始变得极为贫乏。叙述性主题不再出现，取而代之的是单个传统的图案。最普遍的形象就是女性头部的侧面轮廓，和简单的几何图形和花卉装饰图案。公元前3世纪初期，描绘有人物形象的陶器逐渐消失，并在公元前2世纪被简单涂色的陶器取而代之。

伊特鲁里亚青铜生产也经历了同样的发展过程。铜镜上的肖像画变得越来越简单，雕刻技术也变得粗陋不堪。仅仅50年，伊特鲁里亚的艺术品就已经从公元前4世纪末期的精美绝伦沦落为公元前3世纪的贫乏粗陋，譬如拉撒和狄奥斯库里的铜镜。

这一时期留下来的大型公共纪念碑寥寥无几。值得一提的只有公元前2世纪后半期的大型神庙——如阿雷佐神庙、塔拉莫神庙和博尔塞纳神庙等建筑上的三角楣饰和黏土饰带。对这一时期神庙的黏土装饰的研究，更加证明了这一时期艺术生产活动的逐渐衰落——这也是这段时期艺术生产的标志性特征。对这段时期装饰艺术的研究表明，当红陶装饰需要更换时，工匠们通常不会进行独立创造，而是根据现有物品套模。这种二次模开始成为公元前2世纪的标准做法。烘焙会使黏土物品的尺寸变小，这是烘焙程序的自然效果，根据已有物品套模制作出来的物品自然会越来越小。

THE ETRUSCANS HISTORY AND SOCIETY
Giuseppina Carlotta Cianferoni

The Greek name for the Etruscans was *tyrrhenoi*. The romans called them *Tusci* or *Etrusci*. The Etruscans, it would seem, called themselves *Rasenna*.

Of all the inhabitants of ancient Italy, the Etruscans are the culture that has most stimulated the popular imagination and continued to promulgate an image redolent of fascination and mystery. But if we carefully examine this historical fascination and correlate its physical manifestation with other ancient societies, it becomes clear that we cannot continue to refer to "the mysterious Etruscans." The Etruscans are, after all, the best known culture of pre-Roman Italy.

The boundaries of Etruria proper are defined by two rivers, the Arno and the Tiber. It included a part of what is now Umbria, Tuscany, and the part of Latium north of Rome, where the right bank of the Tiber was considered Etruscan. The Etruscans also expanded into Campania in the south and into the Po River valley (Etruria Padana) to the north, and their monuments and other reflections of their art and culture can be encountered in both of these regions. But when we talk about Etruscan art, we have to be careful not to assign an ethnic definition to this term; it simply serves to indicate a certain artistic production that accompanies the formation of culture in the Italian peninsula from its first appearance in the ninth century until its dismantlement by the Romans in the first century B.C.E.

It is important to remember that the Etruscan city-states were quite independent and at the same so resistant to unified action that they were unable to organize themselves against a common enemy, Rome, which was thus able to conquer the Etruscan cities one by one.

The discoveries and research of the last few years has definitely demystified a culture that, through ardiaeological research in spite of the scarcity of Greek and Roman literary sources, turns out to be both rich and nuanced, allowing the Etruscans, once again, their historical place in the first millennium B.C.E. Archaeologists have long debated the origin of the Etruscans. In antiquity the prevailing opinion was that the Etruscans originally came from Asia. According to this theory, the Etruscans were the heirs of *Pelasgi* who reached the *Tyrrhenian* coast lead by Tyrrhenus, son of Athys, the king of Lydia. This population had been obliged to leave its homeland owing to a terrible famine.

This theory was prevalent into the modern era, but a second hypothesis was put forward at the beginning of the 19th century. This theory, which can be considered a kind of natural extension of the first one, deems the Etruscans the protagonists of an impressive migration from the north. According to this hypothesis, Etruscans would have come into Italy from the trans-Alpine region.

These two theories share the assumption that this populations origin results from migration. But a third theory that does not trace Etruscan origins from abroad suggests instead that Etruscans origins are to be found on Italian soil. This thesis of autochthonous origin is strongly supported by an ancient source, Dionysus of Halicarnassus.

Today, all these hypotheses are considered obsolete, thanks to the work of one of the greatest archaeologists of the 20th century, Massimo Pallottino, who pointed out that each of these theories have insurmountable limits. Indeed, in his opinion, Focusing on the origin of a population is the wrong premise. The issue is one of Formation, not of origin. The specific nature of any culture will always result from different elements. Thus, the only way to trace culture formation is through investigation of the various ethnic and cultural influences that, once assimilated, made its development possible.

As with origin, the Etruscan language has long been regarded as a mystery, but this is not at all true. The Etruscan language is not difficult to read because, with some adjustments, it uses the alphabet brought to Italy by the first Greek colonizers. To read it, we must take into account that, generally, the writing goes from right to left and, in the earliest texts, there is no separation among words. Only later, the partition of any phrase begins to be distinguished by means of dots, or, rarely, by spaces.

Unfortunately, problems arise when we try to interpret the Etruscan language. This is because, unlike Greek, Etruscan is a dead language that has not been spoken for 2,000 years. Moreover, documents at our disposal are Few and of poor quality. Indeed, in the overwhelming majority the extant inscriptions are short and repetitive, for they are nearly exclusively funerary in nature. These inscriptions usually provide only the name of the deceased, or the name of the object on which the inscription is found.

THE ORIGINS OF ETRUSCAN CIVILIZATION (NINTH — LATE EIGHTH CENTURY B.C.E.)

The beginnings of the Etruscan civilization go back to the ninth century B.C.E. coinciding with the earliest manifestations of Villanovan culture, named after Villanova, a town near Bologna that was the first site to produce finds characteristic of this period. The archaeological documentation for the Villanovan period comes almost exclusively from cemeteries. We have ample knowledge of how the "cities of the dead" were constructed, but we know very little about the dwellings of the living.

There are numerous reasons for this lack of information, but probably, the most important factor is the historical methodology of archaeological investigation. In the past, archaeologists focused primarily on the excavation of tombs and sanctuaries, thus privileging objects with certain historical and artistic value and neglecting settlements, a methodology that reflects little interest in aspects of daily life. Furthermore, many Etruscan centers continued to thrive into the Roman and Medieval periods; indeed many are still inhabited today. This is why the fragile structures of Etruscan settlements have been almost completely erased from memory.

Villanovan settlements were usually built on large, easily defended high areas that were located near rivers or springs, to provide easy access to water sources. These villages were made up of small autonomous groups of a limited number of huts that were oval or rectangular in shape.

From what remains of the ground plans, it seems as if the huts were distributed without any apparent order. That they were far apart, suggests that land used for agriculture or reserved for domestic animals was subdivided. Only the foundations remain. The huts can only be recognized by the

foundation cuttings and post holes, as well as by layers of habitation debris overlying more or less undisturbed soil.

Analysis of these fragmentary remains reveals a variety of floor plans. Round, oval, square and rectangular plans have been documented, seemingly with no chronological difference; all can be found at the same time, and the same variety is reflected in an assemblage of hut urns from the same period. These urns, funerary models that were in use from the tenth to the eighth century, constitute the most important documentation available for the reconstruction of Proto-historic habitations. The material used in the construction consisted of cane or branches covered with clay. The thatch roof was held up by a wooden framework in a form that resembles a tortoise shell.

As to the tombs, the prevailing funeral rite was cremation; the ashes and the bones, for the most part, were deposited in biconical-shaped clay urns covered with "bowl-lids" turned upside down or by a bronze or clay helmet. Sometimes the ash urns were shaped like huts in an attempt to symbolically represent the dwellings of the living. Objects that were with the deceased at the time of the cremation were placed inside the urns, while vessels containing household objects were placed beside the cinerary urn in small holes dug into the rock or covered with stones. The evolution of "Villanovan" culture during the two centuries of its development is marked by an event of vital importance that took place in the first half of the seventh century B.C.E.: the beginning of Greek colonization in Campania with the foundation of the Euboean center of Pithecusae (Ischia) and the Chalchidian colony of Cumae. As a result of contact with the Greek world, not only many foreign objects imported into Etruria, but also many artisans and merchants set up businesses, attracted by the outstanding economic potential of Etruscan cities that controlled rich mining areas such as the deposits in the Tolfa Mountains of Latium or the Colline Metallifere and the Tuscan island of Elba. Contact with another civilization accelerated the growth of technical knowledge, which affected agriculture and artisan production. New types and methods of cultivation, particularly the cultivation of grapes and olives, were introduced jointly with important technical innovations such as the potter's wheel. This led to a progressive transformation of the social structures of the Villanovan world and gave rise to a complex culture evidenced by numerous and thriving productive activities. The workshops, already skilled in working bronze and in ceramic production, rapidly took advantage of the contributions of the Greek world, wisely combining these with local forms and decorative repertoire. In this context, the structures of the city asserted themselves with ever more vigor, and concomitantly there must have been growth of private possession of land.

This transformation is well documented in Villanovan tombs, particularly in those of the most important centers of coastal Etruria. In the earliest phases of Villanovan society, the ninth century B.C.E., there is a uniform, "egalitarian" aspect to the household goods that are left with the dead, reflecting a society that was not substantially differentiated, but later on in the Villanovan period the more heterogeneous household goods that are found in tombs reflect the progressive organization of communities into distinct classes, among which a new class of rich aristocrats stands out as the chief protagonist of the splendid flowering of the Orientalizing period occurring in the following century. From earliest prehistory, leaders were represented as warriors. Even on the Tyrrhenian coast of west-central Italy, from the beginning of the early Iron Age, as documented by funerary inclusions, the role of the warrior was exalted. Prominent males were usually depicted as warriors and their grave goods feature both weapons and armor. Thus, the aristocratic classes that emerged in the eighth century were distinguished by their wealth and warrior ideology. The working of wool was a hallmark of women, much as weapons were the hallmark of masculine pursuits; if childbearing and educating were the destiny of women, then the spinning of wool is also an important signifier.

This difference between the ancient roles accorded to women and men is well attested to in the funerary assemblages where we find the remains of implements and tools that characterize duty in life. The most common elements in the tombs of females are the spindle whorls and spools indicating the activities of spinning and weaving; these are commonly found in Proto-historic graves. Often

there is more than one example, and occasionally even 50 or more examples. The spindle whorls are very diverse typologically, including globular, truncated conic, or biconical, faceted, and those with incised and impressed decorations. The spools, which comprise fewer types, are differentiated by concave or flat ends that are rarely decorated. Occasionally documented are loom weights in the shape of a truncated pyramid. The often large number of spindle whorls recovered in an assemblage has led to the suggestion that they are connected not only to the making of thread, but also to textile weaving. The distaff must have been associated with the spindle, but is found only in wealthy graves, and was made of bronze, bone or glass. In other graves, distalfs must have been made of wood, as with the spindles, since no trace of them remains.

PRINCE CULTUR
(LATE EIGHTH - FIRST QJARTER OF THE SIXTH CENTURY B.C.E.)

The orientalizing period, that is the period falling between the last decades of the eighth and the first quarter of the sixth century B.C.E., can be considered historically the most emblematic. This is when the Etruscans appear imperiously on the Mediterranean scene and assume a dominant position in the dynamic relations among Greece, the Italian Peninsula and various Eastern peoples. The most obvious and best known aspect of this phase is the widespread presence of luxury objects that are either imported from the Near East and Greece or produced locally following eastern prototypes. The objects include gold and silver articles, richly decorated silver and bronze vessels, objects sculpted in ivory, faience vases and beautiful figurative ceramics.

Contact with Greek colonies (eighth to seventh centuries B.C.E.) introduced to Italy the use of terracotta roof tiles for covering houses. These tiles can be documented to at least as early as the second half of the seventh century. With time, the crude foundations came to be replaced with stone, and walls were made of unfired brick and lattice work. The predominant type of structure was the long house, with rooms along the sides. During the course of the sixth century B.C.E., these rooms were typically oriented around a central area that was either coveted (an atrium) or open to the sky (a courtyard). The most important private houses and public buildings displayed roofs that were initially decorated with akroteria (ridge statues), figural antefixes and painted tiles. Later roofs were decorated with friezes depicting stories from the life of the owner of the house, such as scenes of banquets, hunting, family assemblies and military exploits.

In the first half of the eighth century, the indigenous peoples established relationships with the Greeks and Phoenicians. As a result, they began to adopt Greek and Phoenician decorative motifs and artistic techniques. Soon afterwards they began to embrace their culture as well. Writing, a new way of dining, and a heroic funerary ideology were all introduced into the indigenous society. In short, they began a new way of aristocratic living that deeply changed the character of their society.

The world described in the Homeric poems is structured around the rites of the dinner table. Highly symbolic foods, such as meat and wine, were reserved for special circumstances and consumed in certain rituals. Meat was eaten only occasionally by the general population. According to the literary sources (especially those relative to Archaic Greece), the gesture of consuming meat and the offering of a sacrifice were indistinguishable, and together they are identified as elementary forms of socialization. Dining occasions were not rare; rather they were a common occurrence regulated by a complex of calendar festivals.

In the historic period, the true banquet with the consumption of meat and drink was decidedly distinct from the symposium, which was generally accompanied by speeches and other social rituals. The symposium appears to us as a convivial entertainment centered upon the consumption of wine. Between the eighth and seventh centuries B.C.E., the custom of the symposium, an important moment for socialization and relationships, was considered the original expression of a type of aristocratic life connected to the emergence of a true and distinct aristocracy. This social class came to be recognizable, definable and distinguishable.

By the end of the eighth century a series of noteworthy

vases, cups (kant/mrai) or drinking cups, pitchers (oinoc/voai) for pouring, and containers (/eraters) for mixing wine and water document the widespread custom of drinking wine even at Funerary ceremonies in Etruria.

Wine and oil, which previously were imported from Greece but soon began to be produced locally, figure among the most valuable products; in Fact, in the sixth century B.C.E., special cultures of grapevines and olives were introduced in Etruria.

The evidence of tomb typology and grave goods suggests that from a socioeconomic and cultural point of view, the Etruscan world in this period was characterized by distinct divisions of social classes, determined by the birth of dominant family groups and based on a structure headed by an elite group that are referred to as "Princes." On one hand, the Princes based their power on land ownership, since they had the opportunity to exploit the resources of the soil primarily through agriculture but also pasturage, hunting and fishing. On the other hand, there was the privilege that gave them control of the primary communication routes and, as a result, of commercial exchanges with distant regions. A later source of wealth came from the exploitation of mineral resources; it is not by chance that the centers making the greatest progress were those that maintained close contact with important mining areas.

Tombs constitute our primary source of knowledge about the Etruscan elite of the Orientalizing period, and characteristic of this period are chamber tombs destined to accommodate many members of the same family. Initially these chamber tombs were individual, as had usually been the case in the Villanovan period, with the chamber in the form of a box made of smooth flat stones over which a burial mound was placed, sometimes delimited by a circle of stones. Beginning in the first half of the seventh century B.C.E., the dimensions of the chambers increase and, as a result, the burial mounds become ever more imposing; in the second half of the seventh century B.C.E., the burial mounds can exceed 10 meters. In the more monumental examples, a long dromos (entry corridor) leads to a large main chamber, with circular or quadrangular floor that is covered with a covered dome or vault.

In southern Etruria, where tufa and limestone which are easier to work are abundant, tombs are generally excavated out of the ground. In northern Etruria, however, monumental tombs are more commonly constructed in their entirety. The great burial mounds, situated in prominent positions and of large dimension, are imposing and a clear indicator of the importance of a i-amily's wealth. The interior structures are frequently architectural masterpieces with a variety of typologies and solutions that indicate not only the great ability of their builders but also the taste of a demanding and refined patronage.

At some northern Etruscan centers there is evidence of another variety of "princely" burial: the a circolo tomb, burials that can be either individual or collective, placed within circles of stones set vertically into the earth.

In any case, the assortment of goods placed in a tomb, often rich in luxurious objects of carved ivory or bone, amber, gold, silver and ceramics, constitutes a statement of the identity of the deceased.

Vessels, especially those used in symposia, reflect productive and recreational activity; weapons in iron and bronze indicate heroic ideals; some insignia, such as the scepter or the faxes lictariae, refer to civic power; others, such as the pyxis, the fhbellum (Fan) or the censer, refer to religious ceremonies.

Arms and armor assume more decorative characteristics. People from various communities are buried with high, crested helmets; large, circular embossed shields; short swords; and heavy spears with bronze points, intended for hand-to-hand combat. Later on in the seventh century, based primarily on the iconographic evidence, it would seem that Greek hoplite armature was known. By the end of the sixth century, some military weapons were being copied from the Greek hoplite type: Corinthian helmets, twohandled shields, greaves, short swords and at least three spears. The hoplite phalanges were marched to the sound of musical horns, like the one From the tomb of the chariots in Populonia, which dates to the second quarter of the seventh century B.C.E. and probably identifies the prince who was buried there as a military leader.

The funerary goods of some women might include a pair of horse bits and, by the end of the eighth century, even a chariot that might have been used for transportation during the Funeral; in this period it is likely these women had only two-horse chariots. The horse bits in the tombs of Females could imply a calash, while the bits in the men's tombs could indicate a war or hunting chariot. Undoubtedly, the chariots from the women's tombs were associated with individuals in the highest levels of society, perhaps the companions of the warrior-rulers.

Female clothing generally appears to be richer than men's and sumptuous parure: characterize some assemblages. A woman adorned with precious belongings was herself an asset to be exhibited as a status symbol of her Family group. The remaining female belongings assume a role essential for exchange with other aristocratic groups. These objects of exchange include worked precious metal and amber, and some types of charm bracelets or ornament for clothing. Marriage appears to have been an upper class instrument for creating alliances among communities or Families.

Perhaps the greatest sign of the wealth and splendor achieved by the Etruscan aristocracy of the Orientalizing period is represented by the magnificent pieces of gold work included in princely tombs. These are true works of metalworking art that bear witness to the high level of craftsmanship achieved by the Etruscan artisan, and in bronze as well: toreutics, an art at which the Etruscans were masters.

In fact, the working of metals is traditionally considered one of the greatest expressions of Etruscan art: the Attic poets of the fifth century B.C.E. spoke highly of the Tyrrhenian bronzes, and in Augustan Rome, the tyrrena sigilla still enriched the great local treasures.

A later sign of the social distinction of the Etruscan elite is that they demonstrated a knowledge of writing and used it as much to leave an enduring mark in the form of funerary inscriptions as to indicate the relevance of an object, sometimes to describe a donor or the giver of a religious offering, other times to indicate the recipient of a gift. And, not only did they take pride in writing but also in teaching it, as is indicated by the presence of an alphabet on vessels and other objects such as the Famous ivory writing tablet Found in the "Circolo degli Avori" of Marsiliana d'Albegna.

URBAN SOCIETY
(END OF THE SEVENTH — FOURTH CENTURY B.C.E.)

By the end of the seventh century the urban structure of the major Etruscan centers had been more or less defined: walls now enclosed the larger villages, within which were public buildings, temples and private dwellings. As was the case in Greece, the acropolis was intrinsic to the political life of the city; it was in a dominant, easily defended position and had a secure water supply; and, being a temple site, it was also afforded divine protection.

During the second half of the seventh century the quality of construction changed: rustic dwellings made of perishable materials such as wood, woven cane and vegetable fibers (used for roofing) were replaced by houses with elevated sections made of unbaked bricks, or those sturdily constructed with grid-like supporting structures made of wood and clay-coated cane, and gabled roofs covered with terracotta tiles. These houses were also characterized by open spaces surrounding a patio where much of the day was spent.

A greater distribution of wealth, which in the preceding period had been in the hands of a small number of aristocratic families, led to the formation of a middle class; involved mainly in commerce and the crafts, it soon began to have a notable influence on the economy and politics of Etruria. This social transformation is well represented by the evolution of the necropolis, which replaced the great funereal mounds of the princely class. Tombs now shared architectural characteristics derived from domestic construction and were reserved for entire families.

The urban age also saw the methodical mining of metals and a more systematic organization of commercial activity. Merchants from western Greece, principally from the cities of Samos, Miletos and Phocaea on the Asia Minor coast, dominated trade (albeit as intermediaries) from the end of the seventh century and throughout the sixth century B.C.E. They brought precious merchandise and also perishables such as perfume and cloth, amphorae for the transport of wine and oil, and domestic ceramics, the latter fabricated in Corinth and in eastern Greece until the middle of the sixth century, and in Athens until the first half of the following century. At the same time, master craftsmen from other regions continued the tradition of establishing themselves in Etruria, significantly impacting all sectors of craft production from ceramics to frescos and architectural terracottas.

Export commerce was primarily destined for the southern coast of France and consisted of wine, bronze vessels, exquisite earthenware pottery and Etruscan imitations of Corinthian ceramics. This merchandise also reached the shores of Corsica, Sardinia, Carthage and Greece's Sicilian colonies. Control of commercial traffic in the Tyrrhenian Sea was also consolidated thanks to a strong alliance with Carthage and an expansionist policy toward other populated regions of Italy; the Etruscan presence in northern Italy (Etruria Padana) was reinforced through colonization and to the south, according to contemporary literary sources, Rome was attacked by Porsenna, the king of Chiusi. The outcome of this confrontation has remained unclear, but it is probable that the city was held by the Etruscans for an indeterminate period of time; in this context, it is important to remember that Roman kings Tarquinius Priscus, Servius Tullius and Tarquinius Superbus were of Etruscan origin.

At the beginning of the fifth century B.C.E., Etruria was still an expansionist state, but by century's end it had declined notably. In the latter part of the sixth century, the Etruscans had been at the gates of Rome, but in a little more than a hundred years (396 B.C.E.), Rome conquered the Etruscan city of Veii and began its victorious march through central Italy. One of the causes of Etruria's decline was, without a doubt, the loss of control of the Tyrrhenian trade routes due to the rise of Carthage and subsequently Syracuse. The battle of Cumae (474 B.C.E.) between the Etruscan fleet and that of Syracuse's allies. The Cumaeans, proved to be the deciding factor; and with the latter's victory, the Etruscans ceased to be intermediaries in Tyrrhenian commerce and had their naval power significantly weakened. The defeat resulted in the closure of Etruria's Tyrrhenian ports; Greek commerce, dominated by Athens, reoriented itself toward the rich markets of the Adriatic, in particular the port of Spina, situated at the mouth of the river Po.

The loss of supremacy in the Tyrrhenian Sea adversely affected the southern coastal Etruscan cities dependent on maritime commerce, but others whose products were destined for different regions, or whose economy was agriculturally based, suffered less severe consequences. Nevertheless, there were special cases such as that of Populonia, which, toward the end of the sixth century, developed an extensive metallurgical industry that attracted the attention of the Greeks, as did the mines of Elba.

The plight of the cities also had an impact on middle-class Etruscans involved in activities such as commerce and artisan production, and their social position gradually began to erode. Power reverted completely to the aristocracy, which resolved certain internal problems with the help of Etruria's neighbors: slave revolts in Areuo were suppressed, first with aid of Tarquinia and later of Rome.

Meanwhile, other clouds had appeared on the horizon. In Campania, the city of Capua, one of the powerful Etruscan centers of the previous century, fell into the hands of the local population and then to the *Samnites*, who descended from the Apennines in 430 B.C.E. In the north, pressure from the *Celtic* tribes that had previously occupied substantial areas of Lombardy finally forced Etruria Padana into submission; it would subsequently serve as a launching area for a series of invasions that eventually (391 B.C.E.) threatened Rome. Archaeological documentation tells us that by the beginning of the fourth century Gauls were already present in the region; lesser Etruscan population centers disappeared and larger ones began to display Celtic characteristics.

HELLENISM AND ROMANIZATION
(334 B.C.E. —FIRST CENTURY B.C.E.)

The hegemony of Etruscan aristocracy came to a slow and inexorable end. Historians recognize its starting point in the failure of Etruria to face the rising power of Rome. The striking effects of Roman expansion on the Etruscan world became more and more readily apparent.

Veii was the first Etruscan city to fall into Roman hands in 396 B.C.E. The period after the conquest was one of relatively calm relations between Etruscans and Romans, in part because of a common threat from the north, the Gauls, who even managed to occupy Rome, albeit temporarily, in 387 B.C.E. Shortly thereafter, Rome's aggressive politics began to be felt again. Etruscan cities tried in vain to resist the Roman advance, at first facing the Romans alone (in the Rome-Tarquinia war of 358-351 B.C.E.) and later allying with Umbrians, Samnites and even Gauls, but Rome prevailed both times.

Between 283 B.C.E. and 282 B.C.E. the Romans broke the Etruscans' last resistance, gradually subjugating all their settlements. The last to fall was Caere (Cerveteri) in 273 B.C.E., after whose submission Etruscan cities slowly established treaties of alliance with Rome. These treaties contained specific obligations for both parties: the Romans were to provide support, as well as political and moral solidarity for the local ruling elite, while Etruscan cities were required to remain loyal to Rome and support Roman military initiatives. We know, for example, that the Etruscans contributed equipment and provisions to Scipio's expedition against Carthage. The list is preserved by Livy and is an exceptional resource for understanding the economy of the Etruscan cities in the third century B.C.E. Caere provided cereals and victuals of all kinds; Tarquinia, linen cloth for the sails; Arezzo, weapons, working tools and cereals; Perugia, Chiusi and Roselle supplied cereals and wood for shipbuilding; Populonia, iron; and Volterra, grain and fish.

The conquest of southern Etruria deprived the landed aristocracy of much of its land, led to a rapid decline of the most important centers, and produced a progressive deterioration of artistic production. It was only in Tarquinia, in the workshops where sarcophagi were manufactured, that elite artistic production survived. Furthermore, the economic slump that followed impoverished the middle classes in general and, above all, those who were involved with trade or were part of the artisan class. These people were then obliged to find different means of subsistence, and, in most cases, they became professional soldiers. Already in the fourth century B.C.E., we find the massive presence of Etruscan mercenaries in the ranks of the Carthaginian army.

As further consequence of the slump that hit the Etruscan middle class, immigration led many Etruscans to settle in distant lands to find a better future. Evidence for this immigration includes, for example, the late Etruscan *cippi* discovered in Tunisia as well as the so-called Liber Linteu: from Zagreb. We still do not know how this linen book made its way from Italy to Egypt, where it was used as a mummy wrapping.

The situation of the northern Etruscan hinterland was inherently different. Here cities enjoyed a general well-being and their territories teemed with manufacturing establishments and settlements where agriculture production attained great intensity. The protagonists were the class of free or semi-free workers who owned small or medium-sized properties. This production allowed a larger population—a new social stratum—access to a broader range of artistic goods and material culture. Thus, artistic and craft production of the Hellenistic period tends to assume an increasingly industrial character, leading to a kind of standardization of workshop production: ceramics, votive terracottas, and even bronzes are now produced serially. Typical of this mass production are the cinerary urns produced in the workshops of Volterra, Chiusi and Perugia and the sarcophagi that continued to be produced at Tarquinia and Tuscania.

As far as pottery is concerned, we can see a drastic impoverishment of the subjects depicted on it.

Narrative compositions areno longer present, and their place was taken by single conventional figures. The most common images were those of profile female heads and simple geometric and floral decorations. At the beginning of the third century B.C.E., figural pottery gradually disappeared and simply painted ceramics took its place in the second century.

Etruscan bronze production underwent a similar development. The iconography of mirrors became simpler while the technical quality of the engraving became very shoddy. In the span of 50 years, Etruscan art passed from the wonderful objects of the end of the fourth century to impoverished third-century works such as the Lasa and Dioscuri mirrors.

Very little remains of the great public monuments of this period. We can cite only the pediments and clay friezes of large temples such as those at Arezzo, Talamone and Bolsena, which date to the second half of the second century B.C.E. The study of fictile decoration from temples of this period has provided more evidence for the progressive decline that marks the artistic production of this period. Careful study of the decorations reveals that when terracottas needed to be replaced, they were not made from scratch, but rather, artisans would take molds from existing objects. Such secondary molds became the norm in the second century. Owing to the natural effect of the firing process, which reduces the size of a clay object, molds that are repeatedly taken from the finished product rather than made from scratch will produce progressively smaller objects.

日常生活与宗教仪式

佛罗伦萨国家考古博物馆　朱塞平娜·卡洛塔·钱菲诺尼博士
伊特鲁里亚文明考古学家　罗萨尔巴·赛特索尔蒂

男性的世界:武器

在远古时期，盔甲在社会群体中扮演着重要角色，但到后来，盔甲开始为军事领袖特有，甚至成为了逝者所从事职业的象征。维兰诺万式的盔甲包括：圆顶或带顶饰的青铜头盔（殉葬品中黏土制作的头盔则是用作藏尸罐的盖子）、覆盖有青铜片的皮革盾牌、用来保护心脏部位的方形铜片（护心镜），矛头、斧、剑，均旨在提升逝者的尊贵地位。珍贵的武器则强调了逝者的崇高地位。这类武器通常参与了某一场富有英雄气概的搏斗或"肉搏战"——原因不同于有组织的武装团伙间的混战。

公元前7世纪中期，受到希腊军事战略的影响，新的军事技术被引进伊特鲁里亚。他们发明了重装方阵战术和骑兵使用的武器盔甲，例如带护鼻、护面甲和皮革衬垫（这一点可根据沿头盔边缘所打的无数小孔推测）的柯林斯式青铜头盔，以及装饰有精美的浮雕箔片的大圆盾和保护胫骨和小腿的护胫甲。人们曾在东方化时期的伊特鲁里亚领主墓葬中出土过整套盔甲装备，其中最值得一提的，就是波普洛尼亚的Flabelli墓葬中出土的全套盔甲几乎是最精美的，也是保持较完好的。

这些几乎都是致命武器，包括长矛、剑、斧、标枪，以及一些作为青铜武器的替代品的铁制武器——毫无疑问，青铜兵器的攻击力和抵抗力要更强。有些剑还保留有汽化的痕迹，这是在多碳的环境中加热造成的，是为了加强武器的强度。

类似内加（Negau）式的锥形头盔于公元前6世纪中期登上历史舞台。这种头盔可以让脸部自由转动，且通常装饰得比较精美。后来锥形头盔被圆顶头盔取而代之，这种头盔有一个位于中央的纽扣、护颈、光滑的护面甲或"三个饰钉"，此外还装有符合人体形状的肩带以将头盔固定。

这类武器均带有明显的表明士兵特定社会等级的标志，从头盔内部铭刻的文字可看出这点。这类铭文包括多种文字，除伊特鲁里亚语之外，还包括拉丁语、凯尔特语等。据东正教相关规定，"贵族"或军事首领，可在战场上或阅兵时乘坐一辆双轮马车。这些做法都是为了向同僚和下级强调其社会地位。从东方化时期的领主坟墓中，我们已经获得了有关这类交通工具的丰富资料，还包括马匹遗骸上精美繁复的马饰，这些马饰通常与二轮马车放在一起。马饰主要包括马勒上的纹章，或精美的铁质或铜质马衔，类似

切尔韦泰里（南伊特鲁里亚，今拉齐奥）老城的伊特鲁里亚墓葬：表现了圆形大盾牌的浮雕细节。男性墓室墙壁上常常雕塑或绘制各类武器。
Etruscan tomb from the old city of Cerveteri (Southern Etruria, now Lazio): detail of the bas-relief representing large round war shields. Very often male chamber tombs were decorated with various kind of weapons reproduced on the walls in the form of sculptures or painted decorations.

维图罗尼亚的波基奥·艾拉·盖迪亚（Poggio alla Guardia)大公B式环形墓出土的马饰。

双轮马车通常由一个配有小车轮的黄铜车厢组成，最古老的马车由木头制作，配有各种青铜装饰，包括各种类型繁多的马蹄铁。双轮马车只可容纳一到两人，车辆较轻，所以速度较快，适合做中短途旅行，可由两匹或者三匹战马驱使——这是伊特鲁里亚当时的惯例。

女性的世界

伊特鲁里亚上层社会妇女的地位较高，在家庭和社会中享有与男性平等的权利。因为享有这一特权，妇女也必须成为积极的社交人士，并通常和丈夫一起参与贵族阶层组织的各种活动，包括宴会、交际酒会、婚礼和舞会表演。这一习俗使伊特鲁里亚妇女饱受各种恶毒且令人沮丧的攻击，这些攻击贯穿了整个古代文学，尤其是希腊文学——这段时期恰逢两国为争夺西地中海交通控制权而成为商业对手。其中最恶毒的一次攻击来自公元前4世纪的作家特奥波姆泊（Teopompo），他写道："她们不挨着自己的丈夫坐着，反而紧贴着第一位来宾；谁想健健康康，她们就举杯祝谁健康"，哲学家亚里斯多德也说过——可能是过于受特奥波姆泊的影响，"第勒尼安人和妇女们同桌宴饮，还和她们裹着同一件斗篷睡在一起。"亚里斯多德是暗示她们可以向在场的任何一个男人献身。希腊社会的妇女境地就截然不同，事实上，阿提卡陶器装饰图案上以客人或表演者身份出现的女性形象都不是合法妻子，而是奴隶出身，甚至是妓女。特奥波姆泊还这样描述伊特鲁里亚妇女："她们酒量很好，而且非常漂亮。"事实上，因为伊特鲁里亚妇女出席公众场合的机会数不胜数，所以她们日常生活中的大部分时间都花在了美容和保养上面。她们穿着贵重的服饰，最初是羊毛服饰，丰富的考古记录证明了这一点。据考古资料记载，在远古时期，妇女们穿着厚重的羊毛长袍，通常还在背部罩上斗篷。后来，公元前6世纪出现了一种轻便得多的新服饰。这是一种亚麻制作的宽大、多褶，长及脚部的短袖外衣。这种长袍曾经风靡了很长一段时期且没有经历较大变化，它着重凸显了女性优雅的体型，尽管依照伊特鲁里亚风俗仍需在肩膀披上或围上一件斗篷，并在胸前或头部两侧垂下两块，但仍不影响这种修饰体型的效果。这一时期，伊特鲁里亚普遍穿着一种鞋头高高翘起的尖头鞋"卡尔凯·莱旁迪"（*calceirepandi*，鞋尖翻卷上来的意思），不过很快这种鞋就被一种有交叉绑带的鞋所代替。

伊特鲁里亚的服饰和发型各种各样，塔尔奎尼亚母狮之墓中的壁画又一次证明了这点。壁画中一位装扮华丽的舞者穿着短袖外衣，披着镶蓝边的宽大红斗篷，头顶一种叫做"托托鲁斯"（*tutulus*）的圆锥形帽子，大大的耳环与透明的短袖外衣相映成趣。画面上还有另外一位舞者。这位舞者赤裸着身子，棕色的长发打着卷儿披在前额和肩膀上。

发型也随着时尚品味的变化而变换。整个东方化时期，妇女们都将头发从额前分为两股，编成两根粗粗的发辫，然后在脑后并作一根发辫，正如壁画中所示。后来，不论男女普遍都将头发随意披散在肩头，或使用发夹或丝带将头发束在脑后。但随着颇具女神气质的希腊式风格的出现，这一习惯又得到改变。女人们开始将精美繁复的头纱顶在头上。两只红绘式陶器再现了这种发型，一只是来自托库的奥伊洛克壶（oinochoai）上红绘伊特鲁里亚人物形象，另一只是波普罗尼亚的坎达罗斯杯（kantharos）上的多个优雅的红绘人物形象。

华贵的服饰还需要补充搭配各种贵金属制作的精美首饰，这些首饰包括发针、各种造型和尺寸的扣环、镶有宝石的光彩夺目的指环，形状大小各异的配有别致挂件的项链、管状耳环，和通常饰有带骨头、象牙和琥珀托座的宝石手镯。造粒技术（将镀金的小圆球焊接在首饰表面，组成各种繁复的装饰主题）和水印制作技术（公元前8世纪由被带入伊特鲁里亚的东方匠师们从别处借鉴而来）的运用的确打造了不少真正的艺术杰作。

我们现在可以了解伊特鲁里亚社会的新趋势和时尚品味了，尤其是女性的服饰和时尚。被罗马击败之前，石棺上装饰的宴会场景均间接展示了数不胜数的女性形象。沃尔泰拉的骨灰瓮和瓮盖上的图案也描绘了死者穿着华丽的服饰，披挂着各种首饰的样子。这些场景均炫耀了逝者及其家族成员的财富。沃尔泰拉出土的一只骨灰瓮的瓮盖上则描绘了一位斜倚着身子的女性形象。这个骨灰瓮是在公元前2世纪末放入的。

伊特鲁里亚的贵妇们可享受十分完善的美容和保养：包括身体的护理、个人的清洁和化妆美容等。文献记载的美容用品包括一些饰有精美图案的象牙梳，如马尔斯里拉（Marsiliana）一个领主墓葬中出土的象牙梳，还有亮闪闪的配有骨面把手的铜镜。这些物品在公元前6世纪下半叶的伊特鲁里亚十分风行，有些是用作梳妆打扮的工具，另一些则饰有具艺术价值的浮雕画——这使它们显得比较复杂精美，正如本次展出的某些展品所示。

这些物品中还包括一些小瓶子。这些形状大小各异的小罐是用来盛放涂在皮肤上的香水或香膏的。这些小瓶可分为多种类型：包括圆瓶（盛放香精的瓶子）和细长瓶（alabaster），均塑造成动物或人物形象，通常饰有精美的雕刻图案或绘画图案。在东方化时期，这些物品主要由陶器制作，但也存在大量雪花石膏小瓶。这些小瓶，还包

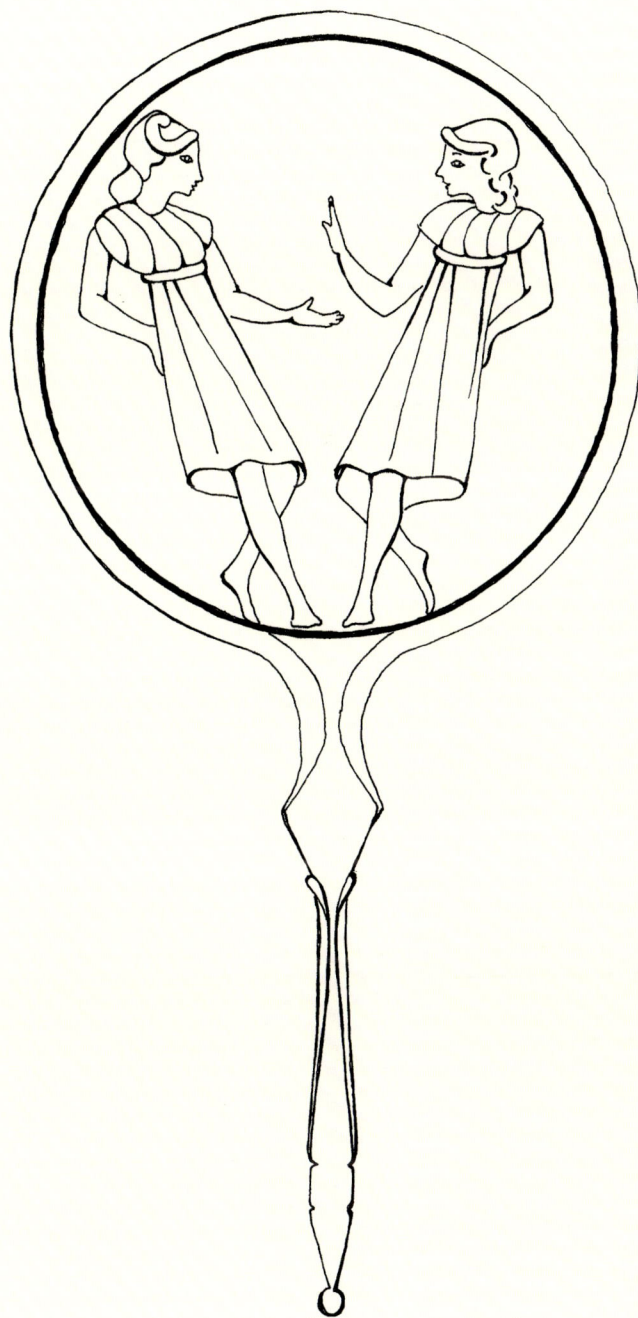

伊特鲁里亚铜镜图案（背面）
Relief of an Etrurian mirror (back)

括一些首饰、高脚玻璃杯，和用来盛放各种身体护理品的首饰盒等等，成为女性墓葬殉葬品的一大特征。本展展出的最古老的一些香水瓶是伊特鲁里亚人依照科林斯样式制造的。随着时间的流逝，香水瓶的形状也有所变化，新的式样开始出现。不过，这类小尺寸香水瓶仍然一直存在。

出席公众场合和享受自由并不能使伊特鲁里亚的贵妇摆脱所有女性的社会职责，譬如养儿育女和管理家庭事务。她们还需要负责纺纱和织布。荷马史诗曾经描绘过这样的妇女形象。例如，根据诗歌的描述，有侍女服侍的潘尼洛普（Penelope）就需要从事同样的活动。纺纱工和织布工在年龄和社会地位上有着显著区别。纺纱工是送葬队伍中的重点，负责织品（frame）的制作——这也是整个制作过程的收尾阶段，也是最复杂、最富创造力的阶段，因此纺纱工人地位仅次于上层社会的妇女，或家里的女主人。

宴会和社交酒会

"他们每天摆两次奢华的酒席，他们铺上刺绣着花朵图案的桌布，他们使用各种形状的银质酒杯，还有许多奴隶服侍。"古代历史学家如是描述伊特鲁里亚奢华无度的宴饮习惯，言语之中不无谴责之意，这时的伊特鲁里亚已经是罗马帝国的一部分。这类人生来就是为了寻欢作乐，享受奢华无度的生活。史料中透露的敌意，一定程度上来自经济上的敌对状态——这是因为争夺西地中海贸易路线控制权而造成的。伊特鲁里亚文化中传达出来的贵族形象，都是对夸耀财富的无节制的沉迷，以及贵族统治的必要性。

人们聚在一起饮酒的宴会和社交酒会都被列为上层社会最重要的体现：是贵族集团聚集起来加强相互联系、交换贵重礼物、分享欢聚时光或自我庆贺的场合。同时，宴会也被视为死后灵魂生活的预示，逝者生前在宴会中使用的所有物品和家具都将陪伴他进入坟墓，从而象征性地将生与死联系起来。古时候的伊特鲁里亚人是坐着进餐的，沃尔泰拉境内的蒙特斯库达伊奥（公元前7世纪上半叶）曾出土了一只著名的骨灰瓮，瓮盖上就描绘了类似的场景。画面中的主角是一位坐在高背宝座上的男子，男子前面摆放着一张三脚桌。桌上摆放着一堆蛋糕，以及各种类型的托盘。男子旁边坐着一位妇女，原本这位妇女应当手持一把扇子、一只大酒杯和一个迪诺斯瓶（dinos），但目前仅存的只有酒杯了。

自公元前7世纪末开始留下的数不胜数的图像学证据表明伊特鲁里亚人在进餐时，或者单独一人或者成双成对地躺在床上，一只手肘靠着枕头，身上则裹着毯子，根据借来的关于伊特鲁利亚环境的模型，这一习惯延续了几个世纪，希腊化时期的骨灰瓮的瓮盖展示了这一点，上面描绘了无数斜躺着身子的男性和女性形象。

在他们面前盛满食物的小圆桌或小矩形桌下面，通常蹲着一只猫或狗，随时准备享用任何抛到地上的残羹剩饭。

有关富裕阶层所拥有的权力，我们已经掌握相当多的信息，这些信息主要来源自辉煌壮丽的墓葬绘画，包括伊特鲁里亚南部雄伟的贵族坟墓中刻在石头上的壁画，一些文学作品也记叙了相关信息。最近，人们对伊特鲁里亚出土的一些遗骸上——甚至包括一些不太富裕的阶层的遗骸——的牙齿进行科学研究，确定了伊特鲁里亚人的饮食习惯。

伊特鲁里亚宴会（壁画）
Etrurian banquet (fresco)

大大小小的罐子可用来烹煮食物，而整套的青铜罐和红陶罐则是款待客人时使用的，且各种不同的罐子有着不同的用途。厨房里会用到火盆，依照伊特鲁里亚传统，人们会模仿金属火盆制作一些沉重的布凯罗黑陶火盆，并将同样材质的小壶、盘、勺、碟、杯以及许多其他工具一起作为殉葬品陪葬，正如本展中的此类物品所示；人们还会用到沉重的金属壁炉——这类壁炉和我们今天使用的壁炉类似，他们将壁炉竖起来以安放木头或长长的铁质肉叉，这样可用来烤肉。

伊特鲁里亚人尤为注重烹饪及其准备工作，这些活动主要由男性负责，因为和荷马时代的英雄人物一样，伊特鲁里亚男性与动物献祭紧密相连。屠宰动物时，要使用各种形状和长度不同的刀具和一口大锅，这种大锅传统上是用来盛放和搅拌烹饪时所需液体的。人们将肉在沸水中煮散，然后用一只带有长叉的工具将肉块叉出，再放到大锅烹煮。

奥维多（Orvieto）戈利尼一世（Golini I）坟墓中的壁画（G·加提临摹了这幅壁画，所以这一场景现在得以保存下来，目前这幅画保存在佛罗伦萨国家考古博物馆里）栩栩如生地描绘了公元前4世纪中期伊特鲁里亚人准备一场盛宴的场景。这幅画以地狱为背景，冥神哈德斯和冥后珀尔塞福涅均在场。画中，被屠宰的动物悬挂在钩子上（包括一整头牛，一只鹿、一只兔子和几只鸟），桌子后面的仆人们正忙着将盛满小圆面包、鸡蛋、石榴和葡萄的盘子端给客人，一个碾谷的巨臼安放在一个三脚架上，画面中还有一只煮着食物的烤箱：所有这些活动——根据文学作品的记载，都是在笛子吹奏出的音乐的伴随下进行，而且音乐的节奏也标志了烹饪工作所处的不同阶段。

贵族以外的其他阶层则消耗大量的小麦和豆类，而不是肉。最近几十年以来，植物学家对伊特鲁里亚人的遗骸进行的研究也证明了这一点。根据拉丁学者朱文诺（Juvenal）的记载，小麦粥是此群体喜爱的食物，罗马饥荒或战争时曾向伊特鲁里亚购买当地盛产的软质小麦。他们很少吃肉，所吃的肉类也仅限于羊肉、猪肉和鸟肉。牛则被视为珍贵的动物，主要用于农业耕种。社交酒会时要举行一场复杂的仪式，这要用到大量容器，每一种容器具有不同功能，东方化时期的领主墓葬中的各种陶器证明了这一点。整个公元前6世纪伊特鲁里亚人都饮用葡萄酒，葡萄酒最初是从外国进口的，后来当地也开始生产。最初，由于葡萄酒是一种珍贵的异域饮料，所以只有有地位的人才能享用。事实上，尽管葡萄酒仍然主要为上层阶级所饮用，但其他社会阶层也形成了饮用葡萄酒的习惯。因为葡萄酒度数很高，所以人们并不直接饮用纯葡萄酒。依照从希腊社会借鉴来的做法，葡萄酒必须兑水稀释，冬天则兑着雪水饮用。稀释的比例则由主持社交酒会的人确定。调酒工作在双耳喷口罐中进行，这是一种有着两只弧形把手的大型器皿。炊具、滤网和过滤器则用来将饮料从喷口罐中舀出，并将其中的杂质滤出。与今天我们饮用的葡萄酒非常不同，古代的葡萄酒要添加蜂蜜以增加甜味，并使用香料、水果甚至玫瑰花瓣调味。现在看来，伊特鲁里亚生产的种类繁多的葡萄酒，以及鲁尼生产的葡萄酒均被古人认为是最好的葡萄酒。而维奥的葡萄酒呈红色，则是出了名的口感差。

在某些场合，搓碎的奶酪也和蜂蜜、大麦一起，添加进味道已经很浓郁的葡萄酒中。殉葬品中出现的无数磨碎机揭示了这一点：这种饮品称为凯可因（kykeion），源于荷马时代，但口感并不怎么好。最后，经过冷却后，由奴隶们将调好的葡萄酒用各种不同规格的酒壶（奥伊洛克壶和欧铂瓶）倒入客人的杯子，这是一件需要相当技巧的工作。

各年代将上述两种宴会服务称为"使来自世界各地的材料聚集一堂"。在远古时代（公元前6世纪上半叶至公元前5世纪后期），珍贵的伊特鲁里亚酒杯（如本展所示，包括一只欧铂瓶、一只酒杯和一个盘子）是模仿了柯林斯陶器华丽的式样和装饰图案，而具有闪亮黑色表面的布凯罗陶器——一种典型的伊特鲁里亚陶器，则是模仿贵重金属器皿的风格。

几只优雅的倒酒的容器（陶酒坛）、一只小勺、一只酒杯、一只彩绘长柄碗、两只杯子，还有一只坎达罗斯双耳酒瓶，都是为了向酒神狄俄尼索斯（伊特鲁里亚神话中

塔拉莫纳奇奥神庙的考古区域
Talamonaccio Archaeological area
by the temple of Talamonaccio

的弗福伦斯，根据神话传说，这位神灵赐予了人类葡萄藤和葡萄酒）和制定了社交酒会规则的斯姆波斯阿卡表示敬意。与希腊化时期的餐具不同，这些餐具包括大量的黑彩酒杯。自公元前4世纪末期开始，人们开始模仿最贵重的金属制作的餐具制作这类黑陶，和这类金属器皿一样，这种黑陶表面也呈现出微妙的光泽。此外还包括许多尺寸各异的陶盘，有些陶盘盘面装饰着繁复精美的图案。还有些杯子、欧铂瓶、倒酒的陶酒坛、一只碟、一只饮酒用的双耳大饮杯，以及两只拉格罗伊壶（lagynoi）。还有一只优雅的双耳喷口罐，喷口罐的两只把手塑造成蛇的形状，这是沃尔泰拉一家著名的工坊生产的。社交酒会上用来打酒和滤酒的工具，辛普拉勺（simpula）和可拉漏斗（cola），都与青铜制作的此类工具十分相似。

宴会和社交酒会上的娱乐活动包括音乐和舞蹈，我们所掌握的丰富的考古文献证明了这一点。文献中记载了竖琴和"欧罗斯（aulos）"的演奏者，欧罗斯是一种类似长笛的乐器，可由多种材料制作，包括木头、骨头或象牙，亦可做成双筒。塔尔奎尼亚的墓室壁画用鲜亮、欢快的色调描绘了人们在宴会上欢歌笑语的场景，特里克林欧（Triclinio）、吉欧克里瑞（Giocolieri）和雷欧帕蒂（Leopardi）的墓室也绘有这种场景。即使在古代记载中，这种在音乐的伴奏下展开当日活动的习俗也被认为是伊特鲁里亚生活中最时髦的部分。事实上，亚里士多德曾经说过欧罗斯的伴奏十分广泛（其他作家也多次引用），这种乐器常用来为拳击、笞打伴奏，甚至如上文所述，和奥维多戈利尼一世陵寝中的壁画所示，为烹饪活动伴奏。

伊特鲁里亚的宗教活动

伊特鲁里亚人对宗教的虔诚在古代世界是广为人知的。拉丁作家塞内卡（Seneca）曾试图解释这种现象，他写道："这就是伊特鲁里亚人和我们的区别……我们认为闪电是云层撞击引起的结果，而他们却认为制造闪电是云层撞击的原因。因为他们认为任何事情都是神的旨意，他们不相信事物发生之后才会产生意义，反而认为事物的发生是为了传达某种意义。"

对于伊特鲁里亚人的同时代人——尤其是罗马人而言，他们不仅是一个十分尊重神圣预兆的民族，而且还尤其精通对这类预兆的解读，这主要得益于他们精深的占卜技术。因此，伊特鲁里亚的牧师（aurispici）十分受人敬重，甚至连罗马人在遇到疑难问题时也会向伊特鲁里亚牧师请教。最普遍的占卜活动包括对闪电和鸟类飞行的解读，以及对献祭动物内脏的观察。的确，这种对宗教仪式和宗教技术性习俗的重视似乎是伊特鲁里亚人神圣意识的重要特征，而且我们已经知道——和往常一样，这些信息来自拉丁资料，因为伊特鲁里亚文献已经不幸全部丢失——《圣书》里规定了宗教行为的标准，而且该书记载了伊特鲁里亚人所有的宗教规则。

例如《祭司书》记载了观察献祭动物内脏的所有必要做法。肝脏是这类观测活动中用到的最主要的器官。数不胜数的考古遗迹，包括装饰精美的铜镜和饰有雕刻图案的骨灰瓮，都描绘了伊特鲁里亚牧师手持动物肝脏的画面，一些陶器和青铜器雕塑也表现了这一情景。这些物品中最著名的一件就是"皮亚琴察的肝脏"，该作品得名于出土的城市皮亚琴察，这是一件绵羊肝脏的青铜雕塑，表面被分割为40份，每一份上都雕刻有主宰它的神灵的名字。

星象观测是伊特鲁里亚占卜习俗中另外一个重要分支：《闪电书》记载了对闪电的解读，并认为闪电是神灵意志的最高表现。

伊特鲁里亚宗教为多神教。事实证明，对伊特鲁里亚神灵名称的语言学分析对确定它们的起源十分有用。一些神的名字很明显是从希神名称演变而来的，例如阿普罗（Aplu），阿耳特美斯（Artumes），埃塔（Aita），珀西派尼（Phersipnai）和赫克勒斯（Hercles）分别从希神名阿波罗、阿耳忒弥斯、哈德斯、珀尔塞福涅和赫拉克勒斯演变而来），此外，还有一些来自印欧神话的名称，包括尤尼（Uni），梅涅瓦（Menerva），塞凡那斯（Selvans），尼顿斯（Nethuns）和撒特（Satre）（分别从朱诺、密涅瓦、西凡那斯、尼普顿和萨杜恩演变而来）。还有一些名字则更像是来自本土语，例如提尼阿（Tinia），图兰（Turan），图美思(Turms)和拉兰（Laran）。

人们很容易发现一些本土神灵与希腊神灵之间的对应关系，正如图像材料所示，每一位神灵都可以找到可识别的希腊神话背景。根据这些证据可推断提尼阿与宙斯、图兰与阿芙罗狄蒂、图美思与赫耳墨斯，以及拉兰与阿瑞斯的部分对应关系。

提尼阿、尤尼和梅涅瓦是最重要的神灵，通常供奉在同一座寺庙。提尼阿为至高无上之神和万神之神，等同于希腊神话中的宙斯和罗马神话中的朱庇特。他是宇宙的统治者，是主宰命运之神，他的象征是闪电。

尤尼是最重要的女神，提尼阿之妻，等同于希神赫拉和罗神朱诺。她主司生育，是

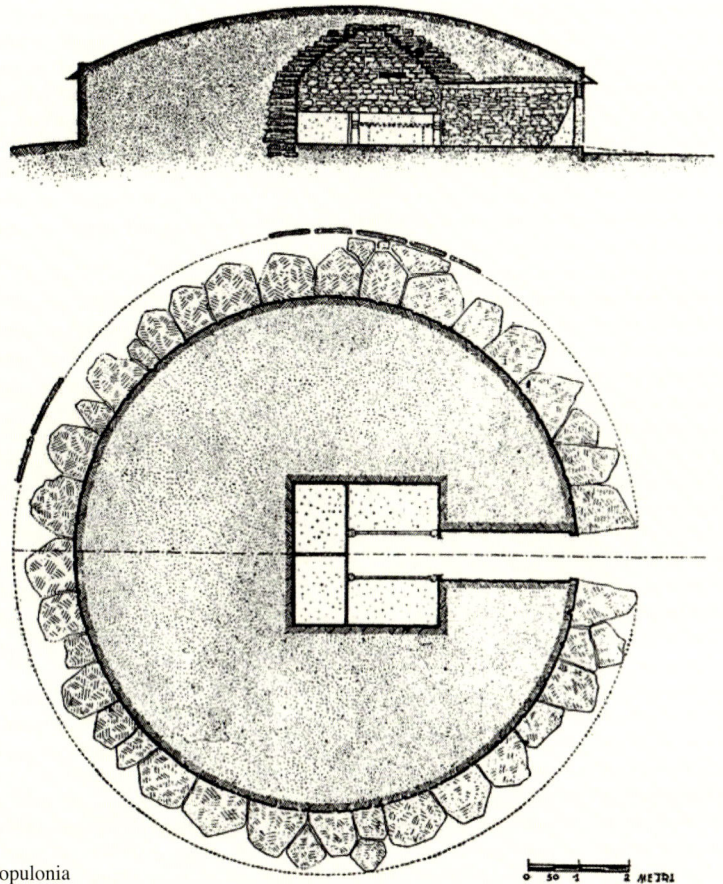

波普洛尼亚的弗拉贝里墓葬图
Drawing of the Flabelli tomb at Populonia

城邦的保护者。梅涅瓦对应希腊神话雅典娜和罗神密涅瓦。她以全副武装的形象出现在希腊神话般的场景中，她的主要象征是头盔、长矛和猫头鹰。祭坛里经常供奉由献给她的人体部位造型的祭品，供奉这些物品可能具有治疗功效。

其他重要的神灵还有主管战争的拉兰（即希腊神话中的战神阿瑞斯和罗马神话中的玛尔斯）、主司爱、美和生育的图兰（希神中的阿芙罗狄蒂和罗神中的维纳斯）、太阳神阿普罗（希神中的阿波罗）及其姊妹月亮神阿耳特美斯（希神中的阿耳忒弥斯和罗神中的戴安娜）、葡萄酒生产的保护者酒神弗兰斯（希神中的狄俄尼索斯和罗神中的巴克斯），以及海神尼顿斯（希神中的波塞顿和罗神中的尼普顿）。

由于伊特鲁里亚文字记载的遗失，考古文献是我们了解伊特鲁里亚的祭祀建筑的唯一途径。在伊特鲁里亚，神庙不仅是祈祷和礼拜的地方，也是聚会场所。

有些神庙坐落在城墙内，是市民们祈祷和礼拜的地方。另外一些则修建在城市外面，甚至是在露天的乡村，通常供奉那些主司健康的神灵。还有一些神庙位于墓地或一些重要交流场所的附近，例如皮尔吉港和格拉维斯卡港。

罗马建筑师维特鲁威曾经写过一篇有关罗马建筑的论文，据他的描述，伊特鲁里亚神庙的布局几乎为正方形，并纵向分为用途不同的两个部分。前半部分为门廊，直通向正门，后半部分则是供奉神灵偶像的房间。伊特鲁里亚神庙一般只包含一个或两个这样的房间，最多三个。

神庙一般建在高高的石头底座或平台上，墙壁用木头或未经烘焙的黏土砖制作——

基本上是易腐烂的材质。瓦屋顶由木制横梁支撑，所有暴露在自然环境中的木制部分均用红陶、瓦檐饰和装饰性石板保护起来，这些保护层均用钉子固定。神庙正门上的山墙也可饰有红陶高浮雕人物形象，而真正的雕像则可用来装饰屋脊。雄伟的祭坛则位于神庙建筑外面。

在所有出土的伊特鲁里亚神庙中，大多数情况下只有地基部分还能看见。不过，考古挖掘进一步为我们提供了更多有关何种神庙供奉何种神祇的信息。有些出土的铭文明确地提到了该庙供奉的神祇，另外一些情况中，神祇的身份可从祭品的性质推测断定。

事实上，在整个古代时期，祭品都与宗教崇拜的氛围紧密相关。在这一方面，伊特鲁里亚的主要避难所——尤其是避难所储藏室挖掘的祭品——提供了十分丰富的资料。由于献给神灵的祭品与日俱增，不得不寻找新的场所存放，因此才建立了这些储藏室。这类储存室存在着很大区别，这与信徒们的经济能力有很大关系。正是这种储存室为我们提供了无穷无尽的证据，并极大地加深了我们对宗教崇拜和宗教习俗的认识。

在最早的时期，祭品几乎都是一些陶器制品，极少数情况下，也有一些代表各种神祇的青铜雕塑，一些代表礼拜者或动物的形象，和一些建筑的隅石或黏土模型。有时，祭品上还刻有铭文，特别指定供奉的神灵或供奉者的名字。供奉现象在古典时期后期和希腊化时期最为显著，而且还出现了一类特别的祭品，使原本丰富的祭品种类变得更加丰富。这类祭品代表人体的不同部位——头、腿、手、脚和内脏——均和祭祀者的健康和生殖状况有着明确联系。这类祭品体现的几乎都是最贫穷的社会阶层对宗教的虔诚，所供奉的物品也是比较普通的当地产品。

阴间世界

伊特鲁里亚人普遍相信逝者死后会在来世超生，并保留生前的习惯。由于这一信仰，逝者被安放在布置得像生前居所的坟墓里，生前使用的一系列物品也一同陪葬。这些物品具有丰富的意义，是其社会地位的象征。由于这个原因，伊特鲁里亚人遵循一系列复杂、特别的葬礼仪式。这些仪式由几个步骤组成，其中三个步骤最为重要：圣餐仪式、瞻仰遗体和悼念死者，送葬游行和葬礼。伊特鲁里亚人逝世后，遗体将会马上展现给家属和其他悼念者瞻仰。主要是为了让妇女们悼念死者并寄托哀思。

遗体的瞻仰可能在帐篷里举行。帐篷四周则用于举办葬礼宴会，还有舞蹈表演和祭祀活动。似乎所有葬礼中的这类活动都大同小异。在大型坟墩的周围和内部还发现了无数祭坛和神龛遗址。这些极有可能是用于礼拜仪式的。

公元前5世纪，随着希腊宗教哲学信条的广泛传播，来世被描述为逝者的最终目的地。逝者携带一些必需品，或步行，或骑马，或乘坐马车，或乘船渡过河流或沼泽，经过漫长的旅途到达这里。从阿里斯托芬创作于公元前5世纪末期的喜剧《青蛙》的一个片段，我们可对这段充满危险的旅行有所了解。在这段文字中，已经经历冥府之旅的赫拉克勒斯，向酒神狄俄尼索斯讲述到达冥府后所遇到的事情："首先，你会遇到一片深不见底的巨大沼泽地。花上两文钱，一个老船夫就会划着一只很小的船将你渡过去……之后，你会看到许多蛇，和一些极其恐怖的妖怪……然后还会碰到许多满是淤泥和粪便

切尔韦泰里古城的伊特鲁里亚人墓葬，死者地宫一瞥，其中心柱以及等高的木排浮雕装饰，如日常所用。这种特别的墓室模仿了生前住所。
Etruscan tomb from the old city of Cerveteri, view of the deposition board for the dead, central pillar and sculpted relief decoration at the same height of the wooden rafts as they were used in domestic buildings. This specific kind of chamber burial imitates the houses of the living human beings.

的河流，一些灵魂深陷其中，他们或者得罪过主人，或者生下儿子而且没有承担相应责任，或者对母亲施加暴力，或者激起父亲的愤怒，或者发了假誓……接下来，你会听到呜咽的笛声，然后看到一道美丽的光芒和一片桃金娘，和男人女人们充满祝福的舞蹈，他们都拍着双手欢迎你的到来。"

阴间的大门是一扇类似城门的门。这是成为这个新世界一员的最后一道关卡。伊特鲁里亚的骨灰瓮上经常刻绘有这类场景，在阴间门口，新来的人受到已经过世的亲人的迎接，如父亲、妻子、丈夫等。

来自另一个世界的生灵担任着保护死者旅途安全的责任，伊特鲁里亚人认为，死者通往阴间的道路十分险恶，潜伏着许多恶魔和残酷的神。这些守护者包括：凯隆（charun），伊特鲁里亚阴间世界最重要的摆渡者，表情贪婪，面带死蓝色，手握一把重锤，可能是用来在死者进入阴间后打开或关闭阴间的大门，或是用来敲进象征死者注定命运的钉子。还有图库耳卡（Tuchulca），它长着秃鹰的面孔和爪子以及驴子的耳朵，周身遍布毒蛇。甚至还有亡灵导神万特（vanth)，这位肋下生翅的女魔承担着一项繁重任务，即宣读卷轴上每位死者死后的命运，还要手举五支火把照亮通往来世的道路。在这些恶魔般的人物面前，每个凡人似乎都显得十分渺小无力。许多陶瓶和住宅壁画上都可找到对这些形象的描绘，而墓葬圆雕则再现了更多神话动物和半人半妖的生灵，譬如半马人、客迈拉（chimeras，一种通常被描绘成狮子、山羊和蛇的组合体吐火的雌性怪物）和斯芬克斯(有翼的狮身女怪，传说她常叫过路行人猜谜，猜不出者即遭杀害)，这些雕塑放置在坟墓入口以保护坟墓安全。

两位神灵守护着阴间：冥神埃塔（Aita，希神中的哈德斯），在伊特鲁里亚人的想象中，冥神头戴狼皮头饰，手持一根顶端盘蛇的节杖；还有头发中盘旋着许多蛇的冥后珀西派尼（Phersipnai，希神中的珀尔塞福涅）。塔尔奎尼亚的奥吉之墓（公元前4世纪上半叶，这座墓葬属于城邦最有声望的一个家族，斯普瑞纳斯家族）里的壁画以精湛的技法描绘了这对夫妇的形象。画面中央，一对夫妇正和其他家族成员宴饮，每个形象后面均镌刻有一位圣贤的铭文。画面背景中我们可以看到维利亚Vel（ia），阿尔特·维尔哈之妻）美丽的面孔，柔和色彩和温暖色调的娴熟运用，赋予了她宁静的表情。从技法来看，这无疑属于伊特鲁里亚古典时期后期最著名的杰作之一。尽管该场景发生在家中花园——正如橄榄树幼苗和环绕里层画面上方的葡萄藤所暗示，但背景中隐约可见一朵乌云，同时出现的还有哈德斯和珀尔塞福涅。葡萄藤和宴会赋予了阴间以永恒的维度，并暗示这个家庭中的尊贵成员生前是献身于公共事务。

贸易与航海

伊特鲁里亚航海业可追溯至远古时期，伊特鲁里亚原史时期留下的许多船只形状的物品似乎可证明这点。事实上，根据古代文献的描述，伊特鲁里亚人擅长制造船只，是富有进取精神的贸易商和优秀的航海员，有足够的能力建立真正的海上统治权；第勒尼安海（希腊人称之为第勒诺伊海）以第勒尼安人命名，这并不是事出偶然。

自公元前8世纪至整个公元前7世纪结束，西地中海的海面上一直活动着在伊特鲁利亚登陆的水手，他们是被"金属山脉"——拉齐奥的托尔发山脉，和波普诺尼亚的厄尔巴岛——唯一俯瞰大海的伊特鲁里亚城镇，所蕴含的丰富而珍贵的金属矿藏吸引而来的。

装饰华丽的希腊花瓶在托斯其的港口登陆；来自近东的异域产品，如绘有图案或饰有雕刻图案的鸵鸟蛋、象牙雕、彩釉陶器和镀银酒杯等。伊特鲁里亚工匠成功地模仿并改进了这些产品，以满足贵族阶级持续的需求——对于他们而言，唯一的生活方式就是享受奢华和财富。

公元前7世纪末期，伊特鲁里亚的商贸活动大大增强，这一时期见证了大量商品的贸易往来，这些商品远销法国南海岸、西班牙、科西嘉、撒丁岛、西西里和意大利南部。主要的贸易产品包括大量葡萄酒，人们将葡萄酒盛放在安夫拉双耳酒罐，并巧妙地堆放在船舱；还有一些布凯罗黑陶和伊特鲁里亚生产的柯林斯式陶器，这些是饮酒用的器皿。不过，不可否认的是，这些船只也会进行海盗行为，甚至有些被历史学家称为"第勒尼的西西里人"——这种称号几乎等同于海盗。

接着，他们开始沿海岸线航行，利用托斯卡纳群岛、科西嘉岛和撒丁岛的天然港口网提供的便利，将船只航行到最遥远的海岸。伊特鲁里亚船只基本可分为两类：战船和运输用的货船。从考古遗址出土的船只缩尺模型，以及最近从海底打捞的数不胜数的船只遗骸，我们已经收集了有关这些船只面貌的宝贵信息。

这些战船模型通常为两层，船只底下则是一个九头怪蛇——这是米卡里画师创作的一个黑色形象。船上的铺板用绳索固定，划船的水手则分为两组：一组在甲板上，一组在甲板下。船头竖立着一个可俯瞰主甲板的脚手架，柱身则固定在船舷上。桅杆为横帆桅杆，仅用帆缆固定。水手们的盔甲表现出典型的公元前6世纪后期的盔甲特征，头戴配有肩带的阿提卡式头盔。在战场上和紧急情况下，敏捷与速度是最基本的首要条件。

运输货物的船只与战船结构不一样。货船体积更大，船的龙骨更为圆滑。船身和船尾均呈曲线形，用于装载双耳酒罐和其他货物。这为我们提供了一个公元前6世纪的地中海地区用于交换和贸易的商品样本。在吉格里奥岛外的坎普瑞斯湾，我们发现了一艘可能是从萨摩斯岛出发的希腊船只遗骸。船上所载货物包括希腊双耳酒瓶、来自各个地区的陶器、铜砖和铅砖、木雕家具、乐器、伊特鲁里亚双耳酒瓶、布凯罗黑陶，此外，当然还有一些盔甲和武器，其中包括一只青铜头盔。这说明船只上配有一支武装护卫队。

EVERYDAY LIFE AND RITUALS

Florence Archaeological Museum
Doctor Giuseppina Carlotta Cianferoni
Archaeologist expert of Etrurian Civilization
Rosalba Settesoldi

The men's word: weapons

During the most ancient period, armor played a prominent role within social groups and later became a particular responsibility of military leaders, even a symbol of profession practiced for the deceased. The armor of the late Villanovan period was characterized by bronze helmets, dome or crested, that were replicated in clay and used as a cover of ossuaries, leather shields covered with a bronze plate, square plates used to protect the heart (kardiophylax), cusps of the spear, axes, and swords, all of which enhanced the prestigious position of the deceased. The preciousness of the weapons underlined the role of superiority. Weapons of this type characterized a heroic fight, or a "melee", which was very different from those conducted by organized bands of armed men.

By the peak of the seventh century, through the influence of Greek strategies, technical changes are introduced. They developed the technique of hoplite phalanx and the use of cavalry for moving weapons, such as Corinthian-type bronze helmets with a cheek and nose guard and, presumably, leather padding (as the numerous holes arranged along the margins seem to imply), and large round shields beautifully decorated with embossed foil and greaves to protect the shins and calves. Complete outfits were found in the tombs of the Etruscan princes from the Oriental Period:it is worth remembering, for example, that these are among the most beautiful partly intact pieces found in the tomb of the Flabelli in Populonia.

These objects are mainly lethal weapons such as spears, swords axes, javelins, and weapons of iron, replacing those of bronze, which undoubtedly provided greater strength and impact resistance. Some swords also bear traces of carburetor, caused by heating in an environment rich in carbon, and provided additional hardening of the weapon.

The cone-like helmet comes into play in the middle of the sixth century, like "Negau". These helmets allow for cheek movement, and are often decorated. They are later replaced by dome helmets, with a central button and neck roll, also providing a smooth cheek or a triple stud; the armor also maintains anatomically shaped shoulder straps to enhance security.

These weapons show the obvious signs of a "craft" that is associated with a certain caste of soldiers, as seen from the inscriptions inside the helmets. These inscriptions are written in a number of languages, in addition to Etruscan, such as Latin, Celtic, etc. According to Eastern sources, the "Signore", or the military captains, had a two-wheeled horse-drawn chariot that was brought out on the battlefield or during military parades. The purpose of these demonstrations were to reiterate their social status to their peers and subordinates. From the princely burials of the Oriental Period, we have acquired an abundance of information on this type of locomotion and also on the elaborate trappings found on the remains of horses, often placed together with the carts. These are mainly bridle medallions or refined horse bits made of iron or bronze, similar to those from Circle B of the necropolis at Poggio alla Guardia, Vetulonia (last quarter of the eigth-early seventh- century).

Typically, the two-wheeled chariot was composed of a bass chest with small wheels; the oldest specimens were made of wood with fine finishes in bronze, followed by elaborate types of horseshoes formed by elastic straps, with low banks and a high front. This vehicle was designed for one or two people. It was light and consequently fast, suitable to cover short and medium distances at a run that could be done by two or even three horses, which was the fashion in Etruria.

The Feminine Sphere

The Etruscan women who belonged to the upper classes relished a certain position in the family and in society of complete equality with men. By virtue of this privilege, a woman must be an active socialite and, often alongside her husband, be involved in all the manifestations of his own aristocratic class such as the banquet, the symposium, weddings, and dance performances. This custom exposed the woman to venomous and mournful criticism that echo throughout ancient literature, but especially in Greek literature, probably around the time before there was commercial rivalry for dominance of the western Mediterranean routes. In one of the more malevolent languages, the fourth century writer Teopompo reports: "they are not at the table next to their husbands, but close to the first comer, and they make a toast to the health of those who they want to be healthy", and then again the philosopher Aristotle, who became perhaps too influenced by Teopompo, said: "the Tyrrhenians feast together with women lying under the same cloak". Aristotle is alluding to the fact that they would give themselves to any of the men present.The situation in Greece was different, in fact, where female figures that appear, for example, in Attican ceramic decorative repertoire as guests or performers, are not legitimate wives but rather women of servile extraction and even prostitutes. Teopompo again states of Etruscan women the following: "They are strong drinkers and very beautiful to look at." And in fact, since their public appearances were numerous, they devoted most of their daily life to the importance of their beauty and physical appearances.They wore valuable clothing, initially wool as evidenced by the rich archaeological record that conveys the female figure dressed in a heavy woolen tunic often accompanied by a mantle that fell down the back, in the most ancient period. Later, during the sixth century, a new and much lighter dress made contact with the Greek harbor. The chiton was a wide, pleated, long garment made of linen cloth that ended at the feet. The dress, that will remain at the height of fashion for quite some time without undergoing substantial changes, placed greater emphasis on the elegant female form, though it was still partly covered by a cloak on the shoulder or across it, according to the Etruscan fashion, with the two flaps that hung on the chest or head. In this period, the typical Etruscan footwear were the *calceirepandi*, with the tips raised up. They were soon replaced by footwear with intertwined laces.

The variety of dresses and hairstyles is exemplified, once again, by the wall paintings of the Tomb of the Lionesses in Tarquinia where there appears a sumptuous dancer dressed in a chiton with a large red cloak trimmed with blue and *tutulus*, adorned with large earrings that contrast with the transparent chiton, and with the other dancer. This one is nude and was given long blond hair styled in curls on the forehead and in long locks over her shoulders.

Even the hairstyles adapt to changes in fashion. Throughout the oriental period, women wore their hair parted on the top of the head in two big bands, collected in the back in a long braid, the same way as those on display. Subsequently, it was firmly established that both men and women may keep their hair loose on their shoulders or pulled back with pins or ribbons. The custom changed, however, with the emergence of Greek fashion which carried with it a goddess-like style. The female hairstyles were done with elaborate mantles like those that adorn the top of the female face. These hairstyles are represented on the two oinochoai, the red Etruscan figures of Torcop or those red elegant figures painted on the kantharos from Populonia.

The sumptuous clothing is made complete with an assortment of precious metals among which are refined by hair pins, buckles of various shapes and sizes used as clasps, gorgeous rings with embossed stones, necklaces in various shapes and sizes enriched with curious pendants, tube-style earrings a kind of purse, and bracelets which were often embellished with precious stones inlaid in bone, ivory or amber. These techniques of granulation (achieved through the welding of small spheres with a layer of gold that make up elaborate decorative motifs) and the watermark (borrowed during the eighth century by skilled Eastern craftsmen who was brought into Etruria) created real masterpieces.

We are now able to grasp the new trends and fashion tastes of the Etruscan society, especially those of the feminine variety. Before the Roman conquest, the numerous feminine depictions were allusive at the banquet displayed on the sarcophagi. The Volterra funerary urns and lids show the dead lavishly dressed and covered with jewels. These scenes flaunt their wealth and that of their family members. On the lid of the funerary urn from Volterra, there is an image of a reclining female figure. This piece is placed at the end of the second century.

Great care was reserved for the Etruscan "Ladies": care of the body, personal hygiene, and cosmetics. Some cosmetics that were documented were ivory combs adorned with elaborate decorative repertoire, like those found in a princely tomb at Marsiliana, or shiny bronze mirrors with the handle covered in bone. These objects become popular in Etruria in the second half of the sixth century: some were for functional use, and others was decorated with engraved scenes of art which makes them more or less complex, as seen on some of the exposed specimens.

Also among the objects were small jars. These were various shaped and sizes, and used for oils and scented balms be spread on the skin. There exist various types: globular (aryballoi) or decidedly more slender (alabaster), configured to animal or human, often ornamented with refined decoration that was carved or painted. In the Oriental Period, these artifacts were made of ceramic or even considerable amounts in alabaster, and they characterized the funerary monuments of the female mound tombs, along with jewelry, goblets, and refined caskets that had to contain all the items needed for the proper care of the body. Those oldest known artifact in the exhibition was produced in Etruria imitating the Corinthian models. As time passed, the forms changd and trade is enriched with new models. However, the small sizes are still maintained.

Public appearances and the pleasure of freedom did not relieve the Etruscan "Lady" from carrying out the duties of women of all ages, such as educating their children and running the home. They were also responsible for the spinning and weaving. The Homeric poems often conveyed the image of women as such. for example, Penelope, who was cared for by her handmaidens, was depicted as has having the very same activities to carry out. There was a distinction of age and social status between spinners and weavers. Spinners highlight the funeral procession: the manufacturing of the frame, which is the terminal phase of the cycle and probably the most complex and creative phase, was only under the jurisdiction of higher-ranking women, or of the mistress of the house.

The Banquet and the Symposium

"They prepare a luxurious table that is set twice a day, they prepare a table-cloth with embroidered floral motifs, they use silver vases of different shapes, and are served by many slaves." The ancient historians reported the sumptuous habits of the Etruscans, not without disapproval, in a period in which Etruria was now part of the Roman world. Traditionally, these people were dedicated to the pleasures and wild luxuries of life. There was certainly hostility derived from the ancient commercial rivalry that had been fighting for control of the trade routes of the western Mediterranean. The culture's transmitted image of posterity, in all its manifestations, was characterized by excessive zeal for ostentation of wealth and the necessity of aristocracy in a narrow social class.

Banquet and symposium, when people gathered to drink together, is ranked among the most important expressions of the higher social class: they were ceremonies for the noble groups to come together to strengthen their ties, to also exchange valuable gifts and to share moments of aggregation and self-congratulation. Also, the banquet was seen as a foreshadowing of the Hereafter, with all the objects and furnishings used by the deceased in their earthly life, thus symbolically linking life and death. During the ancient period they dined seated, as depicted in the scene on the cover of the famous urn of Montescudaio (first half of the seventh century), found in the territory of Volterra, which appears to be the oldest reproduction of a banquet scene. The protagonist is a man seated on a high-backed throne at a table with three legs. On the table are stacked cakes, as well as other type of dishes. Next to him is a woman who was originally depicted as holding a fan and a large vase, a dinos, while only a second vessel remains attached.

Beginning from the late seventh century, there is numerous iconographic evidence showing the guests, either alone or in pairs, lying on a bed (kline) with one elbow leaning on a pillow and wrapped in a blanket, according to a borrowed model of the Etruria environment which continued over the following centuries as shown by the countless recumbent figures of men and women in portraits on the lids of the urns from the Hellenistic age.

It is not uncommon to see in front of them small, round or rectangular, tables covered with food with a cat and dog crouched underneath ready to devour any food remains thrown to the ground.

We derive a substantial body of information about the power of the wealthy class mainly from the depictions in magnificent funerary paintings, from the frescos on the monumental aristocratic tomb stones in southern Etruria, as well as from literary sources. Recently, the scientific analysis done on the teeth from some of these remains was able to determine the diet and feeding practices adopted by the Etruscans, even from the less affluent classes. Pots of varying sizes were used for cooking food while whole service bronze and terra-cotta pots, each with a specific function, were for serving the guests. In the kitchen, there had to be large braziers, which was traditionally reproduced in heavy bucchero in imitation of metal models, shown on display along with small jars, plates, spoons, trays and vases and many other tools that are part of the funeral; heavy iron andirons, similar to those that we still use today for a fireplace, were raised to keep the wood or the long iron skewers supported so that they may be used to roast the meat.

Particular attention was paid to the preparation and the cooking, which were primarily only masculine activities because the male sex is tied to the sacrifice of animals, as it happens for the Homeric heroes. for the slaughter they used knives of different shapes and length and large cauldrons, traditionally considered a vase to hold and mix the liquid for cooking. It seems to have been used for boiling the many pieces of meat which were then extracted from boiling water with a utensil with long sharp prongs.

The frescoes in the tomb of Golini I of Orvieto (fortunately survived from the drawings done by G. Gatti which are kept in the National Archaeological Museum of Florence) offer a lively scene of the preparation of a feast that takes place around the middle of the fourth century. The scene takes place in the Underworld in the presence of Hades and Persephone. It shows slaughtered animals hanging from hooks (including a whole ox, a deer, a hare and some birds), the bustle of servants behind the tables ready to bring platters laden with buns, eggs, pomegranates, and grapes to the guests, the grinding of grain in a giant mortar hoisted on a tripod, an oven cooking food: all accompanied, according to literary sources, with the sound of flute music that marked the various stages of the work of his companions.

The rest of the population consumed wheat and legumes in large quantities, instead of meat. Paleobotanists from Etruscan excavations seem to confirm the studies carried out in recent decades on their remains. According to the documentation of Juvenal, a Latin author, soup of wheat seems to have been the dish preferred by this population, and soft wheat, produced in excess in Etruria, was purchased from Rome during famines and wars. Rare meat consumption was limited to sheep, pigs, or birds. The ox, however, was considered a precious animal as it was used for farm work. The symposium provided for a complex ceremony that involved a large quantity of containers, each of which performed a specific function, as evidenced by the pottery placed in the princely kits from the Oriental Period. The wine, imported at first and then produced locally, was preserved for the entire sixth century. Wine was a precious exotic drink, the consumption of which was reserved for people of rank. Eventually, while still remaining a drink primarily for the upper classes, the consumption of wine became a habit of the lower classes in society as well. Because of its high density, wine in its purity was not consumed. In accordance with the methods borrowed from the Hellenic world, it had to be diluted with water, or with snow during the winter, in percentages that were established from time to time by the one who oversaw the symposium before it could be consumed. The vessel for this task was the crater, a large vessel equipped with two loops. Cookware (simpula), strainers (cola) and filters (infundibula) were used to draw the beverage from the crater and free it from any impurities contained inside. The ancient wine was very different from today's. It was sweetened with honey and flavored with spices, fruit and even rose petals. It seems that in the wide range of wines produced in Etruria, wine from Luni had a reputation among the ancients to be the best. Wine from Veio, with the reddish color, had a reputation of being very poor quality.

On certain occasions, grated cheese was also added to the already strong wine along with the honey and barley. We know this because of the presence of numerous graters among the grave goods: as a drink, the taste was not so inviting, the kykeion, which drew its origins from the Homeric world. In the final stage, after the cooling operation, the drink was poured into the cups of the guests from jugs of different sizes (oinochoai and olpai), a maneuver that required a certain amount of skill on the part of servants.

Different chronological periods refer to the two banquet services exhibited as bringing together material from various origins. In the oldest period (the first half of the sixth to late fifth century) precious Etruscan-Corinthian vases are exhibited (olpe, a kylix, and a plate) that replicate the exuberant forms and decorative repertoire of the pottery product at Corinth, and bucchero vessels, which is a typical Etruscan ceramic style with a shiny black surface (achieved from firing in a kiln) as in imitation of the most precious metal prototypes. Elegant vessels are visible to pour the wine (oinoche), as well as a small dipper, a cup with a kyathos, two glasses, and finally a kantharos, the two-handled cup attributed for the excellence of the god Dionysus (Fufluns in Etruria), who according to mythology gave human beings the vine, the wine, and the simposiarca, i.e. the person that dictates the rules of the symposium. The service, unlike those from the Hellenistic age, includes a significant amount of black painted vases; since the end of the fourth century, a series of this pottery was produced in imitation of the most expensive metal prototypes that gave the subtle sheen to the forms. Also included were plates of various sizes, sometimes decorated with elaborate markings on the inner bottom, cups, olpai oinochoai to pour the wine, a tray, and a skyphos to drink, along with two lagynoi. There is also an elegant krater with handles designed as snakes, produced by a prestigious factory in Volterra. The instruments needed to tap into and filter the wine during the symposium, simpula and cola, are similar to those made in bronze.

The entertainment at the banquet and symposium consisted of music and dance as evidenced by the rich archaeological documentation in our possession. This includes the evidence of harp players or aulos, a flute-like instrument made of various materials including wood, bone, or ivory, that could also have been double-barreled. In this scene, the people rejoice in vibrant and colorful depiction of a banquet in the painted tombs of Tarquinia, like that of the Triclinio, the Giocolieri or the Leopardi. Even the ancient sources refer to this custom as being the height of fashion for the Etruscans, to accompany the activities of the day with music. In fact, Aristotle (later repeated by other writers) reports in detail that the use of the aulos was particularly widespread, so that the sound of the instruments accompanied the boxings, floggings, and even culinary activities as seen in the tomb of Golini I of Orvieto, mentioned above.

Aspects of Etruscan Religion

The etruscans were famous in the ancient world for their deep religious feeling. Attempting to explain this phenomenon, the Latin writer Seneca wrote: "This is the difference between us and the Etruscans [...] we believe that lightning is caused by clouds colliding, whereas they believe that clouds collide in order to create lightning. Since they attribute everything to gods, they are led to believe not that events have a meaning because they have happened, but rather that they happen in order to express a meaning."

To their contemporaries, most notably the Romans, the Etruscans were known not only as a people respectful of divine omens but also as one that was particularly skilled in the interpretation of such omens, thanks to their use of refined techniques of divination. Within this context, Etruscan priests, the aurispici, were highly respected, so much so that the Romans themselves consulted them in times of special difficulty. The divinatory practices most commonly employed were the observation of lightning, the flight of birds, and the examination of sacrificed animal entrails. Indeed, this emphasis on rites and technical aspects of religious practice seems to characterize the Etruscan sense of the sacred, and we have come to know as always, thanks to Latin sources, since the entire body of Etruscan literature has unfortunately been lost that the norms governing religious practice were codified in the Sacred Books, Where the Etruscans had collected all of their religious precepts.

In the Libri Haruspicini, for example, all the practices necessary for the examination of the entrails of sacrificial victims are set forth. The primary organ used in this type of examination was the liver. Numerous archaeological monuments, such as decorated mirrors and sculpted cinerary urns, show this organ in the hands of Etruscan priests, and also actual models in clay and bronze.

The most famous of these, the so-called "Piacenza liver," which takes its name from the city where it was found, is a bronze model of a sheep's liver whose surface is divided into 40 sections, each one bearing the engraved name of the divinity that presides over it.

Another important branch of Etruscan divinatory practices was the observation of celestial omens: the Libri Fulgurales were concerned with the interpretation of lightning, considered the supreme manifestation of the will of the gods.

Etruscan religion was polytheistic. Linguistic analysis of names of Etruscan divinities has proven very useful in the determination of their origin. In addition to a nucleus of gods whose names are clearly of Greek derivation, such as Aplu, Artumes, Aita, Phersipnai and Hercles (derived, respectively, from the Greek names Apollo, Artemis, Hades, Persephone and Heracles), there is a group of names derived from the Italic world, such as Uni, Menerva, Selvans, Nethuns and Satre (derived, respectively, from Juno, Minerva, Silvanus, Neptune and Saturn). Other names appear to have a more properly indigenous origin, such as Tinia, Turan, Turms and Laran.

Some of these latter deities may be easily identified with Hellenic deities, as demonstrated by the iconographic tradition, where each divine figure is found within a recognizably Greek mythological context. Based on this evidence, it is possible to infer at least a partial identification of Tinia with Zeus, of Turan with Aphrodite, of Turrns with Hermes and of Laran with Ares.

The major gods were Tinia, Uni and Menerva, sometimes venerated in the same temple. TINIA was the supreme god, the lord of the gods, identifiable with the Zeus of the Greeks and the Jupiter of the Romans. He was the ruler of the universe and the lord of destiny; his distinguishing attribute was the lightning bolt.

UNI was the most important female divinity, the wife of Tinia, equivalent to the Greek Hera and the Roman Juno. She was primarily revered as the protector of births and the protector of cities.

MENERVA corresponded to the Greek Athena and the Latin Minerva. She appears completely armed in Greek mythological scenes; her main attributes are the helmet, spear and owl. Anatomical votive offerings are commonly found at altars dedicated to her; these probably had a healing character.

Other important divinities were LARAN (Ares of the Greeks and Mars of the Romans), god of war; TURAN (Aphrodite of the Greeks and Venus of the Romans), goddess of love, beauty and fertility; APLU (the Greek Apollo) and his sister ARTUMES (Artemis of the Greeks and Diana of the Romans); FUFLUNS (Dionysus of the Greeks and Bacchus of the Romans), god of wine and protector of wine production; and NETHUNS (Poseidon of the Greeks and Neptune of the Romans), god of the sea.

Due to the loss of the indigenous literary tradition, our only testimony for Etruscan sacred buildings comes from the archaeological record. In the Etruscan world, the temple was not only a place for devotion and prayer but also a meeting place and a gathering place for groups of people. Some temples were located within city walls and reserved for the devotions of citizens, while others were built outside of the city, even in the open countryside, and often dedicated to those divinities charged with protecting health. Still others were located in cemeteries or in the vicinity of important places of communication, such as the ports of Pyrgi and Graviscae.

According to Vitruvius, a Roman architect who wrote a treatise on Roman architecture, Etruscan temples presented an almost square floor plan that was longitudinally divided into two sections, each one intended for a different function. The front section was occupied by a portico

that opened onto the main facade, while the rear section was reserved for the rooms that contained statues of the god or gods venerated in the temple. Temples typically contained one, two or, at most, three of these rooms.

Built on a high stone base or podium, the walls of the temple were made of wood and unbaked bricks, that is, perishable materials. Tile roofs were supported by wooden beams, and all the wooden parts that were exposed to the elements were protected by terracottas, antefixes or decorative stone slabs, which were held in place by nails. The pediments could be decorated with terracotta figures in high relief, while true statues could adorn the ridge of the roof (columen). The altar, which could also be monumental, was located outside of the building.

Of the Etruscan temples that have been excavated, in most cases only the foundations are visible; however, archaeological excavations have deepened our knowledge to the point where it is possible to establish to which divinity a building was dedicated. Some

inscriptions have been found that expressly mention the god or goddess; in other cases, the divinity's identity may be inferred from the presence of votive offerings.

Throughout the ancient world, in fact, offerings to divinities were closely associated with the sphere of cult worship. In this respect, the major sanctuaries of Etruria provide rich documentation, especially as a result of excavations of votive deposits located within sacred areas. These deposits were created when, due to the steadily growing number of dedicatory offerings, it became necessary to find new places for the dedications. Such deposits, closely related to the economic power of the devotee and differing greatly in terms of quality, constitute an inexhaustible testimony that has served to greatly increase our knowledge of cult worship and religious practices in general.

In the earliest period, offerings almost always consisted of ceramic objects and, in rare cases, bronze statues representing the various divinities, figures representing the worshipper or animals, coins or clay models of buildings. Sometimes the offering was enriched with inscriptions that specifically named the god or the worshipper. The phenomenon of devotion becomes even more noteworthy in the late classical and Hellenistic periods, when the vast typology is enriched by a special class of anatomical votive offerings. These objects, which represent various parts of the body—heads, legs, hands, feet and internal organs—are clearly related to the sphere of health and fertility; they are almost always the expression of a religiosity associated with the poorest social classes and with local products of a more modest quality.

The World of The Underworld

The widespread belief among the Etruscans was that the deceased survive after death in the Hereafter, retaining the same earthly habits. Because of this belief, the deceased were placed in their grave, which replicated a typical home, along with a set of objects that had belonged to them in life. These objects represented meaningful symbols of their social status. For this reason, special care was dedicated to the people of this complex ritual of burial. The ritual included several stages, but three of them were the most important: the prothesis, the exposure of the body, and ekphora, the funeral procession and burial. Immediately after death, the body was presented to the late family members and to the rest of the mourners. This was done specifically for the women to be able to mourn and express their sadness.

The presentation of the body took place perhaps

under a tent. Around the tent a funeral feast was held, along with dances and ritual games. These events seemed to have been the same for every funeral. Also found with the burial were numerous remains of altars, or shrines, near or within large mounds. In all probability, these were used for worship.

During the fifth century, following the spread of Greek philosophical doctrines, the Afterlife was described as the point of arrival for the dead. The deceased come fitted with the necessary supplies after a long journey on foot, or by means of horses, wagons, or boats crossing a river or a swamp. We can get an idea of this perilous journey from a passage in the comedy of Aristophanes' Frogs, written at the end of the fifth century. In this passage Heracles, who had already gone down to Hades, tells Dionysus about what awaited as he made his descent into hell: "You will come first to a huge, bottomless swamp. For two mites, an old boatman, in a boat so small, you can carry it... Afterwards, you will see many snakes and very horrible monsters...And then there's so much mud and dung rivers in which souls are immersed, those who have insulted the host, or enjoyed a boy without paying for it, or roughed up the mother, or sent the father into an outrage, or swore falsely ... then Next there will be sigh of flutes and you will see a beautiful light and groves of myrtle, and blessed dances of men and women, all clapping their hands."

The entrance to Hades is a door, often similar to that of a city. It is the last barrier to overcome before being integrated into the new world. This scene is often carved on Etruscan funerary urns, in a rather stylized fashion, where the newcomer is welcomed by

their relatives who have already passed on: a father, a wife, a husband, etc.

Otherworldly creatures were tasked to protect the deceased on their terrible journey into the world of the dead that was believed to be populated by monstrosities and cruel gods: among them were the Charun, the most important Etruscan ferrymen of Hades, with greedy faces the typical bluish color of death, armed with a heavy hammer that was possibly used to open or close the gates of Hades behind the dead after their entry, or to thrust in the nail that symbolized their predetermined destiny. There was Tuchulca, with the face and claws of a vulture and the ears of a donkey, covered with snakes. Even Vanth, the winged female demon who was assigned the onerous task of announcing the deadly fate of each individual written on a scroll, carrying five torches that illuminate the path to The Beyond. All of these monstrous figures, before which mortal individuals do not seem to have any power, are found in an ample variety of

vase paintings, wall paintings in homes, and in funerary sculptures where more fantastic animals and hybrid creatures, such as Centaurs, Chimeras, and Sphinxes, are made in the round and placed at the guarded tomb at the entrance of the structures.

Two deities guard the underworld: Aita (Hades in Greek) that the Etruscans imagined to be bearded with a wolf skin headdress and holding a scepter in his hand topped by a snake, and his wife Phersipnai (Persephone in Greek) with snakes in her hair. A masterful representation of this pair and was restored from the wall paintings of the Ogre Tomb of Tarquinia (in the first half of the fourth century) which belonged to one of the most prominent families of the city, the Spurinas. At the center of the scene, two spouses feast along with other family members, each assigned an inscription of a saint. In the background we see the beautiful face of Vel(ia), wife of Arnth Velha, dashed with the skilful use of light colors and warm tones that give to it a detached serenity of expression. Stylistically, it is certainly one of the most noble of the Etruscan paintings from the late classical age. Despite references to a home garden, such as olive seedlings or a sequence of vines surrounding the upper frame on the inside pictorial cycle, a gray cloud is seen in the background along with the presence of Hades and Persephone. The vine and the banquet projected the Underworld in a timeless dimension, hinting at the privileged members of a family who in life were devoted to public affairs.

Trade and Navigation

The Etruscan maritime vocation goes back to very ancient times as the many boat-shaped artifacts in the Etruscan figurative repertoire of prehistoric times seem to attest.

Ancient sources speak of the Etruscans, in fact, as skilled shipbuilders, enterprising traders, and excellent navigators capable of establishing a real dominion over the sea; it is not by chance that the name of the Tyrrhenian Sea, called Tyrrenoi by the Greeks, originated from the Etruscans.

From the end of the eighth century, and throughout the course of the seventh century, the western Mediterranean was furrowed by sailors who landed on Etruscan shores drawn to the precious mineral resources of the metal-bearing hills of Campigliese, the Tolfa Hills in Lazio, and the Island of Elba at Populonia, the only Etruscan town that overlooked sea.

Ornate vases from Greece arrived in the ports of Tusci; from the Near East, exotic products such as ostrich eggs painted or decorated with engravings, carved ivories, faience pots, and cups of gilded silver. These products are successfully imitated and revised to cater to the constant demands of the aristocratic classes for which luxury and wealth are the only known way of life.

The Etruscan trade intensified at the end of the seventh century, which documents a traffic of traded goods that extended from the southern coasts of France, Spain, Corsica, Sardegna, Sicily, and southern Italy. The essential trade consisted of excess amounts of wine transported in large amphorae, skillfully placed on boats, along with some bucchero and Etruscan-Corinthian ceramics, the function of which was the consumption of beverages. However, it cannot be ruled out that these vessels also carried out acts of piracy such as those usually attributed by historians of the Siceliots of Tirreni, whose name comes to be almost synonymous with pirates.

There they did a coastal navigation, using the network of natural harbors offered by the Tuscan archipelago islands, as well as Corsica and Sardinia, to reach the more distant coasts. Essentially, there were two types of Etruscan ships: warships, and cargo ships, used for transportation. We have gathered valuable information about their appearance by vascular depictions, from scale models of ships found at archaeological excavations or from the numerous remains of wrecks recently recovered from the ocean floor. The model reconstructions of the warships often show boat at two levels shown on a

Hydra, a black figure attributed by the Micali Painter. The planking of the hull is held in place by ligatures while the rowers are arranged in two classes: those on deck and those below deck. A scaffold overlooks the main deck at the bow ,while the shaft is fixed to the beam. The mast is lateral and only held by rigging. The armor of the soldiers is typical of the late sixth century armor, with shoulder straps and an Attican helmet. Agility and speed were basic priorities in battle or in emergency situations.

The ships used for transporting goods were unlike the the warships. They were larger and were equipped with a more rounded keel. The hull and stern curved wide and accommodated the cargo of amphorae and other transported materials. In this regard, we are offered an sample of what can be exchanged and traded at the beginning of the sixth century in the Mediterranean. The cargo of a wrecked Grecian ship, that probably sailed from Samos, was found in the Gulf of Camprese off the Isola del Giglio. Among the cargo were Greek amphorae and pottery of various origins, bricks of copper and lead, carved wooden furniture, musical instruments, Etruscan amphorae, buccheri and, naturally, some armor and weapons, including a bronze helmet. This suggests the presence of an armed escort on board.

语言与文字

威尼斯大学伊特鲁里亚学教授 里亚诺·马吉亚尼

语言学联系

近来，一个曾在罗马境内盛极一时的古文化（几乎每一个意大利的一直都是（*paene omnis Italia fuerit*））又登上了历史的舞台，它的文化特征激起了共和晚期罗马知识分子的好奇心——尽管他们主要的研究对象是复杂的宗教思想，同时，也凸显了它的语言的孤立性与独特性，因为它无法与其他任何语言进行比照。"在语言和习俗方面，与其他任何民族都同。"公元前1世纪后期，哈利卡纳苏斯历史学家狄奥尼修斯这样描述伊特鲁里亚人。

上个世纪以来，人们一直试图将伊特鲁里亚语与其他主要古代语系，包括印欧语系和一些安拉托利亚语联系起来，但都没有取得进展，现代语言研究仅发现了一种与之语系上存在联系的语言。这种语言来自爱琴海北部的利姆诺斯岛（Lemnos），自雅典人占领此岛到公元前500年，岛上居民一直讲这种语言。事实上，岛上发现的为数极少的铭文仅能用伊特鲁里亚语解释。据某些学者称，利姆诺斯语是伊特鲁里亚人（据希腊文献推测，可能是第勒尼安海盗）从意大利来此岛定居（可能是公元前8上世纪末期）的证据。

其他一些学者则认为，利姆诺斯语和伊特鲁里亚语是一种虚构的语言——"元第勒尼安语"演化而来的不同语言，这种语言的构词基础可能来自近东地区的语言。

这个问题十分复杂，而且与意大利的伊特鲁里亚文明的起源和形成等疑难问题密切相关。

文献库

伊特鲁里亚人留下了异常丰富的碑铭遗产，数目比古代意大利境内任何一种语言（不包括意大利南部的希腊殖民地的语言，但碑铭除外）都要多得多，证明了在希腊人狄马拉图斯（Demaratus）被暴君希普赛罗（Cipselo）放逐到塔尔奎尼亚

陪葬石狮，瓦尔维东，托斯卡纳，公元前8世纪

这只狮子匍匐在猎物——一只公羊的头的上方，狮子底下的基座刻有铭文，表示它属于厄尔特·内瓦扎，一位举足轻重的人物。墓葬题献文字通常使用"我属于……"这种格式，或者"xy将我赠与xx……"，表示这是一件某位重要人士赠与死者的礼物。

这座石狮脚下高高的圆形底座上刻有以下铭文："ECA SUUI NEVZNAS ARNVAL NÉS"。

Funerary Lion, Val Vidone, Tuscania, sec. IV-IIII B.C. E.

Crouched on top of his prey, a head of a ram, this animal is placed on a base bearing an inscription indicating that it belonged to Arnth Nevza, a very important person. Writing was normally used for funerary dedication texts such as 'I belong to...' or to indicate a gift to the dead on behalf of some other important person ' Xy gave me to xx...'. The lion has a high round base bearing the following inscription: ECA SUUI NEVZNAS ARNVAL NÉS.

（公元前676）前半个世纪，伊特鲁里亚人就已经形成了一套文字系统，并对附近位于皮特库赛（Pithecusae）和库迈的埃维厄殖民地语言产生了影响。

最古老的伊特鲁里亚铭文出现在塔尔奎尼亚的尤克·克泰尔，可追溯至公元前700年左右，不过，它所体现的语言发展阶段比拼写书（几十年后）中的要更进一步，这时似乎已经有效地复制了一套早期皮特库赛铭文（公元前740年，大约与"内斯特之杯"同时期）中的字母表；例如阿尔贝纳的马塞里亚那城"象牙圈"出土的象牙写字板，就证明了这点。

最古老的伊特鲁里亚字母表复制了范本字母表中的所有符号，包括那些发音古怪而未被伊特鲁里亚人用到的字母，包括β、δ、O、samech（被称为第一代拼写系统，希伯来语的第十五个字母）。这是为了保留一整套指示一系列名称的符号的完整性，如哈利卡纳苏斯的狄奥尼修斯所说，在希腊教育传统中，必须记住全部符号，不能漏记，否则整个系统就会崩溃。这套字母表一直保存至希腊化时期后期。直到第二个阶段，由于公元前7世纪后期一场席卷整个伊特鲁里亚的改革运动的影响，这些从未用过的字母——被称为死字母——才被全部从字母表中移除，这与文字的运用大体上一致（第二代拼写字母）。但是，伊特鲁里亚的语音系统需要再一次调整。

音素f，在希腊语中不存在，但出现在了伊特鲁利亚语中，它的图形标记为8，并被添加到字母表末位（第三代拼写字母）。

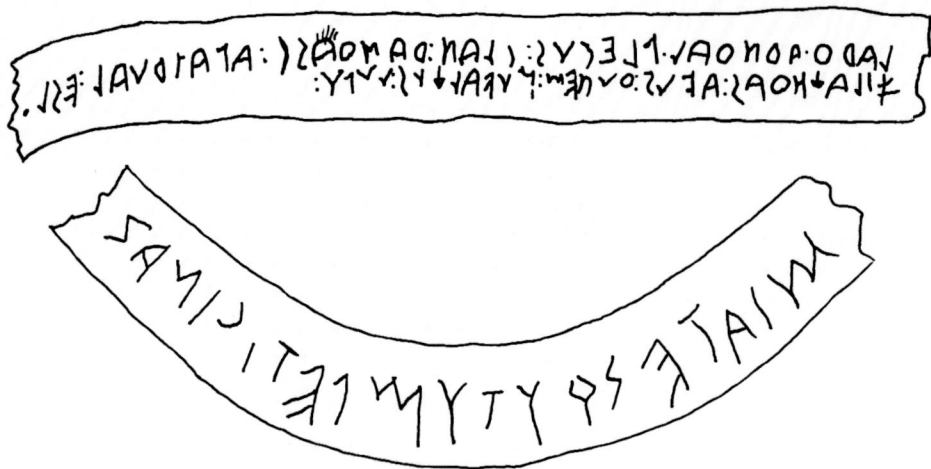

伊特鲁里亚文字的发明和发展上的巨大成功，要得益于foci（写作学校，有时附属于神殿）的出现和发展，它也充当伊特鲁里亚城市之间的信息传播中心。

得益于伊特鲁里亚的调停仲裁，文字书写开始以下地区所采用：菲尔斯克（公元前7世纪）、拉齐奥（公元前6世纪）、威尼托、列昂捷夫、利古里亚（公元前6世纪中期前后）、翁布里亚和奥斯克（公元前6-公元前5世纪）。

语音特征

近几十年来，伊特鲁里亚语音学研究领域已经取得了巨大的进展。对伊特鲁里亚语中来自希腊语的元素的研究起到了至关重要的作用；事实证明，这些元素成为了一笔极其重要的遗产。一方面，它提供了一些在文化传入框架下进口到伊特鲁里亚的物品（如各种器皿）、农产品（例如橄榄）、工具（日晷）的命名，另一方面，为数更多的英雄人物和神的名称进入了伊特鲁里亚语，这是因为希腊神话和意大利国内重要人物的巨大影响，这些人物迅速在当地传统文化中生根发芽，他们的形象经常配着铭文出现在伊特鲁里亚的雕塑花瓶和雕饰铜镜上。研究这些希腊名称在伊特鲁里亚语中的演变，可能帮助我们分析出一套伊特鲁里亚语的语音—音位规则。目前，人们普遍知道伊特鲁里亚语中有四个元音(a, e, i, u)，其中有两个上颚开元音(e, i)，只有一个veral音（u），而希腊语和拉丁语均有两个（o, u）。于是，希腊语中的奥德赛（Odysseus）在伊特鲁里亚语中就变成了乌德赛（Utuse），同样的，阿波罗就变成了阿普罗。

伊特鲁里亚语辅音系统的特征则表现为音位对应关系的缺失，这就是说，希腊语和拉丁语中闭塞音和爆破音均有两套，即哑音（(p, t, k)）和响音（b, d, g），而伊特鲁里亚语未作区分，仅使用希腊语中发哑音的符号。例如，Diphilos就变成了Tiphile，而Ganymedes变成了Catumite。

另一方面，伊特鲁里亚语历史上的一个重要现象及其发生时间已经被研究人员确定。公元前5世纪上半叶，几乎是在整个伊特鲁里亚境内同时发生了一个语言现象——可能是首重音造成的，即被称为"重读音节后的字中音省略"现象，也就是重读音节后的音节中的元音的消失（书写符号的消失）。这种省略之前已经历了很长的一段发展过程；这一位置的元音发音无疑比较困难；因此，该元音在单词拼写中也时有时无，直到公元前5世纪上半叶，这种不确定现象才结束。举个例子，这就是为何神话英雄阿喀琉斯（Achilles，希腊语中为Aquilleús，首音节上的重音可能变为次重音）在古代被写作阿喀尔（Acale）和阿奎尔（Aquele）的原因。但是，自公元前5世纪开始，阿喀琉斯仅以阿克尔（Acle）的形式出现，原(始)音素已经完全省略。一个较为常见的伊特鲁里亚名字阿维尔（Avile）也经历了同样的演变，在古时候可能被写作阿瓦尔（Avale）和阿威尔（Avele），但后来就变成了阿维尔（来自拉丁语Aulus）。

语法特征与句法特征

近年来，研究人员伊特鲁里亚语的语法领域取得了巨大的进步，这主要归功于赫尔穆特·瑞克斯（Helmut Rix）的辛勤工作。今天，随着对伊特鲁里亚语中不同词素的一系列不同格（属格I和II，与格I和II，直接受格，呼格，夺格）的确定，对一些名词、形容词和代名词的演变——和作为源语的希腊语和拉丁语相比较，我们已经有足够了解。

伊特鲁里亚语分主动式和被动式（过去分别用词素－ke和-che实现）和多种语气和时态。副词、介词和后置词也得到了确定。

伊特鲁里亚语的一个特征是其约束性，也就是说在词干基础上添加后缀，这点和现代语言中的土耳其语有点类似。一个很典型的例子便是名词tusurthir，可翻译为"配偶"（或其他同义词）。这个词可这样分析：tus = 床 [?]，tus-ur = 床（复数），tus- ur-thi=在床（复数）上，tus-ur-thi-ri =在床上的那些人（去世的那对夫妇，因为这句铭文雕刻在一间墓室内）。

专有名词系统

语言史上一个具有重大社会意义的篇章，便是人称的指代。在前字母时代（公元前8世纪末期之前），以及在近代的一些边远地区，用来指代个体的系统仅有一个个体的名称，后面加上父亲名称的属格，这一点与希腊语完全相同。Avile Spuries（clan）可翻译为Avile of Spuries（子），与Aias Talamonos(uios)可译为Aias of Telamon（子）一样。很快，这一结构经历了改变，其中父亲的名字可用作形容词。在伊特鲁里亚语中，这一变化通过添加_na后缀实现。于是，上述表达方式的内容可以用"Avile Spurie-na"的形式表达。同样，以Aias Talamonos为例，希腊语中也有同样的构词方式，例如表示父亲的形容词以后缀/io/实现：Aias Telamonios就等同于Aias Telamonios (uios)，而且在文本中可以互相替代。

大约自公元前8世纪末期起，伊特鲁里亚语中的个体指代格式又有了进一步发展，这与伊特鲁里亚的社会政治转型有关（父姓体制的建立）。

该指示方式的第二个元素注定要随着时代的变迁而变化，事实上，在公元前700左右，这个元素突然变成世袭制，于是，个体的指代不再只指示生父，而且还要指示父系。这种指代方式承认了家族集团的血统，是一种更为普遍的指代原型。

于是，专有名词系统变得更为复杂，每个个体由一个名（可供选择的范围越来越小）、一个姓(这一类词有越变越多的趋势)和一个源于父名的姓或名字（生父通常用属格表示）组成的词组表示。

越来越复杂的专有名词系统反映了社会政治结构的日益复杂，而且很快对古代意大利附近的民族和文化产生了影响，尤其是拉丁语和法利希语（Faliscan）。

主要文本

伊特鲁里亚文明留下了较多记载在不同材料上的文本。其中一些较古老的文本包括：一个石灰华板（Cippus Perusinus，公元前2世纪初）、一片巨大的黏土瓦（Tabula Capuana，公元前5世纪），一个铅盘（马利亚诺盘，公元前5世纪），和一本亚麻书（Liber Linteus Zagabriensis，公元前4-3世纪）。

正如我们所知道的，这本亚麻书得以留存至今的经历十分传奇，它先被主人带到埃及，在公元前1世纪时又被裁成细条，成了一具女木乃伊的裹尸布。

除第一个文本之外（一套法律文件中的一份，记载了威尔提那和阿夫那两个家族之间的协议），其他文本都有一个共同特征：即文本都较简短，且都是对宗教仪式的详细记载。这些文本，以及考古文献的有力证据，均证明了伊特鲁里亚人是一个名不虚传的对宗教最虔诚（*gens ante omnes alias deditareligionibus*）的民族。

解释学

伊特鲁里亚文化研究所取得的进步，也较大地推动了人们对伊特鲁里亚文本内容的理解。

这样一种已经消亡，而且基本上与其他已知语言不存在任何联系的语言，像伊特鲁里亚语，给解释学的研究带来几乎无法克服的障碍。

人们曾经尝试采取多种研究手段解决这一问题，包括语源学手段和综合性手段。前者几乎完全无法应用，目前也未能取得任何结果；后者则极为复杂，旨在通过对文本本身和记载文本的材料的研究来解释该文字记录，同时也使用双语对照的方法，基于两种联系密切的文化的语言结构比较相似这一假设展开研究，譬如对属于相同概念类别的某些铭文进行研究。目前获得的最积极的研究成果来自后一研究分支，譬如，人们已经可以肯定地对一系列表示归属的铭文加以解释。

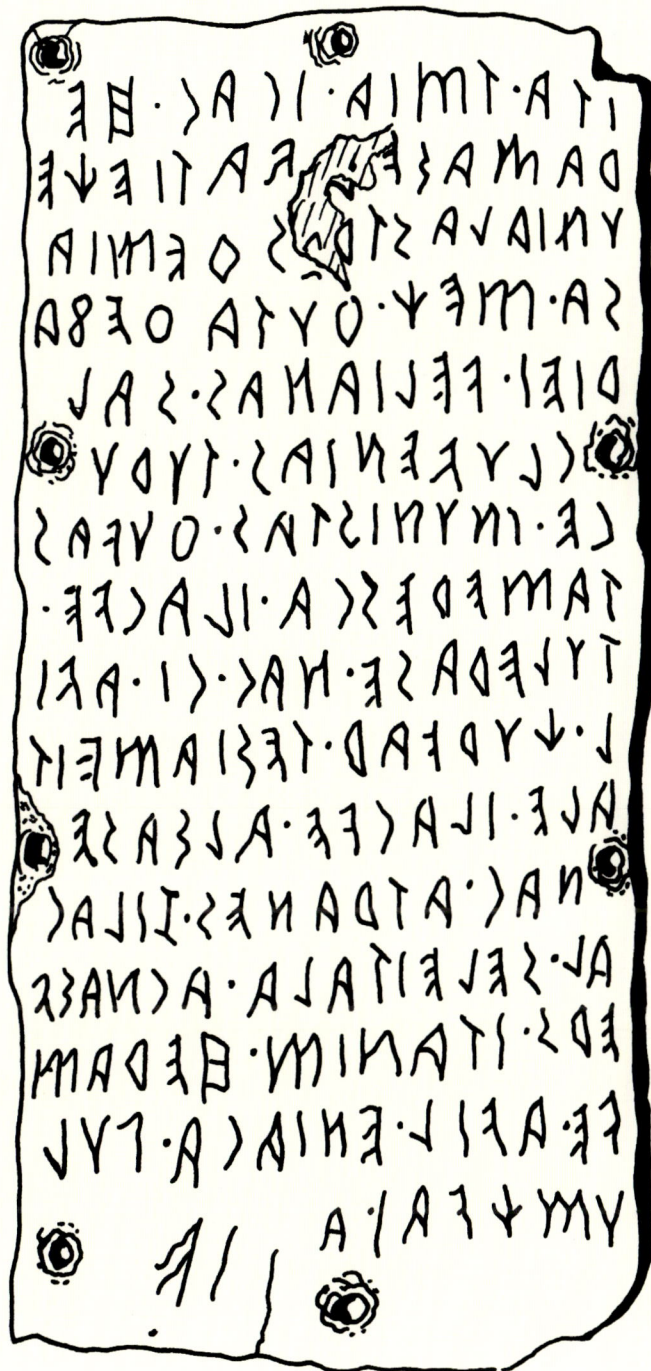

刻有铭文的金箔

皮尔吉，卡瑞，约公元前500年

1964年，卡瑞的一个港口小镇皮尔吉，在一个大型圣殿的挖掘出土过程中，人们发现了三片写满铭文的金箔。

其中两片写着伊特鲁里亚语，而另一片则写着腓尼基语。

圣殿被摧毁时，这三片金箔被人藏在了两座神庙中间的一个小洞里。

卡瑞的领主特发瑞·威利阿纳斯（Thefarie Velianas）的名字出现在伊特鲁里亚语中，他就是这座献给尤尼的神庙的赞助人。

这位神的名字出现在其中一片金箔中，正是这片载有腓尼基语的金箔推动了对伊特鲁里亚语及其数字表示方式的研究和了解。

Gold laminae with inscription

Pyrgi, Caere, 500 B.C.E. ca.

In 1964 in Pyrgi, one of the harbours of Caere, during the excavations planned to bring to light a large sanctuary, three golden laminae were found covered with inscriptions. Two of them bear an Etruscan text while the third a Phoenician one. It's for sure that these laminae were hidden inside a hole which was dug between the two temples when the sanctuary was destroyed. The name of the Master of Caere, Thefarie Velianas, appears in the Etruscan text. He was the one who dedicated a sanctuary to Uni.

The name of this god appears in one fo these laminae which helped to go ahead and deepen the research and the knowledge of the Etruscan language and the name of numbers.

LANGUAGE AND WRITING

Etruscology at Venice "Cà Foscari" University Prof. Adriano Maggian

The CULTURAL ASPECTS OF A CIVILISATION THAT FLOURISHED ON THE CONFINES of the Roman state and recently came to light on the stage of history, in whose hands once paene omnis Italia fuerit, could not fail to arouse the curiosity of the intellectuals of the late Republic who, although especially investigating elaborate religious thinking, also highlighted the isolation and uniqueness of a language that had no comparison with any other. "Unlike any other in terms of language and customs" was how Dionysius of Halicarnassus, the historian who lived in the late first century BCE, defined the Etruscans.

Despite the attempts made since the last century to link Etruscan with the major language families of antiquity, both with IndoEuropean language and with some Anatolian languages, modern research knows only one language genealogically related to it, which was spoken on the island of Lemnos, in the northern Aegean, from before the occupation by the Athenians up to 500 BCE; in fact, the rare inscriptions found on the island can only be explained using Etruscan.

According to some scholars, the Lemnian language is proof of the settlement – perhaps at the end of the eighth century BCE – of Etruscans from Italy (probably the Tyrrhenian pirates known by Greek sources); others prefer to think of Lemnian and Etruscan as separate outcomes of a hypothetical "proto-Tyrrhenian", whose formative base is to be sought possibly in the Near East area.

The issue is complex and is closely related to the very intricate subject of the origins and formation of the Etruscan civilisation in Italy.

DOCUMENTARY BODY

The Etruscans have left a great heritage in inscriptions, an infinitely greater number than all the other languages of ancient Italy (except the Greek of the colonies of southern Italy, but including epigraphic input, however), which demonstrates that half a century before the arrival of Demaratus in Tarquinia, expelled from his homeland by the tyrant Cipselo (676 BCE), the Etruscans had already developed a writing system, returning to that of the neighbouring Euboean colonists, established in Pithecusae and Cumae.

The oldest Etruscan inscription, which appears on the so-called Jueker kotyle of Tarquinia, can be dated to around 700 BCE, nevertheless, it records a stage of writing that is more evolved than that documented by spelling books (a few decades later), which appear to effectively reproduce a type of alphabet used in older Pithecusan inscriptions, at the chronological level of "Nestor's Cup of " (740 BCE); see, for example, the ivory tablet of the Circle of Ivories in Marsiliana d'Albegna.

The oldest alphabetical series reproduce the entire repertoire of the signs of the model alphabet, including those that Etruscan, because of its phonological peculiarities, did not use, such as beta, delta, omicron, samech (called first generation spellers). This is explained by the need to maintain the integrity of the series of signs representing a sequence of names of letters which, in the tradition of Greek education, was maintained until the late Hellenistic age, as recalled by Dionysius of Halicarnassus, had to be memorised in full without the possibility of omissions otherwise the system would collapse. Only in a second phase, and as a result of a reform that was consolidated simultaneously throughout the whole of Etruria in the late seventh century BCE, were the unused letters – called dead letters – deprived of sequence all together, which thus substantially coincided with that used in the practice of writing (second generation spellers). However, the phonology of Etruscan required another adjustment; the phoneme /f/, unknown in Greek but present in Etruscan, is graphically represented by the symbol 8 and is added to the end of the series (third generation spellers).

The remarkable success that shone from the beginning on the writing of Etruria contributed to the formation of foci of development (writing schools, sometimes attached to shrines), which also functioned as centres of transmission to neighbouring towns of Etruria.

Thanks to Etruscan mediation, writing was taken up in the following regions: Felsic (in the seventh century BCE), Lazio (sixth century BCE), Veneto, Leontief, Liguria (around the mid-sixth century BCE), Umbria and Osco (V-V1 centuries BCE).

PHONOLOGICAL ASPECTS

In recent decades there has been great progress in the field of Etruscan phonology. Study of Greek "loans" to Etruscan has been crucial; this is an extremely important heritage which, on the one hand, provides names of objects (e.g. types of vessels), agricultural products (such as olives) and instruments (sundials) imported to Etruria in the framework of the acculturation process, and on the other, a much larger group of names of heroes and deities which, thanks to the huge success that Greek mythology and its protagonists found on Italian soil, soon took root in local tradition, to the point that they often appeared alongside the images and inscriptions on figurative vases and engraved mirrors. Study of the transformations that Greek names underwent in Etruscan has made it possible to state a series of Etruscan phonetic-phonological rules. Currently, it is widely known that the Etruscan system provided for a series of four vowels (a, e, i, u), with two degrees of opening in palatal series (e, i) and only one in veral series (u), instead of the two (o, u) in Greek and Latin. Thus, the Greek name Odysseus is known as Utuse in Etruscan and the theonym Apollo as Apulu.

Instead, the system of consonants is characterised by the lack of correlation of sound; that is to say that while Greek and Latin have two series in the occlusive class, plosives, the obtuse (p, t, k) and the sonorous (b, d, g), Etruscan distinguished one only, shown graphically with the signs used by the Greeks for the obtuse. For example, the name Diphilos becomes Tiphile, and Ganymedes becomes Catumite.

On the other hand, a phenomenon critical for the history of the Etruscan language has been identified and located in time. Thus, in the first half of the fifth century BCE, simultaneously throughout the whole of Etruria, perhaps as a result of the initial marked accent, there took place the phenomenon known as post-tonic vowel syncope, i.e. the fall (absence of graphic display) of the vowel in the syllable following the syllable in which the accent fell. This phenomenon is the conclusion of a process that began long ago; the exact nature of the vowel inserted in that particular position was surely perceived with difficulty; as a result, this was recorded in writing in a non-constant manner until, as has been said, in the first half of the fifth century BCE this uncertain stopped being noted. This is why, for example, the name of the hero Achilles (from the Greek Aquilleús, with probable decrease of the accent on the initial syllable) could be written in the ancient times as Acale and Aquele; however, from the fifth century it appears only in the form of Acle, completely omitting complete the socalled "archiphoneme". A similar process is seen in the well-known local forename Avile, which in ancient times could be written as Avale and Avele, but later only Avle (from the Latin Aulus).

GRAMMATICAL AND SYNTACTIC ASPECTS

In recent years remarkable progress has also been made in the field of Etruscan grammar, thanks mainly to the work of Helmut Rix. Today, a declination of names, adjectives and pronouns, as in Greek and Latin, is quite well known, with the definition of a series of different cases of distinct morphemes (genitives I and II, datives I and II, accusative , vocative, ablative).

The Etruscan word provides for active and passive diathesis (which are effected respectively, for the past, with the morphemes –ke and -che) and a large number of modes and times. Adverbs, prepositions and postpositions have also been identified.

A feature of the language is that it is binding, that is to say that it adds suffixes to a thematic basis, a bit like in Turkish among modern languages. A very significant example is the noun tusurthir which can be translated as "spouses" (or similar), which must be analysed as follows: tus = bed [?]; tus-ur = the beds; tusur-thi = in the beds; tus-ur-thi-ri = those in the beds (i.e. the deceased couple, since the inscription is engraved inside a chamber tomb).

ONOMASTIC SYSTEM

A separate chapter in the history of the language, with profound social implications, is the system of personal designation. In the pre-alphabetic era (before the end of the eighth century BCE), and in more recent periods in marginal areas, the system provided for designating an individual with just one individual name, followed by the name of the father in the genitive, exactly as happened in Greece. Avile Spuries (clan) can be translated as Avile of Spurie (son), just as Aias Talamonos (uios) can be translated as Aias of Telamon (son). Very soon this structure suffered a transformation, in which the father's name was used as an adjective; in Etruscan, this took place through _na suffix. Thus, the content of the aforementioned expression must also be used in the form of Avile Spurie-na. Also in this case, there is a similar formation in Greek, where the paternal adjective takes the form of the /io/ suffix: Aias Telamonios is equivalent to Aias Telamonios (uios), and is used interchangeably in texts.

Linked to the socio-political transformations of Etruria (institution of the family name system), probably from the end of the eighth century, there was further development of the individual designation formula.

In fact, around 700 BCE, the second element of the formula, destined to vary continuously with the change of generations, suddenly crystallized to become hereditary; thus, the individual is no longer designated exclusively by indicating the natural father, but rather by referring to the pater gentis, a more or less real common archetype, recognised in the origin of the family group of which it is part.

Thus, the onomastic system becomes more complex, and each individual is designated by a personal forename (chosen from a range of dwindling options), with the family name (which enters a class that tends to be more and more numerous) and with the patronymic (the natural father is always expressed in genitive form).

This more complex onomastic system, reflecting the greater complexity of the socio-political situation, soon passed to populations and cultures close to ancient Italy and in particular, to Latin and Faliscan.

MAJOR TEXTS

Etruscan civilisation has left a relatively large number of texts, recorded in various materials. Among the older texts, there is a tablet of travertine (Cippus Perusinus, beginning of the second century BCE), a giant clay tile (Tabula Capuana, fifth century BCE), a lead disc (Magliano Disc, fifth century BCE), and a linen "book" (Liber Linteus Zagabriensis, fourth-third centuries BCE).

The latter document, which is quite exceptional, has been preserved, as is known, because it was transported to Egypt by its owner, and given the form of narrow strips to wrap a mummy of a woman in the course of the first century BCE.

Except for the first, which is one of a series of legal documents (since it records agreements between two family groups, the Velthina and the Afuna), the other texts share a common feature: they are small and detailed descriptions of rituals, a circumstance which, together with the evidence of archaeological documentation, confirms the fame of the Etruscans as gens ante omnes alias dedita religionibus (a people dedicated more than any other to religious practices).

HERMENEUTICS

The progress in Etruscan studies has permitted considerable progress in understanding the content of the texts.

A dead language, like Etruscan, substantially lacking kinship with other known languages, poses almost insurmountable problems for hermeneutics. The question has been addressed by putting into practice various methodological approaches, both etymological, which are virtually unusable and so far lack acceptable results, and combinatorial, which are extremely complex and aim to interpret the written document starting just from inside the text and the material in which it appears, without forgetting bilingualism, based on the assumption that cultures living in close contact developed similar schemes of formulae, as is the case with some inscriptions related to the same conceptual category. The most positive results come from this latter branch of studies; for example, it has made it possible to interpret with certainty the series of inscriptions of possession.

索瓦纳古城大墓入口
Entrance of a monumental tomb in the old city of Sovana

图 版
PLATES

维兰诺万文化与随葬品

首先，葬礼包括一个火葬仪式，火葬后的骨灰被保存在双锥状骨灰瓮里。瓮盖分为红陶盖和青铜盖，具体视逝者为男性（133号墓葬）还是女性而定（179、163号墓葬），如逝者为女性，瓮盖则为小碗状或小罐状，如逝者为男性，瓮盖则为头盔状。通常，与这些造型十分独特的骨灰瓮一起下葬的还有一些个人物品。扣针（胸针，男女墓葬皆有）和黏土制作的纺纱或织布的工具，如织布机的纺坠和垫片，则说明坟墓的主人是女性。而葬有男士刀具和武器的坟墓，则说明墓主是男性，而且该男性的社会身份是武士。

我们可以相当肯定地断言，远古时期殉葬品记录了死者的生活和社会地位。生者和死者的世界相互交织，紧密相连。对于没有留下文字记录的文明（例如维兰诺万文化），墓葬比其他艺术形式更加全面地记录了人们的生活和物质文化。同样，当文字记录仍被时间的迷雾笼罩，或只有少数有意义的文字存世时（如伊特鲁里亚后期），这类墓葬品又为我们提供了宝贵的信息。

Villanovan Culture and Grave Goods

First, the burial ritual involved a form a cremation, with the ashes preserved in ossuaries shaped like biconical urns. These had terracotta or bronze lids that, depending on whether the ashes were female (tomb 133), or male (tombs 179 and 163), were shaped like a small bowl or pot, for the women, and like a helmet, for the men. These rather unique ash urns were normally buried with a few, generally personal items. Fibulae (brooches, both for women and men), and clay spinning or weaving tools used as weights or spacers in looms showed the tombs were for women. The presence of razors and weapons for men, defined the tombs as masculine and showed the male social identity as warriors.

We can say fairly confidently that as far back as this ancient period, grave goods documented the life and the social standing of the deceased. The world of the living mixes and lives side by side with the world of the dead. Tombs provide a better record than any other art form of life and material culture of peoples and civilizations that left no written records (as in this stage of Villanovan culture). Likewise, such goods provide valuable information in those cases where the forms of writing used remain shrouded in the mists of time or where few significant texts survive (as with the later Etruscans).

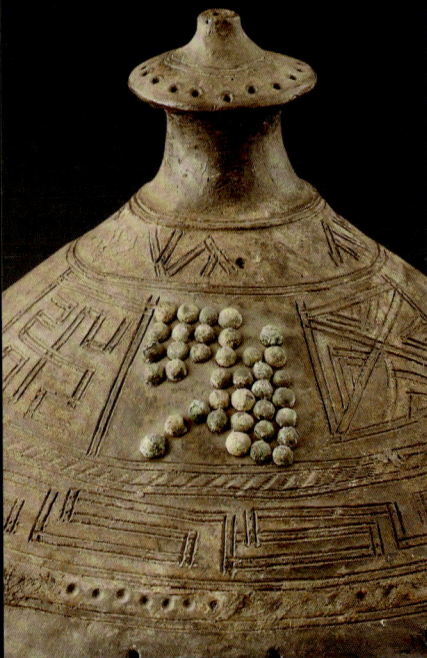

塔尔奎尼业，基尔奇特罗·迪·索普拉，133号墓
公元前9世纪下半叶

Tarquinia, necropolis at Selciatello di Sopra, well tomb nr. 133
Second half 9th century B.C.E.

双锥体盔形盖骨灰瓮
Biconical Ossuary With Covering Helmet

公元前9世纪
褐陶
罐：高33.8、直径19厘米
盖：高15、直径23.4厘米
9th century BCE
Impasto
Ossuary: H.33.8cm, D.19cm ,
Helmet: H.15cm, D.23.4cm

本件为维兰诺万时期
（Villanovan period）的骨
灰瓮，瓶身有环形把手，外
壁刻有几何图案并凿有小
孔。容器上的头盔式盖表明
死者为男性。

Biconical vase fitted with a tortile
loop handle used to hold the ashes
of the deceased in the Villanovan
period. The vessel has engraved
geometric motifs on the surface and
is punch embossed. The presence
of the helmet covering the vessel
indicates that the deceased was
male.

阿斯克斯陶牛首壶
Figure-Shaped Askos

公元前9世纪
褐陶
高15.7、长18厘米
9th century BCE
Impasto
H.15.7cm，L.18cm

陶制容器，有环形柄，便于
盛装和倾倒液体。一端为牛
头造型。阿斯克斯是古希腊
一种扁平带流细颈油壶。

Pottery vessel provided with a 'loop
which was used to contain and pour
liquids. One end is shaped like a
head of cattle.

安夫拉陶瓶
Amphora

公元前9世纪
褐陶
高19.9、直径13.5厘米

9th century BCE
Impasto
H.19.9cm, D.13.5cm

小瓶，用棒抛光，外壁有两
个陶土制环形柄，瓶身刻有
几何图案，一耳残。安夫拉
是古希腊一种双耳瓶。

Small vessel equipped with two
loops of dough polished stick part of
the outfit. The body has, as the urn,
engraved geometric motifs comb.

陶圈足盘
Dish on A Pedestal

公元前9世纪
褐陶
高5、直径14厘米

9th century BCE
Impasto
H.5cm; D.14cm

本件为盛放贡品的小圆盘，
底部有圈足。葬礼仪式上用于
盛放小盘食物，通常是水果，
用于陪伴死者去往来世。

Small circular plate on bottom hem
foot and used to separate the offers.
In funeral rites small portions of
food were placed on it, often fruits,
intended to accompany the deceased
on his journey to the afterlife.

陶圈足盘
Dish on A Pedestal

陶高圈足盘
Dish on A Pedestal

公元前9世纪
褐陶
高8.2、直径12厘米

9th century BCE
Impasto
H. 8.2cm, D.12cm

该圆盘经人工使用黏土捏制
而成，有喇叭状高圈足，表
面用棒抛光。

The dish comes with a high foot horn
was made by hand in dough and
then polished on the surface with a
stick .

青铜盘状搭扣
Disc Fibula

公元前9世纪
青铜
长14、直径6厘米

9th century BCE
Bronze
L.14cm, D.6cm

样式精致的搭扣通常饰以刻纹，是早期装饰的见证。该盘状搭扣似乎为男性专属陪葬品。男子用它在肩膀处扣住长袍。在一边肩膀处扣住长袍或斗篷，通常只需一只扣针。

Fibula from elaborate form that provides a record often decorated with engravings. The fibula seems exclusive male burials. It used by men to pin the robe at the shoulder. Usually just one fibula closed the robe or pinned the cloak on one shoulder.

青铜剃刀
Razor

公元前9世纪
青铜
长12厘米

9th century BCE
Bronze
L.12cm

剃刀呈月牙形，有小手柄，刀身和把手常常分离。青铜剃刀常见于维兰诺万（Villanovan）文化男性的工具箱中。

The razor is one of the objects present in most kits male Villanovan. It has a crescent-shaped body and a small handle often worked separately.

塔尔奎尼亚，塞尔奇特罗·迪·索普拉，163号墓

公元前9世纪下半叶

Tarquinia, necropolis at Selciatello di Sopra, well tomb nr. 163
Second half 9th century B.C.E.

双锥体盔形盖陶骨灰瓮
Biconical Ossuary With Covering Helmet

公元前9-8世纪
褐陶
罐：高39、直径20.5厘米
盖：高27、直径23厘米

9-8th century BCE
Impasto
Ossuary: H.39cm, D.20.5cm
Helmet: H.27cm, D.23cm

本件用于存放骨灰。器物表面通常由几何图案或蚀刻小孔装饰。和上个墓穴中的头盔一样，这个头盔也是骨灰瓮的瓮盖，可能是一件青铜头盔的复制品——青铜头盔则比之前造型较简单的圆锥形头盔更加尊贵。事实上，这件顶部呈半月状的头盔较深，又称顶饰头盔，盔顶有一个饰有羽毛或动物毛皮的羽冠，就像是一束真正的羽毛。与后期羽冠位于接缝处的头盔不一样，这件头盔的羽冠位于前方，因而盔顶的羽毛或毛发清晰可见。这是部落酋长的头饰。

Vessel that originally contained the ashes of the deceased. The surface is often a decoration consists of geometric patterns engraved or etched punch.

As in the case of the previous tomb, this helmet is the cover for the cinerary urn and is probably a replica of a bronze helmet that was more prestigious than the previous simple conical helmet. In fact, this cap is deeper with a half-moon shape at the top, which defines it as a "crested" helmet, with a proper crest to which feathers or animal fur was attached, like a proper plume. Unlike the later periods, however, the crest is at the front and not on the cap's seam, so that the feathers or fur is clearly visible. This is the headdress of a tribal chief.

塔尔奎尼亚，塞尔奇特罗·迪·索普拉，179号墓
公元前9世纪下半叶
Tarquinia, necropolis at Selciatello di Sopra, well tomb nr. 179
Second half 9th century B.C.E.

双锥体碗形盖陶骨灰瓮
Biconical Ossuary With Covering Bowl

公元前9-8世纪
褐陶
高48、直径20.8厘米

9-8th century BCE
Impasto
H. 48cm, D.20.8cm

本件为维兰诺万时期
（Villanovan period）的骨
灰瓮，瓮身有环形把手。骨
灰瓮盖可能为碗型，如本
件，若被埋葬者为男性，则
为黏土或金属制盔形盖。

Biconical vase fitted with a loop
handle used to hold the ashes of the
deceased in the Villanovan period.
The cover could be constituted by a
bowl, as in our case, or by ahelmet
clay or metal, if it was a male burial.

安夫拉陶瓶
Amphora

公元前9-8世纪
褐陶
高9.5、直径9厘米

9–8th century BCE
Impasto
H.9.5cm, D.9cm

瓶身小，用棒抛光，有两个陶土制环形柄，为女性陪葬品。在维兰诺万时期，陶器由妇女制作，并作家用。制作原料为粗糙的黏土和未经过滤的水，因而得名为"混合黏土"。这件陶器由手工制作，表面用棍棒修平，通常饰有蚀刻的几何图案以及冲模和模具印刻的图案。最复杂的陶器上甚至饰有青铜元素，如嵌入黏土混合物中的青铜片或小饰钉。

Small vessel equipped with two loops of dough polished stick part of the support of female burial. In the Villanovan Age, pottery was produced by women for domestic use, made with coarse clay, unfiltered water, defined as a "mixture". This pottery was made by hand and the surface levelled with a stick, often decorated with etched geometric motifs and imprints made with dies and moulds. The most elaborate examples feature bronze elements, such as plate or small studs, inserted into the clay mixture.

安夫拉陶瓶
Amphora

公元前9-8世纪
褐陶
高13.2、直径10.5厘米

9–8th century BCE
Impasto
H.13.2cm, D.10.5cm

瓶身用棒抛光，有手柄，无装饰，与其他陪葬品一起装入骨灰瓮。安夫拉是系列常见的双耳细颈球体瓶。

Jar-handled mixing polished stick, undecorated, that accompanied the urn with other funerary objects.

陶纺轮
Fuserolas

公元前9-8世纪
褐陶
直径2.8-4厘米

9-8th century BCE
Impasto
D.2.8-4cm

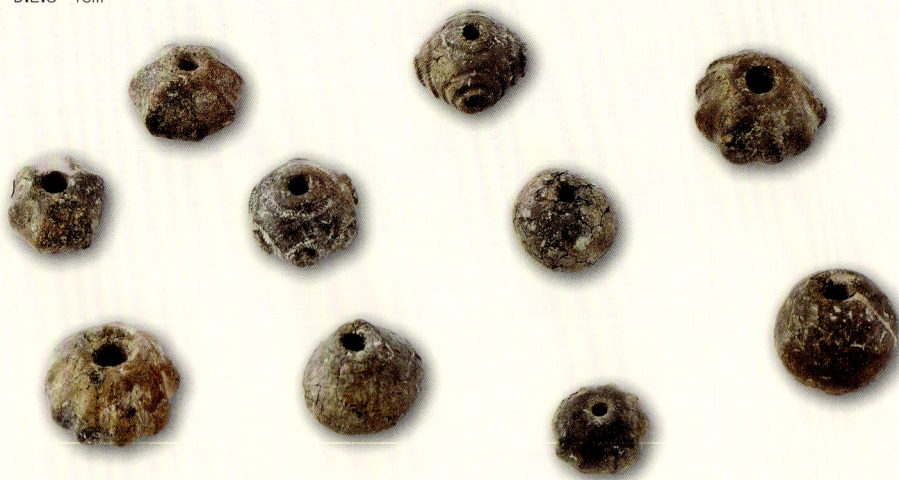

圆形中空，妇女用于纺织。正如其定义"纺轮"所示，使用时将其串在木棒或金属（青铜）棒上，并逐个叠加，具体而言就是将其做成一个锭子。纺线或纱线缠绕在上面，绕成整齐的一捆或一团，以便在织布机上织成各种布料。

Core of small objects of pottery, from its rounded shape and provided with a central through gold, used by women to the spinning of the tissues. The definition "whorls" indicates that these were used by threading them one on top of the other on a wooden or metal (bronze) rod, in the more elaborate examples, to create a spindle. The fabric thread or yarn was wound around these to create neat skeins or balls that would later be used to make fabrics of various kinds on the loom.

玻璃项链珠
Glass Paste Necklace Beads

公元前9-8世纪
玻璃
上：直径1厘米，下：长1厘米

9-8th century BCE
Glass
D.1cm, L.1cm

两颗别致的玻璃制的项链珠：一颗为圆形，刻有黄色"蜻蜓眼"图案，另一颗蓝色的珠子上面饰有白色图案。珠子中空，用于穿线。

Two lovely necklace of glass paste: one round in shape with inserts "eyes" in yellow, the other blue with white inserts. Both have a gold passing through the housing of the wire.

贝壳
Shell

公元前9-8世纪
贝壳
长3.7、宽2.3厘米
9-8ᵗʰ century BCE
L.3.7cm，W.2.3cm

本件为女性陪葬品，形状小巧，无疑为装饰物，从一端的穿孔来看可能是项链的垂饰。

Being a female burial, the small shell undoubtedly represented an ornament, probably a pendant necklace as evidenced by the small gold at one end.

青铜搭扣
Fibulae

公元前9-8世纪
青铜
高1.8-3、长2.8-5厘米
9-8ᵗʰ century BCE
Bronze
H.1.8-3cm，L.2.8-5cm

青铜质拱形小搭扣，用于衣服及装饰物的简单的方格织物。

Group of small arched fibulae of bronze used for simple stop fabrics of the clothes and ornaments as.

精英阶层的殉葬品

一些墓葬品中只有糊状黏土制作的陶器，而另一些墓葬则含有青铜器皿，说明墓主生前的社会地位较高。不管是在这一阶段还是之后，在以商贸为基础的经济体中，金属一直是制作礼品的贵重材料。包含有这类材料的器皿在许多方面与陶制器皿都比较相似，但它们要珍贵得多，因为需要使用铸造和冲压工序将其制作成青铜薄片。墓葬中还有一类武器，这类武器说明男性墓主的社会角色为猎人或武士。

Elite Grave Goods

Unlike the graves goods consisting only of impasto pottery, those with bronze vases were meant for people of high social standing. This metal had always been a precious material, used for gifts in the trade-based economies both in this period and later. Such vessels included certain types that were similar in many ways to the earthenware ones, but they were far more prestigious, having been crafted from hammered or punched bronze sheets. The presence of a few weapons shows the male's social role as a hunter and warrior.

拜赛特，布卡斯公墓，1号墓
公元前8世纪末期至公元前7世纪早期
Bysenthium, necropolis of The Bucacce, tomb nr. 1
Late 8th-early 7th century B.C.E.

斯图拉铜瓶
Situla

公元前8-7世纪
青铜
高19.4、直径16厘米

8-7th century BCE
Bronze
H.19.4cm, D.16cm

这件珍贵的桶形瓶由青铜薄片制成，以提梁抬放，把手呈半圆形，便于抓牢器物。瓶身饰有优美的几何图案。斯图拉是意大利北部出现的一种桶形器。

Precious vase made of sheet bronze, beautifully decorated on the body with geometric motifs executed cantilever. It's provided with a semicircular handle for gripping.

青铜高足杯
Cup

公元前8-7世纪
青铜
高21.6、直径18.8厘米

8-7th century BCE
Bronze
H.21.6cm, D.18.8cm

青铜杯子有喇叭形高圈足，
肩部的环形手柄为后期用铆
钉固定。

Cup on a high splayed foot end plate
made of bronze: The loop has been
fixed at a later date with rivets.

斯图拉青铜瓶
Situla

公元前8-7世纪
青铜
高19.5、直径24厘米

8-7th century BCE
Bronze
H.19.5cm, D.24cm

这件珍贵的桶形瓶由青铜薄
片制成，以提梁抬放，把手
呈半圆形，便于抓牢器物。
瓶身饰有优美的几何图案。
这种形状最为普遍，黏土器
皿中这类形状也最常见。

Precious vase made of sheet bronze,
beautifully decorated on the body
with geometric motifs executed
cantilever. It's provided with a
semicircular handle for gripping. This
shape is one of the most common, as
is that of the clay containers.

安夫拉陶瓶
Amphora

公元前8-7世纪
褐陶
高25、直径18.2厘米

8-7th century BCE
Impasto
H.25cm, D.18.2cm

本件器形优雅，瓶肩装有对
称的弧形把手，瓶腹部饰一
圈密密的竖直棱形纹。

Elegant container equipped with two
ribbon handles decorated on the
shoulder with thick vertical ribbing.

奥拉式斯泰莫斯瓶
Stamnos-Like Olla

公元前8-7世纪
褐陶
高32、直径22.5厘米

8-7th century BCE
Impasto
H.32cm, D.22.5cm

本件有喇叭形高圈足，表面用抛光棒打磨，器身四周的两个插孔和两个环形手柄对称分布。斯泰莫斯是古希腊的贮酒器，奥拉则是古罗马的一种球形水罐。

Developed tank mix with surface polished rod. Presents a high foot horn and, in the most expanded, two loops and two sockets arranged in a symmetrical.

凯特斯陶勺
Kyathos

公元前8-7世纪
褐陶
高8、直径9.1厘米

8-7th century BCE
Impasto
H. 8 cm, D.9.1cm

这种小勺是用来盛舀液体的，它有一个雕塑而成的把手，十分独特。

The small jar used to draw fluid has a peculiar plastic handle with lateral expansions.

伊特鲁里亚式几何纹克拉特陶瓶
Etruscan Geometric Crater

公元前8-7世纪
陶
高27.5、直径21.3厘米

8-7th century BCE
Purified Clay
H.27.5cm, D.21.3cm

维兰诺万时代后期阶段标志着陶器生产发展到另一个重要阶段，即所谓的"意大利——几何"陶器。本件陶器由精炼黏土制作，后用车床或轮制，绘有棕色或红色几何装饰图案。在造型和装饰图案方面——包括新的轮制技术，这种器皿的制作明显受到希腊影响，正如这件克拉特瓶所示。它的形状让人想起古希腊盛酒的双耳喷口瓶。涂料通常为有机材料，大多数情况下为赭石。该巨型酒瓶是宴会上用来调制葡萄酒。克拉特瓶是古希腊一种用于调酒，类似斝的双耳广口瓶。

The last phase of the Villanovan Age marked the start of pottery production that developed significantly over the next period, the so-called "Italo-geometric" pottery. The pottery was made with purified clay and turned on a lathe or wheel, with painted brown and red geometric decorations. They were clearly influenced by the Greeks, both in terms of the shapes and the decorativemotifs and also the new wheel technique, as with this krater, whose shape is reminiscent of theancient Greek kraters used to hold wine. The colours are organic in origin, for the most partochre.Large vase that was used to stir the wine at the banquet.

陶水壶
Jug

公元前8-7世纪
褐陶
高26、最大直径21厘米

8-7th century BCE
Impasto
H.26cm,D.(max)21cm

这件配有弧形把手的陶壶是宴会上用来斟倒饮料的。花瓣状壶口与高耸的圆筒形壶颈和起皱的壶身相映成趣。

Pottery vessel equipped with a 'loop that was used to pour liquids during the banquet. The trefoil mouth insists on a high cylindrical neck and body crushed.

安夫拉陶瓶
Amphora

公元前8-7世纪
褐陶
高19.4、直径16厘米

8-7th century BCE
Impasto
H.19.4 cm, D.16cm

本件器形优雅，瓶肩装有对
称的弧形把手，瓶腹部饰一
圈密密的竖直棱形纹。

Elegant container equipped with two
ribbon handles decorated on the
shoulder with thick vertical ribbing.

青铜手镯
Armilla

公元前8-7世纪
青铜
直径6.7厘米

8-7th century BCE
Bronze
D.6.7cm

本件为青铜手镯，由细青铜线扭绕而成。手镯，通常当做脚镯佩戴，男女通用。

Bracelet made of bronze with a thick bronze wire twisted. Bracelet, often worn as an anklet, used by both men andwomen.

铁矛头
Spearhead

公元前8-7世纪
铁
长30.3厘米

8-7th century BCE
Iron
L.30.3cm

铁匕首
Dagger

公元前8-7世纪
铁
长25厘米

8-7th century BCE
Iron
L.25cm

男性随葬品的武器中常见矛头，多以青铜或铁（如本件）制成，它被固定于木柄上。这段时期，长矛不仅作为攻击性武器使用，也充当狩猎工具——这也是它最重要的功能。狩猎为两项最重要的男性活动之一。

Among the weapons more common in male burials is the tip of the spear, in bronze or iron, such as this, designed to be fixed on wooden handle. During this period, spears were used not only as an offensiveweapon, but first and foremost for hunting, one of the twomost important male activities.

在维兰诺万时期丰富的随葬品中发现有武器，一般显示死者为男性，且生前已有很高的社会地位。

The weapons found in rich funerary Villanovan denote the male of the deceased and the high social position achieved in life.

伊特鲁里亚文明的起源

棚屋状骨灰瓮与房状墓室

早期墓葬中除了有黏土双锥形骨灰瓮，还发现有十分独特的棚屋状骨灰瓮。这些骨灰瓮都是死者生前居住的房屋——或棚屋，更准确的说——的缩小版黏土或木制模型。有时，这些骨灰瓮的墙壁上还涂有涂料。最常见的形状为椭圆形，屋顶是茅草或黏土搭建的，和现在那些边远地区仍然存在的棚屋没什么不同。存在这种相似性的原因在于，即使是最贫穷的社会成员也有能力建造这样的棚屋，尤其是可以就地取材进行建造。棚屋主要用于睡觉，中央有一个火灶，火灶的位置基本与屋顶烟囱的位置相吻合。门是唯一的出入口。

Hut-shaped Urns, Tombs like Houses

The production of impasto biconical urns at the previous burial sites was flanked by the rather unusual creation of hut-shaped cinerary urns. These were small-scale models of their houses or huts, to be more precise made with wood and clay. Sometimes they even had daub walls. Oval was the predominant shape, with a thatch and mud roof, not unlike those still found today in the most remote and diverse corners of our planet. The explanation for such similarities lies in the fact they can be built by even the poorest parts of society, especially as they can be constructed with local materials. The huts were mainly used for sleeping and had a fireplace in the centre that roughly matched the positioning of a smoke vent in the roof. The door was the only opening.

茅屋状陶骨灰瓮
Hut Shaped Urn

公元前9世纪
褐陶
高25、直径22厘米

9ᵗʰ century BCE
Impasto
H.25cm, D.22 cm

来自比森齐奥
波尔图·麦当那1号墓

本件完美而抽象地再现了一间
有着人字屋顶的四方形小屋,
支撑屋顶的横梁在屋顶上方交
错排列,起着装饰效果。

From Bisenzio, Porto Madonna,
tomba 1
The urn perfectly reproduces in
reduced forms hut with a rectangular
plan and gable roof supported by
beams that intersect at the top to
form a decorative pattern.

茅屋状陶骨灰瓮
Hut Shaped Urn

公元前8-7世纪
褐陶
高39.7、底径46厘米
来自维图罗尼亚

8-7th century BCE
Impasto
H. 39.7cm, D.(base)46cm
From Vetulonia

这类特别的物件原用于盛放逝者的骨灰，其造型往往模仿维兰诺万时期的私人住宅，例如本件就模仿带门的圆形尖顶茅屋。

The characteristic object that originally contained the ashes of the deceased in the form reproduces the private house used in the Villanovan period, ie a hut with a ridged roof, door furniture and circular.

茅屋状陶骨灰瓮
Hut Shaped Urn

公元前9世纪
高43、底径50厘米
褐陶

9th century BCE
Impasto
H. 43cm, D.(base)50cm

来自塔尔奎尼亚
波乔·德·因姆皮卡托

这类特别的物件原用于盛放逝者的骨灰，其造型往往模仿维兰诺万时期的私人住宅，例如本件就模仿带门的圆形尖顶茅屋。

From Tarquinia, Poggio dell'Impiccato
The characteristic object that originally contained the ashes of the deceased in the form reproduces the private house used in the Villanovan period, is a hut with a ridged roof, door furniture and circular.

男性的世界：武器

伊特鲁里亚人历来擅长航海，在与希腊和东方的商业往来中，伊特鲁里亚人受到了这些古代文明的深刻影响。这种影响在统治精英阶层中最为明显，著名的伊特鲁里亚贵族几乎总是在不断作战，一方面保护自己的财产和领土，另一方面也要向外扩张，吞并邻国的土地和人民，这在古代各民族中都是司空见惯的。在伊特鲁里亚的君主时代，也就是古希腊时代（公元前六世纪），正是这种争取扩张和成长的力量驱使着伊特鲁里亚人控制了后来的罗马城。所以，战争是人们为了保护自己的身份而进行的一种特殊活动。陪葬品记录了男性战士，尤其是领袖的生活。这些人的陪葬品中除了有实际使用过的大刀长矛等武器外，往往还包括专门用于死后随葬的仪仗武器。

这些武器用青铜片制造，还有各种头盔，甚至一些铠甲。最初，铠甲只是一些圆形的护板，但后来发展成人体形状的贴身外罩，或者在皮制的内芯之外缝上甲片制成（一些铠甲的边缘有小孔就是证据）。盾牌也是由皮革外覆青铜制成的。不过，在许多情况下，内层的结构是木制的，或用有机易腐材料制成，只有少量残片因被覆盖在青铜片之下而得以保存至今，其余大部分经过漫长岁月都已分解消失，不复存在。许多伊特鲁里亚人制造的武器装备都与明显受到希腊影响的物品联系在一起，例如许多按人体体形制成的甲上常常有雕刻。在某些情况下，供显赫人物使用的物品往往直接从希腊购置。

The Men's World: Weapons

The Etruscans were always a sailing people that, through their commercial relationships with the East and Greece, were heavily influenced by these ancient civilizations. Nowhere was this more true than for the ruling elites, the famous Etruscan aristocracies that, as was all too common among ancient peoples, were almost constantly at war both to protect their possessions and territory, and to expand, encompassing neighbouring peoples. During the age of the Etruscan kings, in the archaic period (6th century BCE), it was this drive to grow that led the Etruscans to take control of the town that would one day be Rome. Thus, war was a distinctive element intended to protect their identity. Once again, grave goods document the lives of male warriors, especially the leaders. Their grave goods often included not only the weapons they actually used - spears and knives - but also parade weapons designed specifically to accompany the wealthy in the afterlife.

The weapons were made of bronze sheet and there was also a range of helmets and even some armour. Initially, the latter was nothing more than disks, but later, body-shaped corsets or greaves stitched on a leather core were made (as shown by the presence of holes along the edges of such armour). The shields were also made of leather plated with bronze. In many cases, though, the underlying structure was made with wood or organic, perishable materials that, aside from a few fragments preserved under the bronze sheets, have completely decomposed over time. In most cases, Etruscan-produced items were associated with items that had a clear Greek influence, such as the anatomical greaves that were often engraved. In some cases, for people of special importance, they were imported directly from Greece.

内加式青铜头盔
Negau Type Helmet

公元前5世纪
青铜
高23.75、宽25.5厘米

5th century BCE
Bronze
H.23.5cm, W.25.5cm

来自波普罗尼亚
圣切尔波公墓，36号墓

这件头盔顶部有条突起的棱边，这种形状的头盔在十五世纪十分典型，在伊特鲁里亚以外也有十分广泛的应用。内加（Negau）在今斯诺文尼亚境内。一般来说，头盔的时代变迁更为显著，从最早的顶饰头盔演变为这种十分简单且更接近近代造型的头盔。在现实生活中，领主和伟大首领统治的社会已经一去不返，过去那种装饰繁复且带有华丽头饰的头盔通常被当做军事领袖的标志，而今已经消失。头盔已经演变为简单的金属帽，其作用为保护头部不受伤害，不再是重要人物的标志。

From Populonia, necropoli di San Cerbone, tomba 36
The shape of this helmet spread over the top with a sharp edge is typical of the fifth century. C. and has a wide geographical distribution outside of Etruria.
The helmets, generally speaking, show a greater development over time, from the earliest agesof the crested helmet to these very simple and more recent helmets. In reality, the society ofprinces and great leaders had begun to vanish and these military head coverings that at one time identified primarily military leaders and types and therefore were very ornate with elaborate decoration, had now become simply metal caps to protect the head and no longer identifiedimportant roles in society.

青铜头盔
Helmet

公元前7世纪
青铜
高17.7、直径25.5厘米

7th century BCE
Bronze
H.17.7cm, D.25.5cm

这件漂亮的青铜头盔顶部呈半球状，盔檐则水平展开。这类头盔有时会配有一层皮革套。

Beautiful bronze helmet with hemispherical and stretched horizontally. In some cases these objects present within a leather jacket.

维图罗尼亚青铜头盔
Helmet From Vetulonia

公元前7世纪
青铜
长16、直径29厘米

7th century BCE
Bronze
H.16cm, D.29cm

来自维图罗尼亚
塞克洛·德格利·尤里瓦斯特

这件头盔是伊特鲁里亚时期在维图罗尼亚这座东方化城市发掘的墓葬中最引人注目的一件物品。它无疑问属于一位曾经统治过该地的军事首领。维图罗尼亚在今意大利格罗塞托省（Grosseto）西北。

From Vetulonia, Circolo degli Ulivastri One of the most striking of the burials Orientalizing Etruscan city of Vetulonia. Certainly belonged to one of the warrior princes who ruled the company.

青铜胫甲
Couple of Greaves

公元前7世纪
青铜
长37、宽13厘米

7th century BCE
Bronze
L.37cm, W.13cm

来自维图罗尼亚，塞洛·特里·纳威赛尔人用护胫，保护膝盖以下的小腿部位，里层同样衬有皮革，两侧通常饰有雕刻图案，与小腿相对应。造型上模仿进口的希腊护胫。

From Vetulonia, Circolo delle Tre Navicelle
Anatomical leggings, made to protect the part of the leg below the knee, were also lined in leatherand often decorated with etchings on the side, corresponding to the calf. The shape is thatof the original imported Greek leggings.

青铜胫甲
Greave

公元前7世纪
青铜

长32、宽16厘米
7th century BCE
Bronze
L.32 cm, W.16cm

来自维图罗尼亚
塞克洛·特里·纳威赛尔

胫甲是武士们用来保护小腿的，它与头盔、盾牌和其他进攻性武器一起作为权贵们的殉葬品。

From Vetulonia, Circolo delle Tre Navicelle
The greaves, which protected the lower part of the legs of the warriors, were placed in the burial of persons of high rank, together helmet, shield and other weapons of offense.

青铜剑与剑鞘
Sword and Sheath

公元前9-8世纪
青铜
剑：长36.2厘米，鞘：长30.2厘米

9-8th century BCE
Bronze
Sword:L.36.2cm, Sheath:L.30.2cm

来自维图罗尼亚，塞克洛·塞克洛·特里·纳威赛尔典型的肉搏战武器，通常配有鞘。如本例所示，由青铜甚至象牙制作。装饰有雕刻图案。殉葬品中的剑与鞘标志着逝者的上层社会身份。

From Vetulonia, Circolo delle Tre Navicelle
A typical close combat weapon, which often had a sheath, as in this case, in bronze or even ivory, decorated with etchings. In the grave goods, these distinguished persons of high rank.

青铜矛头
Spearhead

公元前9-8世纪
青铜
长25.5、宽4.5厘米

9-8th century BCE
Bronze
L.25.5cm, W.4.5cm

青铜或铁制作的矛头可有多
种形状，或多或少为细长形
状，有无中间的棱纹皆可。
不过所有矛头底部都配有可
插入木杆的金属箍，金属箍
由轧制的金属片制作。
通常，这些木杆均用非常容
易腐烂的有机材料制作，因
而无法保存至今。盔甲内层
的皮革或织布衬里也是如
此，但不排除有些盔甲底层
仍残余一些纤维的痕迹。

The spearheads, made of bronze or
iron, had a variety ofshapes, more or
less elongated and with or without
a centralrib. All of them, however,
had the lower part, the ferrule,made
of rolled plate, in which to insert the
wooden shaft.
Usually, these have not been
preserved, being made of
veryperishable organic material.
The same is true of leather orwoven
fabrics, with the exception of a few
traces of fibre onthe inside.

青铜矛头
Spearhead

公元前9-8世纪
青铜
长26、宽4厘米

9-8BCE
Bronze
L.26cm, W.4cm

这类矛头有着长刃和有叶状
装饰，可安装在木柄上。

The spearheads of this type have
a long blade and foliated handle
quarry that was attached to a rod of
wood.

费埃索式武士图石碑
Funerary Stele Fiesole Style Representing Some Warriors

公元前6世纪
沙岩
高42.5、长32、厚10厘米

6th century BCE
Sandstone
H.42.5cm, L.32cm, Th.10cm

该类墓碑是安装在伊特鲁里亚东方化时期或更古时期的大型土墩墓上方。墓碑的一面装饰有两位手持武器的武士，这是为了强调逝者较高的社会地位。费埃索（Fiesole）是今佛罗伦萨省的小镇。

Stele of this type were placed on top of the large mound tombs of the Etruscan Orientalizing period and archaic. One of the faces is decorated with two armed warriors, to emphasize the high social status of the deceased.

陶双马双轮战车
Miniature Biga

公元前8世纪
褐陶
高11、长20厘米

8th century BCE
Impasto
H.11cm, L.20cm

来自奥维多，本件陶土模型再现了一辆微缩版的小型战车，这是一种由两匹战马拉的轻快、灵活的战车。它无疑属于一位武士。

From Orvieto
The group represents miniature forms in the clay model of a small chariot, wagon fast and agile used in battle, pulled by two horses. Certainly belonged to a warrior.

战车
Chariot

公元前7世纪
青铜、铁
高140、宽180、直径104厘米

7th century BCE
Bronze and Iron
H.140cm, W.180cm, D.104cm

来自波普罗尼亚，卡里之墓
这辆精美的马车事实上是一
辆真正的双轮战车，来自波
普罗尼亚最大的墓葬。这辆
轻快的战车是领主在军事阅
兵时乘坐的，后来与一系列
种类丰富的殉葬品一起陪
葬，作为墓主权力的主要标
志。战车为木质结构（该木
质框架为现代复原），然后
将其他部件组装上去，并贴
上华丽的金属片作为装饰。

From Populonia, Tomba dei Carri
This beautiful cart, in this case a
real chariot with two wheels, comes
from the most monumentaltomb
in Populonia. This light, fast vehicle
was used by princes during military
parades andthen placed with the rich
array of grave goods as the main
monument to their power. It has
awooden structure (rebuilt in modern
times) to which the various parts
in hammered and richlydecorated
metal plate were attached.

青铜马衔
Couple of Horsebites

公元前7世纪
青铜
长38、铜板高7厘米

7th century BCE
Bronze
L.38cm, H. Piastra 7cm

青铜马衔
Couple of Horsebites

公元前8世纪
青铜
长35厘米

8th century BCE
Bronze
L.35cm

这类物品属于马具中的一部分，马衔有各种不同的形状和尺寸，经常出现在东方化时期的伊特鲁里亚国王墓葬中。

古时候，马匹是克敌制胜的关键元素，乘坐马匹是领袖的特权——不管是单人乘骑，还是成双成对地用作驱使战车（如来自波普罗尼亚的马车所示）。在高级阶层男性的墓穴中，除陪葬有个人使用的防御性和攻击性武器外，还包括青铜或铁质的马具部件和马嚼。与其他文明相比较，这些物品的制作十分繁复精美，因而通过马匹的装束彰显主人的地位。

Such items, which are part of the harness horses, of various shapes and sizes, are very frequent in the depositions of the rich Etruscan princes of the Orientalizing period.

In the ancient world, horses were crucial to conquest, and a prerogative of leaders alone,whether the horses were used singly or as a pair for the famous chariots (like the one fromPopulonia). In the burials of high-ranking males, along with the individual defensive andoffensive weapons, there were also items in bronze and iron from the horse harness, and bits,very elaborately made compared to other ancient civilizations, thus identifying the status of theowner through his horse.

来自维图罗尼亚
波乔·阿拉·噶尔迪亚B

这对马衔呈柱形，一端装饰着一匹栩栩如生的小马。

From Vetulonia, Poggio alla Guardia, Circolo B
These horse bits are the pillar decorated with a plastic figurine of a horse made with a Natural.

女性的世界：饰物和美容

　　上层社会的殉葬品以其珍贵的饰物而闻名。扣针是男女通用的饰品，而男性仅在系带有复杂扣件的皮带时使用扣针。著名的伊特鲁里亚首饰生产主要为妇女服务，包括饰针、一系列形状大小各异的扣针、螺旋状黄金发箍、饰有雕刻图案的薄片手镯，例如armille。最著名的一些伊特鲁里亚人首饰来自极其富有的维图罗尼亚的皮特拉（Pietrera）墓葬，该墓葬出土了许多精致小巧、装饰优美的带饰、项链和耳环。伊特鲁里亚文化早期的首饰的制作工艺和技术极其高超——例如，将极其精细的金粉或金珠焊接在黄金薄片上，即使现代技术也无法完全与之匹敌。单个的坠饰或垂饰通常为儿童饰物。象牙与黄金一样珍贵、难得，它属于进口物品，取材自大象的獠牙。象牙通常以其最原始的状态抵达伊特鲁里亚，然后由依靠为贵族工作为生的工匠们制作成饰物。象牙可制作垂饰和发针。

The World of Women: Ornaments and Beauty

The grave goods of the upper class are notable for their precious ornaments. Fibulae were used by both men and women, while only men used to wear belts with elaborate fastening devices. However, the production of the famous Etruscan jewellery was for women and included pins, an array of various shaped and sized fibulae, twisted golden thread hair spirals, and decorated sheet bracelets, such as the armille. The most outstanding examples of these are those from the wondrously wealthy Pietrera di Vetulonia tomb, which had minute, finely decorated overlapping bands, necklaces and earrings. In the early periods of the culture, jewellery was made with such skill and techniques - like fixing fine gold powder or granules onto a sheet of gold - that it still has not been completely matched by modern technology. Single pendants or bullae were generally for children. Ivory was as precious and sought after as gold. It was imported, having been obtained from elephant tusks. It would arrive in Etruria in its raw state so that it could be worked by the craftsmen who depended on the aristocratic families for their livelihoods. Ivory was used to make pendants as well as hair pins.

青铜搭扣
Buckle

公元前7世纪
青铜
长11厘米

7th century BCE
Bronze
L.11cm

来自维图罗尼亚
塞克洛·特里·纳威赛尔

本件由矩形框架和抓钩组
成，是用来控制马匹的配
件。这是典型的男性墓葬
品，在伊特鲁里亚沿海地
区、丘西（阿雷佐省的小
镇）地区和北部疆域都十分
常见。

From Vetulonia, Circolo delle Tre
Navicelle
Rectangular frame structure with
hooks configured to protome horses.
This is typical objects of male burials
very common in Etruria in the coastal
area, Chiusi and in the northern
territories.

青铜搭扣
Buckle

公元前7世纪
青铜
长11厘米

7th century BCE
Bronze
L.11cm

来自维图罗尼亚
塞克洛·特里·纳威赛尔

本件由矩形框架和抓钩组
成，是用来控制马匹的配
件。这是典型的男性墓葬
品，在伊特鲁里亚沿海地
区、丘西（阿雷佐省的小
镇）地区和北部疆域都十分
常见。

From Vetulonia, Circolo delle Tre
Navicelle
Rectangular frame structure with
hooks configured to protome horses.
This is typical objects of male burials
very common in Etruria in the coastal
area, Chiusi and in the northern
territories.

来自丘西

这件青铜腰带搭扣展现了十分精美复杂的图案，方框中间是一只动物形象。这件作品说明创作者是一位精通金属加工的行家。

From Chiusi
This belt buckle in bronze presents an elaborate decoration traf gold with a figure of an animal at the center of the frame. Opera refers to an artisan an expert in metalworking.

青铜腰带
Belt

公元前8世纪
青铜
长12、宽29厘米

8th century BCE
Bronze
L.12cm, W.29cm

来自波普罗尼亚
S·塞邦公墓，36号墓

Early 8th century B.C.E.
这类腰带被称为"菱形腰带"，得名于其特别的形状，通常见于男性墓葬，但有些情况下，女性墓穴的殉葬品中亦可见此物。一般说来，伊特鲁里亚文明最早阶段中，衣物上的饰物和个人物品在墓葬中都较为常见，但后期，装饰品和首饰逐渐成为特定的女性物品。

From Populonia, necropoli di S.Cerbone, tomba 36
This type of belt, defined as "a losanga (lozenge)" because of its special shape, was usedin male graves although in some cases, it has also been found in female grave goods. In general,ornaments from garments and personal items were commonly and typically used in the earliestphases, then gradually ornaments and jewellery become more specific to the feminine sphere.

青铜弓形扣针
Segmental Arch Fibula

青铜
长4.5厘米

Bronze
L.4.5cm

来自维图罗尼亚
塞克洛·特里·纳威赛尔

伊特鲁里亚饰针有着多种造型和大小，通常穿有小块琥珀或玻璃涂层小珠作为装饰，在古代作为纽扣扣牢衣襟，通常沿着一侧肩膀固定。

From Vetulonia, Circolo delle Tre Navicelle
The fibulae, of various shapes and sizes, often decoratedwith little amber or glass paste beads threaded along the pin,were used in ancient times as real buttons to close the twoedges of the garment, usually along the shoulders but alsoon the side.

青铜扣针
Fibula

公元前7世纪
青铜
高 4.8、长10厘米

7th century BCE
Bronze
H.4.8cm, L.10cm

来自维图罗尼亚
塞克洛·特里·纳威赛尔

这类环形扣针，甚至包括尺寸较大的扣针，通常有一个装饰精美的弓形搭扣，譬如本例就采用了雕刻装饰。

From Vetulonia, Circolo delle Tre Navicelle
Rings of this type, even of large dimensions, often have the decorated arch, as in this case, by incisions.

青铜扣针
Fibula

公元前7世纪
青铜
长14厘米

7th century BCE
Bronze
L.14cm

这种青铜制作的水蛭形饰针是典型的女性装饰品，即使她们知道还有更为珍贵的金属饰针，像本件这种弓形的、雕刻有图案的扣针和平板式扣针，在很长一段时间内十分盛行。

The leech fibulae of bronze or craft, typical ornaments related to women, totaled over a period of time rather wide, even if they know precious metal versions, plain or decorated with carvings on the arch like this.

青铜扣针
Fibula

公元前7世纪
青铜
高4.5、长8.5厘米

7th century BCE
Bronze
H.4.5cm, L.8.5cm

来自维图罗尼亚
塞克洛·特里·纳威赛尔

这类环形扣针，甚至包括尺寸较大的扣针，通常有一个装饰精美的弓形搭扣，譬如此例就采用了雕刻装饰。

From Vetulonia, Circolo delle Tre Navicelle
Rings of this type, even of large dimensions, often have the decorated arch, as in this case, by incisions.

青铜扣针
Fibula

公元前7世纪
青铜
长15厘米

7th century BCE
Bronze
L.15cm

这种青铜制作的水蛭形饰针是典型的女性装饰品，即使她们知道还有更为珍贵的金属饰针，像本件这种弓形的、雕刻有图案的扣针和平板式扣针，在很长一段时间内十分盛行。

The leech fibulae of bronze or craft, typical ornaments related to women, totaled over a period of time rather wide, even if they know precious metal versions, plain or decorated with carvings on the arch like this.

银扣针
Fibula

公元前7世纪
金
长11.5厘米

7th century BCE
Gold
L.11.5cm

来自阿尔贝纳的马塞里亚那城，塞克洛·德·佩拉左特
这一时期各种款式的波浪状弓形搭扣，在埃特鲁斯坎（意大利中部的古国）的北部地区的男性葬礼十分常见。

From Marsiliana d'Albegna, Circolo di Perazzeta
Fibulae of this type, with wavy bows, include a wide range of variants. Widespread especially in northern Etruria where they are often found in male burials.

金弓形扣针
Fibula With Engraved Arch

公元前7世纪
金
高1.6、长3.6厘米

7th century BCE
Gold
H.1.6cm, L.3.6cm

来自维图罗尼亚

这种黄金制作的水蛭形饰针是典型的女性装饰品，在很长一段时间内十分盛行，包括平板的或雕刻有装饰图案的，例如本饰针，即使他们知道还有更为珍贵的金属饰针。

From Vetulonia
This gold fibula is a typical ornament used by women, used over a long period of time. It can be plain or decorated with carvings on the arch like this.

金弓形扣针
Fibulae With Granulation Decoration

公元前7世纪
金
高3.2、长9.4厘米
7th century BCE
Gold
H.3.2cm, L.9.4cm

来自维图罗尼亚
瑞博斯提戈里奥·德·费布罗尼

这只饰针在针弓和针托上均饰有相似造型和大小的装饰图案，并运用了独具一格的"颗粒"工艺，即将一颗颗黄金珠子焊接在光滑的底座上，并组成各种不同的装饰图案。这只扣针上，我们可以分辨出人物形象和动物形象。

From Vetulonia, Ripostiglio dei Fibuloni
This fibula, similar in shape and size, are both decorated on the arch and on the bracket with the peculiar technique of "dust", very small beads of gold welded on a smooth base comprising various decorative motifs. We distinguish theories of human figures and animals.

金弓形扣针
Fibulae

公元前7世纪
金
高1.5、长5.5厘米
7th century BCE
Gold
H.1.5cm, L.5.5cm

来自维图罗尼亚
波乔·阿拉·嘎尔迪亚

这种黄金制作的水蛭形饰针是典型的女性装饰品，在很长一段时间内十分盛行，包括平板的或雕刻有装饰图案的，例如本饰针，即使他们知道还有更为珍贵的金属饰针。

From Vetulonia, Poggio alla Guardia
This gold fibula is a typical ornament used by women, used over a long period of time. It can be plain or decorated with carvings on the arch like this.

金发箍
Couple of Plait Holders

公元前7世纪
金
直径4厘米

7th ce4
D.4cm

这种螺旋状线圈或粗或细，
有时饰有图案，有时则素
面，通常为光滑的线圈造
型——如本件所示，用于束
住发辫末梢，男女通用。

Thicker or thinner twisted wire,
decorated or plain, frequently
smooth wire as in this case, wasused
to fasten the end of a braid, by both
men and women.

金手镯
Couple of Armillae

公元前7世纪
金
直径9.5厘米

7th century BCE
Gold
D.9.5cm

来自维图罗尼亚

这两只手镯被认为是伊特鲁
里亚珠宝首饰中的杰作。手
镯运用了精美的浮雕装饰工
艺和伊特鲁里亚工匠从东方
借鉴而来的金银丝细工艺。

From Vetulonia
These two bracelets are considered
as two masterpieces of Etruscan
jewelry. They have a refined
embossed decoration and filigree
techniques borrowed from Etruscan
craftsmen from the Orient.

青铜手镯
Armilla

公元前7世纪
青铜
直径8.5厘米

7th century BCE
Bronze
D.8.5cm

来自维图罗尼亚，
塞克洛·特里·纳威赛尔

手镯，有些情况下也做脚镯
使用，男女通用。

From Vetulonia, Circolo delle Tre
Navicelle
Bracelet, anklet too in some cases,
common to both womenand men.

青铜手镯
Armilla

公元前7世纪
青铜
直径10厘米

7th century BCE
Bronze
D.10cm

人们普遍认为本件是个人袖
口的饰品，通常见于东方化
时期的富有女性陵墓中。

The cuff is wide certification among
personal ornaments that denote
wealthy funerary female Orientalizing
Period.

金手镯
Couple of Armillae

公元前7世纪
金
长33.5-34.7、宽6.2厘米

7th century BCE
Gold
L.33.5-34.7cm,W.6.2cm

来自维图罗尼亚

这对手镯由精美的金箔制作
而成，表面的条纹造型两端
均饰有人头装饰和其他图
案。出土于伊特鲁里亚城
市——维图罗尼亚的一座重
要的国王陵墓。

From Vetulonia
Bracelet made of fine gold foil
divided into bands decorated at the
ends with human heads and other
reasons obtained cantilever. Come
from an impressive princely tomb of
the Etruscan city of Vetulonia.

维图罗尼亚金项链
Necklace With 36 Pendants From
Vetulonia

公元前7世纪
金
高2、宽1厘米

7ᵗʰ century BCE
Gold
H.2cm,W.1cm

来自维图罗尼亚

在伊特鲁里亚的城市维图罗
尼亚有大量的古墓，在最有
名的皮特拉（Pietrera）的
墓中，出土了这件珍贵的用
金箔打造的项链坠饰。

From Vetulonia
The precious necklace pendants
equipped with gold foil decorated
with busts of women come from the
tomb of Pietrera, one of the most
prestigious burial mounds of the
Etruscan city of Vetulonia.

公元前7世纪
金
长32、宽0.8厘米

7th century BCE
Gold
L.32cm,W.0.8 cm

来自维图罗尼亚
图穆罗·德拉·皮特瑞拉

这条精美的串珠项链由一串
近似球体的小珠子组成，珠
子上包裹一层有压印纹饰的
金箔。

From Vetulonia, Tumulo della Pietrera
The refined necklace is composed
of a sequence of vague spheroidal
obtained with a gold foil embossed
decoration.

金耳环
Couple of Earrings

公元前6世纪
金
高3.5、宽2厘米

6th century BCE
gold
H.3.5cm,W.2cm

据考证，这类水蛭造型的耳环来自公元前7世纪的伊特鲁里亚。这种花朵元素组成的图案有着各种不同的形状和大小。

Earrings leech as these are attested in Etruria from the seventh century BC. The decoration consists of floreal elements applied that have different shapes and sizes.

金耳环
Earring

公元前6世纪
金
高2.5、宽2.3厘米

6th century BCE
Gold
H.2.5cm, W.2.3cm

据考证，这类水蛭造型的耳环来自公元前7世纪的伊特鲁里亚。这种花朵元素组成的装饰图案有着各种不同的形状和大小。

Earrings leech as these are attested in Etruria from the seventh century BCE. The decoration consists of floreal elements applied that have different shapes and sizes.

金耳环
Couple of Earrings

公元前6世纪
金
宽1.5厘米

6th century BCE
Gold
W.1.5 cm

这种保龄球袋式的耳环是整个伊特鲁里亚古风时期最为流行的一种饰品，传播了一种装饰模式。

The earrings of this type, bowling bag, are among the most prevalent in Etruria throughout the Archaism. Report a decoration mold.

金耳环
Couple of Earrings

公元前6世纪
金
高1.5-2、直径1.8-2厘米

6th century BCE
Gold
H.1.5-2cm, D.1.8-2cm

来自锡纳纶伦加

这些耳环的边缘饰有一串珍珠，主体饰以花蕊母题，一只耳环用金箔做成花朵，另一只耳环上则饰花蕊图案。

From Sinalunga
Earring decorated on margin with floral motifs in golden foil, printed on the ring. One of these earrings is decorated with flowers.

美人鱼金簪
Golden Pin With A Mermaid

公元前6世纪
金
长6.6、宽1.8厘米

6th century BCE
Gold
L.6.6cm,W.1.8cm

来自波普罗尼亚

这只金簪来自伊特鲁里亚的著名城市波普罗尼亚，金簪头部饰有一个展翅的狮身人面像图案。

From Populonia
The pin from the prestigious Etruscan town of Populonia has his head decorated with a winged sphinx made cantilever.

狮身鹰首金戒指
Ring With A Griffin

公元前6世纪
金
直径2.4厘米

6th century BCE
Gold
D.2.4 cm

来自维图罗尼亚

这枚珍贵的图章戒指采用了尖顶造型，戒面饰有神话动物，本件可能来自国外。

From Vetulonia
The precious signet ring shows an ogival decorated with a fantastic animal. Likely imports.

维图罗尼亚金坠饰
Pendant From Vetulonia

公元前7世纪
金
直径3厘米

7th century BCE
Gold
D.3cm

这件圆形坠饰是用金箔制成的，其顶部的金横管则是用以串线。

Bulla circular foil made of gold provided at the top of a small tube with gold transverse through for the insertion of the wire.

在希腊化时期，即伊特鲁里亚文明的最后一个阶段，首饰的类型和装饰图案发生了重大改变。复杂精密的造粒技术和撒粉工艺（或许对于处于经济衰退时期的伊特鲁里亚社会，这种工艺过于昂贵，而且这一期间制作的陶器也越变越小）开始日益少见，早期贵族殉葬品中常见的尊贵至极的奢侈品也有所减少。

During the Hellenistic stage, the last stage of the Etruscan civilization, the jewellery showed a major change in the types and the decorative motifs. The sophisticated granule and powder techniques (perhaps too costly in a moment of economic recession for the Etruscan society, as is also visible from the pottery getting smaller) became less common and there was a decrease in the most prestigious luxury items that were always found among the grave goods of the wealthiest from earlier times.

金王冠桂枝
Laurel and Olive Branches Diadem

公元前2世纪
金
长26-33厘米
2th century BCE

Gold
L.26-33cm

来自沃尔泰拉

本件用于额头发佩饰。由金箔作成橄榄枝的椭圆形的树叶和叶茎。这典型的希腊化时期风格。
这类叶状王冠是首饰中最尊贵的类型，由十分精细的黄金薄片制作，在男性和女性墓葬中均有出现，可能仅作丧葬用途，并作为重要的殉葬品陪葬，代表墓主崇高的社会地位。

From Volterra
Ornament used to adorn the hair on the forehead. It consists of a series of small oval shaped leaves made with a thin gold foil welded to a stem. Typical of the Hellenistic period. The leafy crown is one of the most prestigious forms ofjewellery, made from very fine plate. They are documentedin male and female tombs, probably made only for funeraryuse as a main item in the grave goods, reflecting the highsocial status of their owners.

金王冠桂枝
Laurel and Olive Branches Diadem

公元前2世纪
金
长26—33厘米

2th century BCE
Gold
L.26-33cm

金头带装饰
Diadem

公元前4世纪
金
高6、长26厘米

4th century BCE
Gold
H.6cm, L.26cm

本件用于额头发佩饰。由金箔作成橄榄枝的椭圆形的树叶和叶茎。这典型的希腊化时期风格。

Ornament used to adorn the hair on the forehead. It consists of a series of small oval shaped leaves made with a thin gold foil welded to a stem. Typical of the Hellenistic period.

女性常在前额佩戴这类物品作为发饰。它由一片薄金箔制作，金箔上浮雕菜叶图案图案。这是典型的希腊化时期头饰。

Object used by women to adorn the hair on the forehead. It made with a thin gold foil embossed with vegetable elements. Typical of the Hellenistic period.

狮头形金耳环
Couple of Earings Lion Head Shaped

公元前4–3世纪
金
直径2厘米

4–3th century BCE
Gold
D.2cm

这对耳环出土于一座珍宝极为丰富的女性墓葬。这类耳环在公元前4世纪后期和公元前3世纪前期的伊特鲁里亚和大希腊时代的塔兰托地区十分常见。

The pair of earrings comes from a female burial particularly rich in precious objects. The type is very common in Etruria and Magna Graecia species in Taranto between the late fourth and early third century. B.C. E.

金耳环
Couple of Earrings

公元前4世纪
金
直径2厘米

4th century BCE
Gold
D.2cm

耳环是"簇镶"耳环中造型最简单的一对,"簇镶"耳环是公元前4世纪最普遍的一种陪葬品,其装饰造型十分多样。

The pair of earrings is a more simplified version of the greatest earrings "cluster" popular among the grave goods of the fourth sec.a. C. variously decorated.

宝石金戒指
Ring

公元前4世纪
金、宝石
直径2.7厘米

4th century BCE
Gold and Agate
D.2.7cm

这只精美的图章戒指饰在压花金底座上镶一枚硬质宝石(绿宝石)。

Refined signet ring decorated with ogival knurled file that contains a hard stone (beryl).

金耳环
Earring

公元前4世纪
金
高3、宽2厘米

4th century BCE
Gold
H.3cm,W.2cm

这只设计繁复精美的簇镶耳环是一座公元前4世纪女性墓塚中发现的一件稀世珍宝。这只耳环的独特之处在于该首饰的底座上井然有序地镶嵌的一系列金珠。

The elaborate earring cluster is large fortune in the fourth century funerary female. B.C.E. The decoration is characterized by a sequence of beads which are generally placed at the base of the jewel.

金耳环
Couple of Earrings

公元前4世纪
金
长6.4厘米

4th century BCE
Gold
L.6.4cm

这类管状耳环通常配有各种形状的耳坠，在希腊化时期（公元前323-公元前146年）广泛流行。根据这类耳环出土的地理分布推断，在伊特鲁里亚北部地区有一个生产点。

The type of these earrings tube, often accompanied by variously shaped pendants, is widespread in the Hellenistic period. The geographical distribution of findings suggests a manufacture in northern Etruria.

金耳环
Couple of Earrings

公元前4世纪
金
高7.3厘米

4th century BCE
Gold
H.7.3cm

这类管状耳环通常配有各种形状的耳坠,在希腊化时期（323-146 BCE）广泛流行。根据这类耳环出土的地理分布推断，在伊特鲁里亚北部地区有一个生产点。

The type of these earrings tube, often accompanied by variously shaped pendants, is widespread in the Hellenistic period. The geographical distribution of findings suggests a manufacture in northern Etruria.

以下物品展现了一些伊特鲁里亚女性的形象，以及伊特鲁里亚女性发型和饰品的历史变迁。通常，这些红陶面孔最生动地再现了古代社会的流行风尚和装束。彩陶上绘制的人物形象也展示了当时的女性面孔和面貌，譬如波普洛尼亚的陶酒坛和康塔罗斯酒杯（用于倒酒和饮酒的陶器，可能由女性使用）。

The following pieces show female images and the development of their hairstyles and ornaments over time. Terracotta faces are often the most telling testimony of the fashions and costumes in an ancient society. The images on painted pottery also provide insight into female faces and looks, such as on the oinochoe and the kantharos from Populonia (pieces of pottery used to pour and drink wine, probably used by women).

陶女子头像
Archaic Female Head Antefix

公元前6世纪
红陶
高20.5、底座长15.5厘米

6th century BCE
Terracotta
H.20.5cm, L.(base)15.5 cm

这尊红陶女性供奉头像的头发在前额分成若干股卷发，并在脑后挽成一束。她佩戴的是簇镶式耳环，头戴珍贵的瓦檐状带饰。该像为古风时代（约公元前8–6世纪）风格。

Female terracotta votive head with face framed by hair on the forehead divided into wavy locks collected at the back. The ears are decorated with cluster earrings while on the chest is visible a valuable necklace with embossed pendants.

陶女子供奉头像
Votive Female Head

公元前4世纪
红陶
高25、宽21厘米

4th century BCE
Terracotta
H. 25cm, W.21cm

这尊红陶女子供奉头像的头发在前额分成若干股卷发，并在脑后挽成一束。她佩戴的是簇镶式耳环，胸前可分辨出佩戴着一条装饰有浮雕图案吊坠的项链。头像造型的供奉雕塑展示了伊特鲁里亚文明末期，即公元前4世纪的饰品和发型。

Female terracotta votive head with face framed by hair on the forehead divided into wavy locks collected at the back. The ears are decorated with cluster earrings while on the chest is visible a valuable necklace with embossed pendants. The votive heads are indicative of the ornaments and hairstyles of the last phase of the Etruscan civilization, the 4th century B.C.E.

陶女子供奉头像
Votive Female Head

公元前4世纪
红陶
高28.5厘米

4th century BCE
Terracotta
H.28.5cm

这尊红陶女子供奉头像的头发在前额分成若干股卷发，并在脑后挽成一束。她佩戴的是簇镶式耳环，头上则佩戴着珍贵的带状头饰。

Female terracotta votive head with face framed by hair on the forehead divided into wavy locks collected at the back. The ears are decorated with cluster earrings while on the chest is visible a valuable necklace with embossed pendants.

美容也极大地促进了伊特鲁利亚一个重要冶铁部门分支的发展，即制造表面极其光滑锃亮的铜镜供女性们欣赏自己的容貌。这种配有把柄的铜镜是最古老的一种铜镜，与东方世界制造的其他铜镜（包括中国铜镜）没什么不同。镜子上通常雕刻有希腊神话和伊特鲁利亚神话中的情节，和一些日常生活中的场景。有些镜子配有骨头或象牙雕刻的手柄，而不是青铜手柄。

The feminine world of beauty care was also the trigger for a major metal production sector in Etruria, namely the creation of bronze items, with their perfectly smooth and polished surfaces, that first enabled women to look at themselves. The mirrors with handles are the most ancient type and are not unlike some other made in the Orient (also Chinese). They were often engraved with episodes from the Greek and Etruscans myths and scenes from daily life. Some had a bone or ivory handles, instead of bronze.

青铜镜
Mirror

公元前4世纪
青铜
宽24、直径12厘米

4th century BCE
Bronze
L.24cm, D.12cm

青铜镜
Mirror

公元前4世纪
青铜
宽27、直径13厘米

4th century BCE
Bronze
L.27cm, D.13cm

青铜镜在很长一段时间内都是典型的伊特鲁里亚女性陪葬品。这类青铜镜表面光滑，通常绘有一张采用磨光工艺制造的装饰精美的面孔，常配有繁复精致的神话场景。有些青铜镜在出土时仍保留有原先的骨柄或象牙柄。

The mirrors bronze characterize the Etruscan burial female for a long period of time. Consist of a smooth part and a polished face often finely decorated with elaborate mythological scenes. Some retained at the time of discovery still have the original neck bone or ivory.

青铜镜在很长一段时间内都是典型的伊特鲁里亚女性陪葬品。这类青铜镜表面光滑，通常绘有一张采用磨光工艺制造的装饰精美的面孔，常配有繁复精致的神话场景。有些青铜镜在重见天日时仍保留有原先的骨柄或象牙柄。

The mirrors bronze characterize the Etruscan burial female for a long period of time. Consist of a smooth part and a polished face often finely decorated with elaborate mythological scenes. Some retained at the time of discovery still have the original neck bone or ivory.

红绘式奥伊洛克陶壶（托扩普族）
Red Figure Oinochoe (Torcop Group)

公元前4世纪
陶
高17、最大直径15厘米

4ᵗʰ century BCE
Ceramics
H.17cm, D.(max)15cm

来自波普罗尼亚

瓶身和颈部装饰的女性面孔表现出典型的托扩普人的特征，托扩普人是公元前4世纪下半叶开始出现的族群。红绘式风格即在黑底上彩绘，是希腊瓶画的主要风格之一，流行于公元前5世纪。伊奥洛克式陶壶是古希腊流行的三叶口的单柄长颈酒壶。

From Populonia
The female faces that stand out on the body and neck of this vessel are characteristic of Group Torcop whose activity arises in the second half of the fourth century. B.C.E.

红绘式伊奥洛克陶瓶（托扩普族）
Red Figure Oinochoe (Torcop Group)

公元前4世纪
陶
高30.5、最大直径13厘米

4ᵗʰ century BCE
Ceramics
H.30.5cm, D.(max)13cm

瓶身和颈部装饰的女性面孔表现出典型的托扩普人的特征，托扩普人是公元前4世纪下半叶开始出现的族群。

The female faces that stand out on the body and neck of this vessel are characteristic of Group Torcop whose activity arises in the second half of the fourth century. B.C.E.

伊特鲁里亚红绘式陶壶
Etruscan Red Figure Oinochoe

公元前4世纪
陶
高36、最大直径18厘米

4th century BCE
Over painted red figures ceramic
H.36cm, D.(max)18cm

本件是用来盛放液体——尤其是红酒的器皿，瓶身精美装饰中的红绘式人物表现出希腊化时期的典型特征。

The vessel, intended for liquids, especially wine, the body has a refined decoration with red figures typical of the Hellenistic period.

黑绘式坎达罗斯陶杯
Overpainted Black Painted Kantharos

公元前4世纪
陶
高15、直径16.2厘米
4th century BCE
Over painted red figures ceramic
H.15cm, D.16.2cm

来自波普罗尼亚

这只伊特鲁里亚酒瓶十分独特：瓶身两侧分别装有两只造型对称的环形把手，瓶颈两侧则装饰着两张使用色彩叠印工艺绘制的女性面孔。坎达罗斯是古希腊双耳酒杯。

From Populonia
Etruscan vase characterized by the presence of two symmetrical loops, decorated on the neck by two female faces addressed realized with the technique of superimposition of colors.

饰物与香氛：香水瓶

这些有着细小喷嘴的小型器皿挂在腰带上，用来盛放香膏和香水的。这些瓶子通常没有把手，并常塑造成小动物的形象——如小鹿、小猪，或做成极小的细颈双耳瓶的样子。于是，墓葬品又一次展现了当时的服饰和装饰面貌。贵族女性的坟墓里陪葬有装满香水的小瓶或造型各异的小罐，以陪伴她们踏上来生的旅途，男性墓葬中的武器亦是如此。这类器皿的种类很多。有些是从东方和希腊进口，还有一些是模仿外国式样和装饰图案制作的本地陶器。伊特鲁里亚—柯林斯瓷器的生产就说明了这点，这些瓷器明显受到了希腊城市柯林斯生产的小型器皿的影响。柯林斯是伊特鲁里亚最大的进口来源地之一（位于雅典之前，东方国家之后）。

Ornaments and Scents: Unguentaria

These small containers, with a narrow spout, were carried on the belt and held ointments and scents. Often they had no handles and were shaped like little animals - fawns or small boars - or tiny amphorae. Once again, grave goods provide insight into the costumes of that age. In the tombs of wealthy women, small unguen- taria or variously shaped tiny pots full of scents were placed to accompany women in their journey into the afterlife, like weapons for men. The variety of vessels was quite substantial. Some were imported from the East and Greece and were often combined with local pottery that imitated styles and decorations from abroad. The Etruscan-Corinthian production is a good example of this, with the evident influence of the small vessels imported from the Greek city of Corinth, which was one of the main exporters to Etruria (sitting ahead of Athens, but after the East).

吕底亚式陶瓶
Lydion

公元前326–350年
陶
高10、直径6厘米
Third quarter 4th century BCE
Purifed Clay
H.10cm、D.6cm

本件用来盛放珍贵的香精油，似乎是制作于希腊–东方地区。瓶身饰有一道黑色颜料涂上的条纹装饰。吕底亚式香水瓶源自小亚细亚的吕底亚（Lydia）

The jar containing the original precious perfumed essences, seems made of Greek-eastern area. It has a band painted on the body with black paint.

狮身人面陶香水瓶
Sphinx Shaped Perfume Flask

公元前6世纪
陶
高6.4、长6.5厘米

6th century BCE
Ceramics
H.6.4cm, L.6.5cm

来自维图罗尼亚，勒米格利
亚瑞，费古洛墓

本件是伊特鲁里亚－科林斯
地区用来盛放香油或香膏的
容器，公元前6世纪在伊特
鲁里亚广泛生产。

From Vetulonia, Le Migliarine, tomba
del Figulo
The container is intended to contain
oils or scented balms, belongs to the
large production of plastic ointment
Etrusco-Corinthian widely in Etruria
in the sixth century. B.C. E.

人形陶香水瓶
Figure Shaped perfume flask

公元前6世纪
陶
高10.5厘米

6th century BCE
Ceramics
H.10.5cm

来自维图罗尼亚
勒米格利亚瑞，费古洛墓

本件是伊特鲁里亚－科林斯
地区用来盛放香油或香膏的
容器，公元前6世纪在伊特
鲁里亚广泛生产。

From Vetulonia, Le Migliarine, tomba
del Figulo
The container is intended to contain
oils or scented balms, belongs to the
large production of plastic ointment
Etrusco-Corinthian widely in Etruria
in the sixth century. B.C.E.

陶祖形香水瓶
Phallus Shaped Perfume Flask

公元前6世纪上半叶
陶
高5.6、宽3厘米

First half 6th century BCE
Ceramics
From Vetulonia, Le Migliarine, tomba del Figulo
H.5.6cm, W.3cm

腿形香水瓶
Leg Shaped Perfume Flask

公元前6世纪上半叶
陶
长21、宽5.5厘米

First half 6th century BCE
Ceramics
L.21cm, W.5.5cm

来自维图罗尼亚
勒米格利亚瑞，费古洛墓

本件是伊特鲁里亚－科林斯地区用来盛放香油或香膏的容器，公元前6世纪在伊特鲁里亚广泛生产。它和下面的展品一样，都来自1883年维图罗尼亚出土的一座陵墓。

The container is intended to contain oils or scented balms, belongs to the large production of plastic ointment Etrusco-Corinthian widely in Etruria in the sixth century. B.C. E. This, like the following, was recovered in a tomb excavated in 1883 Vetulonia.

来自维图罗尼亚
勒米格利亚瑞，费古洛墓

本件是伊特鲁里亚－科林斯地区用来盛放香油或香膏的容器，公元前6世纪在伊特鲁里亚广泛生产。

From Vetulonia, Le Migliarine, tomba del Figulo
The container is intended to contain oils or scented balms, belongs to the large production of plastic ointment Etrusco-Corinthian widely in Etruria in the sixth century.B.C.E.

科林斯式阿博洛斯香水瓶
Corinthian Globular Aryballos

公元前6世纪上半叶
陶
高7.8厘米

First half 6th century BCE
Ceramics
From Vetulonia, Le Migliarine, tomba del Figulo
H.7.8cm

来自维图罗尼亚
勒米格利亚瑞，费古洛墓

阿博洛斯带纹球形香水瓶，以前用于存放精油，其形制最早见于希腊。从希腊柯林斯进口的物品深刻地影响了伊特鲁里亚的器皿生产，主要表现为对柯林斯陶器的模仿。

Aryballos globe decorated with simple bands. Originally used to preserve wood and scented oils. The specimen was manufactured in Greece. one of the shapes typical of the Greek city of Corinth,whose imports were to affect the Etruscan production that developed to imitate this.

雪花石膏平底瓶
Flat Bottom Alabastern

公元前6世纪上半叶
陶
高18厘米

First half 6th century BCE
Ceramics
H.18cm

除了通过贸易往来进入伊特鲁里亚的东方和希腊物品外，大多数墓葬中包括大量由伊特鲁里亚工匠制造的盛放香水和香膏的容器。伊特鲁里亚—柯林斯陶器这一定义就有效地解释了这一本土制造的现象，这些陶器造型各式各样，包括人型和动物造型，都是模仿从柯林斯（希腊城市，与伊特鲁里亚有着紧密的贸易联系）进口的香膏瓶和香水瓶制造的。这些陶器都来自权贵人物的墓葬，均证明了伊特鲁里亚曾制造受东方风格启发的奢侈品。

In addition to the objects that came from the East and Greece with trade flows, most of the grave goods have a great number of containers for scents and ointments produced by the Etruscans. The definition of Etruscan-Corinthian pottery is useful to explain that this local production, with variously shaped objects - including anatomical and animal ones - was done in imitation of the containers for balms and scented oils imported from the Greek city of Corinth, with which the Etruscans had major trade links. They come from prestigious grave goods and are a testimony of luxury goods with an oriental inspiration.

来自波普罗尼亚，库拉特瓦墓穴

阿博洛斯瓶或各种球形、梨形的饰有带纹、动物纹和植物纹的小瓶，早先用于装芳香精油，伊特鲁里亚时期的工艺主要吸收了希腊科林斯地区的样式。

From Populonia, tomba dei Colatoi Aryballoi or alabastra of various shapes and sizes like these, globular or pear-shaped, decorated with simple bands, colorful, animals or plant matter, it was originally used to preserve wood and scented oils. Manufactured in Etruria for the entire period imitating Greek models of the city of Corinth.

雪花石膏平底瓶
Flat Bottom Alabastern

公元前6世纪上半叶
陶
高18厘米

First half 6th century BCE
Ceramics
H.18cm

来自波普罗尼亚库拉特瓦墓穴

阿博洛斯瓶或各种球形、梨形的
饰有带纹、动物纹和植物纹的小
瓶，早先用于装芳香精油，伊特
鲁里亚时期的工艺主要吸收了希
腊科林斯地区的样式。

From Populonia, tomba dei Colatoi
Aryballoi or alabastra of various shapes
and sizes like these, globular or pear-
shaped, decorated with simple bands,
colorful, animals or plant matter, it was
originally used to preserve wood and
scented oils. Manufactured in Etruria for
the entire period imitating Greek models
of the city of Corinth.

阿拉巴斯塔陶香水瓶
Alabastron

公元前7-6世纪上半叶
陶
高12厘米

End 7th–first half 6ᵗʰ century BCE
Ceramics
H.12cm

来自波普罗尼亚

阿博洛斯瓶或各种球形、梨形的饰有带纹、动物纹和植物纹的小瓶，早先用于装芳香精油，伊特鲁里亚时期的工艺主要吸收了希腊科林斯地区的样式。

From Populonia
Arybolloi or alabastra of various shapes and sizes like these, globular or pear-shaped, decorated with simple bands, colorful, animals or plant matter, it was originally used to preserve wood and scented oils. Were manufactured in Etruria for the entire period imitating Greek models of the city of Corinth.

科林斯式阿博洛斯香水瓶
Aryballos

公元前6世纪上半叶
陶
高8.5厘米

First half 6ᵗʰ century BCE
Ceramics
H.8.5cm

来自波普罗尼亚

阿博洛斯瓶或各种球形、梨形的饰有带纹、动物纹和植物纹的小瓶，早先用于装芳香精油，伊特鲁里亚时期的工艺主要吸收了希腊科林斯地区的样式。

From Populonia
Arybolloi or alabastra of various shapes and sizes like these, globular or pear-shaped, decorated with simple bands, colorful, animals or plant matter, it was originally used to preserve wood and scented oils. Were manufactured in Etruria for the entire period imitating Greek models of the city of Corinth.

梨形陶香油瓶
Pear Shaped Aryballoi

公元前6世纪上半叶
陶
高11厘米

First half 6th century BCE
Ceramics
H.11cm

来自波普罗尼亚，库拉特瓦墓穴

阿博洛斯瓶或各种球形、梨形的饰有带纹、动物纹和植物纹的小瓶，早先用于装芳香精油，伊特鲁里亚时期的工艺主要吸收了希腊科林斯地区的样式。

From Populonia, tomba dei Colatoi
Aryballoi or alabastra of various shapes and sizes like these, globular or pear-shaped, decorated with simple bands, colorful, animals or plant matter, it was originally used to preserve wood and scented oils. Were manufactured in Etruria for the entire period imitating Greek models of the city of Corinth.

梨形陶香油瓶
Pear Shaped Aryballoi

公元前6世纪上半叶
陶
高10厘米

First half 6th century BCE
Ceramics
H.10 cm

来自波普罗尼亚，库拉特瓦墓

阿博洛斯瓶或各种球形、梨形的饰有带纹、动物纹和植物纹的小瓶，早先用于装芳香精油，伊特鲁里亚时期的工艺主要吸收了希腊科林斯地区的样式。

From Populonia, tomba dei Colatoi
Aryballoi or alabastra of various shapes and sizes like these, globular or pear-shaped, decorated with simple bands, colorful, animals or plant matter, it was originally used to preserve wood and scented oils. Were manufactured in Etruria for the entire period imitating Greek models of the city of Corinth.

阿拉巴斯塔陶香水瓶
Alabastron

公元前6世纪上半叶
陶
高9.2厘米

First half 6th century BCE
Ceramics
H.9.2cm

来自波乔·索玛维拉

阿博洛斯瓶或各种球形、梨形的饰有带纹、动物纹和植物纹的小瓶，早先用于装芳香精油，伊特鲁里亚时期的工艺主要吸收了希腊科林斯地区的样式。

From Poggio Sommavilla
Aryballoi or alabastra of various shapes and sizes like these, globular or pear-shaped, decorated with simple bands, colorful, animals or plant matter, it was originally used to preserve wood and scented oils. Were manufactured in Etruria for the entire period imitating Greek models of the city of Corinth.

阿拉巴斯塔陶香水瓶
Alabastron

公元前6世纪上半叶
陶
高9厘米

First half 6th century BCE
Ceramics
H.9cm

来自波乔·索玛维拉

阿博洛斯瓶或各种球形、梨形的饰有带纹、动物纹和植物纹的小瓶，早先用于装芳香精油，伊特鲁里亚时期的工艺主要吸收了希腊科林斯地区的样式。

From Poggio Sommavilla
Aryballoi or alabastra of various shapes and sizes like these, globular or pear-shaped, decorated with simple bands, colorful, animals or plant matter, it was originally used to preserve wood and scented oils. Were manufactured in Etruria for the entire period imitating Greek models of the city of Corinth.

阿博洛斯条纹陶香水瓶
Aryballos

公元前6世纪上半叶
陶
高8.5厘米

First half 6th century BCE
Ceramics
H.8.5cm

来自波普罗尼亚，库拉特瓦墓

阿博洛斯瓶或各种球形、梨形的饰有带纹、动物纹和植物纹的小瓶，早先用于装芳香精油，伊特鲁里亚时期的工艺主要吸收了希腊科林斯地区的样式。

From Populonia, tomba dei Colatoi Aryballoi or alabastra of various shapes and sizes like these, globular or pear-shaped, decorated with simple bands, colorful, animals or plant matter, it was originally used to preserve wood and scented oils. Were manufactured in Etruria for the entire period imitating Greek models of the city of Corinth.

阿拉巴斯塔陶香水瓶
Alabastern

公元前6世纪上半叶
陶
高11厘米

First half 6th century BCE
Ceramics
H.11cm

来自波普罗尼亚，库拉特瓦墓

阿博洛斯瓶或各种球形、梨形的饰有带纹、动物纹和植物纹的小瓶，早先用于装芳香精油，伊特鲁里亚时期的工艺主要吸收了希腊科林斯地区的样式。

From Populonia, tomba dei Colatoi Aryballoi or alabastra of various shapes and sizes like these, globular or pear-shaped, decorated with simple bands, colorful, animals or plant matter, it was originally used to preserve wood and scented oils. Were manufactured in Etruria for the entire period imitating Greek models of the city of Corinth.

阿拉巴斯塔陶香水瓶
Alabastern

公元前6世纪上半叶
陶
高9厘米

First half 6th century BCE
Ceramics
H.9cm

来自波普罗尼亚，库拉特瓦墓

阿博洛斯瓶或各种球形、梨形的饰有带纹、动物纹和植物纹的小瓶，早先用于装芳香精油，伊特鲁里亚时期的工艺主要吸收了希腊科林斯地区的样式。

From Populonia, tomba dei Colatoi
Aryballoi or alabastra of various shapes and sizes like these, globular or pear-shaped, decorated with simple bands, colorful, animals or plant matter, it was originally used to preserve wood and scented oils. Were manufactured in Etruria for the entire period imitating Greek models of the city of Corinth.

双锥形阿博洛斯陶香水瓶
Biconical Shaped Aryballos

公元前6世纪上半叶
陶
高6厘米

First half 6th century BCE
Ceramics
H.6cm

来自波普罗尼亚，库拉特瓦墓

阿博洛斯瓶或各种球形、梨形的饰有带纹、动物纹和植物纹的小瓶，早先用于装芳香精油，伊特鲁里亚时期的工艺主要吸收了希腊科林斯地区的样式。

From Populonia, tomba dei Colatoi
Aryballoi or alabastra of various shapes and sizes like these, globular or pear-shaped, decorated with simple bands, colorful, animals or plant matter, it was originally used to preserve wood and scented oils. Were manufactured in Etruria for the entire period imitating Greek models of the city of Corinth.

蛋形阿博洛斯香水瓶
Egg-Shaped Shaped Aryballos

公元前6世纪上半叶
陶
高8.5厘米

First half 6th century BCE
Ceramics
H.8.5cm

来自波普罗尼亚，库拉特瓦墓

阿博洛斯瓶或各种球形、梨形的饰有带纹、动物纹和植物纹的小瓶，早先用于装芳香精油，伊特鲁里亚时期的工艺主要吸收了希腊科林斯地区的样式。

From Populonia, tomba dei Colatoi
Aryballoi or alabastra of various shapes and sizes like these, globular or pear-shaped, decorated with simple bands, colorful, animals or plant matter, it was originally used to preserve wood and scented oils. Were manufactured in Etruria for the entire period imitating Greek models of the city of Corinth.

动物纹阿博洛斯陶香油瓶
Globular Aryballos Decorated With Animals

公元前7世纪末至公元前6世纪上半叶
陶
高8厘米

End 7th-first half 6th century BCE
Ceramics
H.8cm

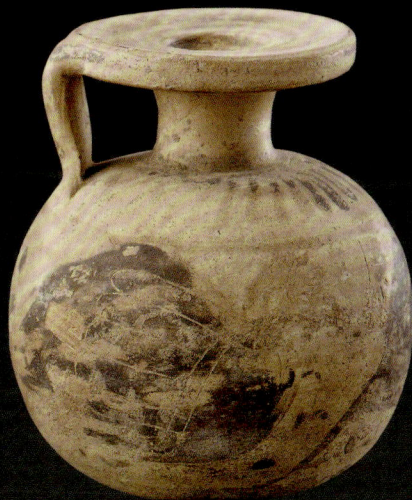

来自波乔·布库

阿博洛斯瓶或各种球形、梨形的饰有带纹、动物纹和植物纹的小瓶，早先用于装芳香精油，伊特鲁里亚时期的工艺主要吸收了希腊科林斯地区的样式。

From Poggio Buco
Aryballoi or alabastra of various shapes and sizes like these, globular or pear-shaped, decorated with simple bands, colorful, animals or plant matter, it was originally used to preserve wood and scented oils. Were manufactured in Etruria for the entire period imitating Greek models of the city of Corinth.

派克斯陶盒
Pyx

公元前6世纪上半叶
陶
高15厘米

First half 6th century
BCE
Ceramics
H.15cm

来自波乔·布库
这种球形的容器通常带盖，
与女性用品相关，极有可能
用于美容用品的包装储放。

From Poggio Buco
Globular container generally
equipped with a lid, linked to the
world of women. Probably contained
cosmetics.

派克斯陶盒
Pyx

公元前6世纪上半叶
陶
高15厘米

First half 6th century BCE
Ceramics
H.15cm

来自波乔·布库

这种小的、形状奇特的香料器
皿，主要吸收希腊东部的工艺
特点，后传入伊特鲁里亚。

From Poggio Buco
The peculiar form of this little vessel
for perfumes mimics prototypes
manufactured in eastern Greece and then
imported into Etruria.

猴形陶香水瓶
Monkey Shaped Perfume Flask

公元前6世纪上半叶
陶
高9.8、宽5.5厘米

First half 6th century BCE
Ceramics
H.9.8cm, W.5.5cm

来自波乔·布库，卡门拉2号墓

本件是伊特鲁里亚－科林斯地区用来盛放香油或香膏的容器，公元前16世纪在伊特鲁里亚广泛生产。

From Poggio Buco, tomba a camera 2
The container is intended to contain oils or scented balms, belongs to the large production of plastic ointment Etrusco-Corinthian widely in Etruria in the sixth century. B.C.E.

兔形陶香水瓶
Leveret Shaped Perfume Flask

公元前6世纪上半叶
陶
高5.7、长8厘米

First half 6ᵗʰ century BCE
Purifed Clay
H.5.7cm, L.8cm

本件是伊特鲁里亚－科林斯
地区用来盛放香油或香膏的
容器，公元前16世纪在伊特
鲁里亚广泛生产。

The container is intended to contain
oils or scented balms, belongs to the
large production of plastic ointment
Etrusco-Corinthian widely in Etruria
in the sixth century. B.C.E.

兔形陶香水瓶
Leveret Shaped Perfume Flask

公元前6世纪上半叶
陶
高7.5、长19.7厘米

First half 6ᵗʰ century BCE
Purifed Clay
H.7.5cm, L.19.7cm

来自维图罗尼亚
勒米格利亚瑞，费古洛墓

本件是伊特鲁里亚－科林斯
地区用来盛放香油或香膏的
容器，公元前6世纪在伊特
鲁里亚广泛生产。

From Vetulonia, Le Migliarine, tomba
del Figulo
The container is intended to contain
oils or scented balms, belongs to the
large production of plastic ointment
Etrusco-Corinthian widely in Etruria
in the sixth century. B.C.E.

波普罗尼亚的阿斯克斯鹿形陶瓶
Crouching Deer Shaped Askos From Populonia

公元前300-325年
陶
高16、长15、宽3.5厘米

Last quarter 4th century BCE
Ceramics
H.16cm, L.15cm, W.3.5cm

来自波普罗尼亚

本件盛放液体，它栩栩如生地再现了一只卧鹿的形象。这只有着长角和尖耳朵的鹿的身上装饰着棕色的斑点。这件器皿原本是一个伊特鲁里亚雕塑作品系列中的一件，该系列中鹿的形象十分普遍。

From Populonia
The vessel, intended for liquids, Replay realistic forms the figure of a crouching deer with horns and pointed ears. The coat was made with thick dashes brown and brown spots. It belongs to a series of Etruscan vases plastic production, including the figure of the deer is very common.

阿斯克斯陶壶
Askos

公元前3-2世纪
黑陶

3-2th century BCE
Black Paint

这件阿斯克斯矮陶瓶造型十分独特，其顶部装有一只供抓握的把手和两个开口，一个用来灌注，另一个则可倾倒。本件无色、没有黑彩或是红彩。

The askos is a vessel with a very peculiar form. At the top is a handle for gripping and two openings used for introducing a liquid. It can be made from achromatic, black paint or red paint pottery.

马头形陶香水瓶
Horse Head Shaped Perfume Flask

公元前6世纪上半叶
陶
高9.5、长9.6厘米

First half 6th century BCE
Purifed Clay
H.9.5cm, L.9.6cm

来自维图罗尼亚
勒米格利亚瑞，费古洛墓

本件是伊特鲁里亚-科林斯地区用来盛放香油或香膏的容器，公元前6世纪在伊特鲁里亚广泛生产。

From Vetulonia, Le Migliarine, tomba del Figulo
The container is intended to contain oils or scented balms, belongs to the large production of plastic ointment Etrusco-Corinthian widely in Etruria in the sixth century. B.C.E.

与希腊文明和意大利南部的西方希腊殖民地的联系使伊特鲁里亚人形成了一些习俗，例如举办宴会（吃烤肉，效仿古代的荷马），以及后来的社交酒会（在社交宴会的不同阶段饮酒）。这些"礼仪"悄悄走进日常生活和葬礼宴会中，并不可避免地对殉葬品也产生了影响。实际上，许多有关荷马时代宴飨的重要证据来自伊特鲁里亚。正如丘西地区的墓葬所揭示的，这类宴会中，客人们通常是坐着而不是半躺着的——与接下来一个时期（即公元前6世纪之后）的希腊习俗相同。历史上，社交酒会在伊特鲁里亚社交生活中占据着重要地位，伊特鲁里亚墓室中的壁画——如曼特罗契的塔尔奎尼亚墓的山墙装饰上描绘的形象，以及用来标记坟墓的墓碑雕塑——如砂岩制作的费埃索石碑，均说明了这一点。

Contact with Greek civilization and the Western Greek colonies of southern Italy enabled the Etruscans to acquire customs such as the banquet (eating roasted meat, from the ancient Homer) and later the symposium (drinking wine during the various stages of social eating). These "rites" found their way into both dayto-day activities and the funeral banquet, with the consequent influence on the grave goods. The symposium acquired a fundamental role in Etruscan social life and became one of the most commonly represented subjects across all art forms (and with all material types), including painted pottery, paintings, such as on the tympanum of the tomb in Tarquinia (Monterozzi area), and sculpture, for example, the steles marking the tombs.

费埃索式石碑
Fiesole Style Stele

公元前5世纪
石
高87、宽43、厚10厘米

5th century BCE
Stone
H.87cm, W.43cm, Th.10cm

来自弗洛伦萨境内

这类石碑一般竖立在墓地，用
来描绘一场葬礼或纪念某件重
要事件。石碑上的浅浮雕装饰
可分为两个场景，分别描绘了
一场宴会和一位骑士。

From Florentine territory
Stone stele of this type, stuck upright
in the ground, served to indicate a
burial or commemorate an event.
The decoration carved in low relief is
divided into sections where there are
a banquet and a knight.

墓穴上方的三角楣饰
Pediment From A Decorated Tomb

公元前6世纪
壁画
高59、长322厘米

6th century BCE
Fresco
H.59cm, L.322cm

来自塔尔奎尼亚
曼特罗契公墓，塔拉拖拉

这件三角楣饰是伊特鲁里亚
南部的塔尔奎尼亚地区众多
壁画墓中的一件。这件楣饰
运用鲜亮的色彩重现了葬礼
宴飨的场景。

From Tarquinia, necropoli dei
Monterozzi, Villa Tarantola
The pediment is from one of the
many painted tombs of Tarquinia
Etruscan-south. Is represented with a
brightly colored a funeral feast.

丘西墓葬，波乔·阿拉萨拉

伊特鲁里亚事实上留下了最有说服力的例子，明确地展示了在伊特鲁里亚的宴会上人们都是坐着的，而不是像晚些时候的希腊人那样半躺着。这件青铜薄片制作的藏尸罐安放在王座上，表明并强调了逝者的贵族身份。这件青铜薄片制作的矮桌位于王座的对面，说明逝者是一位社交酒会的客人。人们在矮桌上发现了骨头制作的眼睛，这双眼睛可能是从藏尸罐上的面具上掉下来的，而用易腐烂材料（可能是木头）制作的面具早已灰飞烟灭。在丘西地区，人形藏尸罐的制作尤为流行。

The Chiusi Tomb, Poggio alla Sala

Etruria actually produced one of the most telling examples that clearly shows that Etruscan banquets were seated and not half-reclined as was the case later in Greece. The ossuary made of a bronze sheet located on a sort of throne represents the deceased, highlighting that he belonged to the aristocratic class. This low bronze sheet table was located opposite the throne, indicating that the deceased was a symposium guest. Eyes made of bone were found on the table and were probably from a mask applied onto the ossuary made of perishable material (wood?) that was not preserved. In the city of Chiusi, the fashion of making ossuaries with a human shape was particularly developed.

青铜王座上的瓮棺
Urn on a Throne

公元前7世纪末期
青铜
瓮棺高：48厘米，椅子高：108、座：40×41.5厘米

End 7th century BCE
Bronze
Ossuary: H.48cm,Chair : H.108cm, Base 40 × 41.5cm

来自丘西，波乔·阿拉萨拉
这件独特的物品是一项重要
发现，来自丘西地区最古老
的一座伊特鲁里亚墓室。这
只青铜箔片制作的瓮棺安放
在一把类似王座的青铜椅子
上，是为了强调墓葬主人是
王室的一位重要人物。

From Chiusi, Poggio alla Sala
The unique core findings come from
one of the oldest Etruscan chamber
tombs of Chiusi. The ossuary in
bronze foil was laid on a sort of
throne of bronze to emphasize
belonging to an aristocratic elite of
the deceased.

青铜餐桌
Dining Table

公元前7世纪末期
青铜
高52、长96.5、宽36.5厘米

End 7th century BCE
Bronze
H.52cm, L.96.5cm, W.36.5cm

来自丘西，波乔·阿拉萨拉

王座前方则放着这张独特的青铜餐桌，说明死者是议事会的常客。

From Chiusi, Poggio 0alla Sala
Before the throne was placed this unique table made of sheet bronze that characterizes the deceased as a participant of the symposium.

骨眼睛
Eyes

公元前7世纪末期
骨
长4、宽3.8厘米

End 7th century BCE
Bone
L.4cm, W.3.8cm

来自丘西，波乔·阿拉萨拉

这对骨头做的眼睛可能是安装在骨灰罐或许是某种容易腐烂材质制作的面具上，将骨灰坛拟人化早在公元前7世纪就已流行的一种趋势。

From Chiusi, Poggio alla Sala
These eyes in bone were probably applied on the ossuary perhaps on a mask of perishable materials, a trend that I closed the door to anthropomorphize the urns as early as the seventh century. B.C.E.

象牙骰子
Dice

公元前7世纪
象牙
长2.2-2.3厘米

7th century BCE
Ivory
L.2.2-2.3cm

这对骰子属于某笔十分丰富的收藏的一部分，这笔藏品包括若干陶器和几只盛放包括这两个青铜色骰子在内的各式骰子的容器，这些骰子每面的数值从1到6不等。

Were part of the rich collection that included ceramic vessels and several containers of these two bronze nuts with values from 1 through 6 on the various faces.

社交酒会的物品

社交酒会可用到多种类型的器皿。最大的器皿不仅包括用于盛酒的器皿（调酒缸），还包括盛放用于与酒和蜂蜜混合的水的器皿（双耳瓶）。餐具器皿主要用于倒酒和饮酒（壶、勺和杯），以及盛放食物（如各种尺寸的盘、碟和烧烤盘）。青铜大锅炉是用来烹煮肉类的。金属冶炼和金属加工是伊特鲁里亚最发达、最知名的一种产业，包括炼铁和炼钢，这使得伊特鲁里亚在古代名声远扬，并为他们提供了与外部进行商贸活动的商品。意大利半岛无数首领的殉葬品证明了这类商贸活动的存在，因为这些墓葬中通常包含伊特鲁里亚制作的工具、青铜罐和花瓶。这类物品可能是通过上层社会间的贸易获得的。

Symposium Objects

There are numerous types of vessels. The largest ones were not only used for wine (kraters), but also for water (amphorae) that was mixed with the wine and honey. The tableware vessels were used for pouring and drinking (jugs, dippers, cups) as well as to hold (variously sized plates, trays and baking dishes). Large bronze cauldrons were used to cook meat. Smelting and working metal was one of the most developed and well-known forms of Etruscan production. It encompassed both iron and bronze, bringing the Etruscans fame in ancient times and giving them something to trade with outside of their lands. Evidence of this is found in the grave goods of numerous leaders from across the Italic peninsula, as these often contain Etruscan tools and bronze pots and vases. Such items would have been acquired through upper-class trade.

伊特鲁里亚式斯泰莫斯瓶
Etruscan Stamnos

公元前6世纪
陶
高42.5、直径19厘米

6th century BCE
Black Figures Ceramics
H.42.5cm, D.19cm

来自丘西

古风时期，蓬勃发展的除了
伊特鲁里亚——柯林斯式陶
器外，还包括另一类重要的
陶器种类，即绘有黑绘式陶
器，本件也是模仿公元前
510-500年从希腊进口的陶
器制作的。瓶身的主要装饰
图案为一个手持长矛奔跑的
年轻人形象：这可能描绘的
是一场出征舞表演。这件贮
酒瓶的创作者为米凯里画
师，最著名的伊特鲁里亚黑
绘陶器画师之一。

From Chiusi
In addition to the class of Etruscan-
Corinthian pottery, in the Archaic Age
there was the developmentof another
important class, that of pottery with black
figures, also imitations of vasesimported
from Greece from 510-500. The main
decoration on the vase shows young men
runningwith spears in hand, probably a
Pyrrhic dance scene. The vase is attributed
to the Painter ofMicali,one of the greatest
painters of black-figure pottery in Etruria.

安夫拉陶瓶
Amphora

公元前6世纪
黑陶
高44、直径25厘米

6th century BCE
Black Figures Ceramics
H.44cm, D.25cm

科勒佐恩·瓦格农维勒

这只双耳瓶的比例显得十分修长，瓶上的两只把手连接着瓶口边缘和瓶肩，瓶子两侧均装饰有用黑绘式描绘的一对年轻人。

Collezione Vagnonville
Jar of very slender proportions, with handles set on the edge and on the shoulder, decorated on both sides with pairs of young painted with black paint.

三色彩绘陶盘
Dish

公元前7-6世纪
陶
高4.2、直径25.5厘米

7-6th century BCE
Purified Clay, Dark Red And Brown Paint
H.4.2cm, D.25.5cm

来自波乔·布库，2号墓

在宴会和葬礼中，这类盘子
则用来盛放食物。盘子的装
饰图案较为简洁，包括一条
沿盘子边缘延伸的带状图
案，其中点缀着各种动物形
象和圆形花饰。

From Poggio Buco, tomba II
During the banquet and the funeral
dishes were placed in these foods.
The decoration consists of a strip that
runs along the edge of the pot with
theory of animals and fillers rosette.

欧帕陶壶
Olpe

公元前7-6世纪
陶
高28、直径13.3厘米

7-6th century BCE
Purified Clay, Dark Red And Brown Paint
H.28cm, D.13.3cm

来自波乔·布库
波德·萨顿，7号墓

这只单柄容器是用来在酒会
上倒酒的。瓶身的华丽装饰
图案是伊特鲁里亚人学自柯
林斯制作的器皿。

From Poggio Buco, Podere Sadun,
tomba VII
The vessel is equipped with a loop,
used to pour the wine during the
symposium, an exhibition on the
body exuberant decoration that
the Etruscans recover from vessels
manufactured in Corinth.

基里克斯陶杯
Kylix

公元前7-6世纪
陶
高9、直径14厘米

7-6th century BCE
Purified Clay, Dark Red And Brown Paint
H.9cm, D.14cm

来自波乔·布库，2号墓

基里克斯陶杯是古希腊一种
高脚浅酒杯，杯身的两面向
外凸出，杯肩两侧各有一只
水平伸出的把手。杯上的装
饰图案则让人联想起柯林斯
花瓶的装饰风格。

From Poggio Buco, tomba II
Cup on a high foot and lenticular
body that includes two horizontal
handles on the shoulder. The
decorative repertoire is reminiscent
of Corinthian vases.

切尔韦泰里陶大口坛
Pithos From Cerveteri

褐陶
高86、直径39厘米

Impasto
H. 86cm, D.39cm

一般来说，除了盛水的安夫拉双耳瓶外，另外还有一种尺寸较大的器皿，通常用混合黏土的褐陶（Impasto）制作，因为该材质的持久性较好。这种陶器也可盛放食品。切尔韦泰里市生产的这类器皿的特征为，坛身饰有别致的浮雕图案，这些图案是用模具或一种制作单个楣饰的小型圆筒印刻，图案风格基本相似。

本件既属于典型的切尔韦泰里（Cerveteri）陶器，约产于公元前7世纪后期和公元前6世纪中期。条状装饰图案下则是一系列栩栩如生的神话动物和竖弦纹。切尔韦泰里是罗马省的一个镇。

Generally speaking, along with the amphorae which contained water, there are also other large containers of considerable size, often made with the clay mixture because of its greater durability. These could also contain foodstuffs. The production of these containers in the city of Caere is characterized by the special relief decoration obtained with moulds or with a small cylinder used to create a single frieze with figures that are all similar.

The great vessel belongs to a class typically Caeretan produced between the late seventh and the mid-sixth century. B.C.E. Under a corrugated band is a frieze obtained through a kind of cylinder with a sequence of animals, also fantastic.

陶奇罗瓶
Ziro

公元前6世纪
褐陶
高71、直径29—51厘米

6th century BCE
Impasto
H.71cm, D.29—51cm

这类大型器皿是用来储存食物的。本件的外表面饰有浮雕图案。

These large vessels were for preserving foodstuffs. The specimen shows the outer surface is decorated with a relief pattern.

欧帕陶壶
Olpe

公元前6世纪
陶
高32、直径14.5厘米

6th century BCE
Ceramics
H.32cm, D.14.5cm

来自波乔·布库

这只欧帕瓶的瓶身上饰有相
互交织的拱形图案，这是典
型的伊特鲁里亚－柯林斯装
饰风格。欧帕瓶原是米诺斯
的一种单柄瓶。

From Poggio Buco
The olpe has on the body is
decorated with interlaced arches
typical of the decorative repertoire
Etrusco-Corinthian.

安夫拉陶瓶
Amphora

公元前6世纪
陶
高34、最大直径23厘米

6ᵗʰ century BCE
Ceramics
H.34cm, D.(max) 23cm

这只配有双耳的器皿是用来
盛放饮料的，在伊特鲁里亚
的宴会上几乎都能看到它的
身影。

Vessel containing liquid with two
loops, almost always served in
Etruscan banquet.

布凯罗黑陶：典型的伊特鲁里亚陶餐具

如前所述，伊特鲁里亚的餐桌上装点着希腊陶器，起初是黑绘陶器，后来又有了红绘陶器，当然，还包括一些伊特鲁里亚人模仿希腊装饰图案的风格制作的陶器。此外，他们的餐桌上还有地地道道的伊特鲁里亚陶器，即布凯罗黑陶（薄胎灰陶）。制作过程中使用了一种特殊的焙烧工艺，以在使用棍棒抛光前使黏土变黑。造型上，布凯罗黑陶延续了之前的典型传统，除模仿希腊陶器造型之外，布凯罗黑陶的制作还受到金属器皿的启发。装饰图案则为蚀刻或使用模具制作的几何图案或人物形象。

Bucchero: typical Etruscan tableware pottery

As mentioned, Etruscan tables were adorned with Greek pottery, initially with black figures and later with red ones and they also had pottery decorated with Etruscan designs that had been created in imitation of the Greek styles. In addition to this, such tables might well have pottery that was exclusively Etruscan, namely bucchero pottery, which was made using a special firing process that turned the clay black before it was smoothed with a stick and polished. The shapes were typical of the previous tradition along with shapes that imitated the Greek vases that, in turn, had been inspired by metallic objects. Decorations were geometric and with figures, either etched or mouldd.

克拉特陶瓶
Crater

公元前6世纪
黑陶
高36、直径36厘米

6th century BCE
Bucchero
H. 36cm, D.36cm

来自波乔·布库
克拉特陶瓶是酒会庆典上最
重要的酒器，它是一种用来
按比例在酒中兑水的容器。

From Poggio Buco
In the ceremony of the symposium
the crater, the container in which the
wine was mixed with water according
to specific proportions, was the most
important vessel.

陶炭盆及配件
Foculo (Miniature Brazier) With Equipment

公元前7世纪
薄胎灰陶
高31.7、长73、宽43厘米

7th century BCE
Bucchero
H.31.7cm, L.73cm, W.43cm

来自丘西

这些使用布凯罗陶（一种薄胎灰陶）工艺制作的炭盆是典型的丘西地区的物品，它们只是用作陪葬。这组数量丰富的小炭盆及一起出现的陪葬品似乎很明显地反映家居和其他的室内活动。

From Chiusi
These braziers made bucchero, typical of the Chiusi, had a destination only funeral. The rich collection miniature accompanying the funeral deposition seems to be rather a clear reference to the home and other activities of the house.

这些使用布凯罗陶（一种薄胎灰陶）工艺制作的炭盆是典型的丘西地区的物品，它们只是用作陪葬。这组数量丰富的小炭盆及一起出现的陪葬品似乎很明显地反映家居和其他的室内活动。

These braziers made bucchero, typical of the Chiusi, had a destination only funeral. The rich collection miniature accompanying the funeral deposition seems to be rather a clear reference to the home and other activities of the house.

陶杯
Cup

公元前7世纪
薄胎灰陶
高3、直径10.5厘米

7th century BCE
Bucchero
H.3cm, D.10.5cm

陶圈足盘
Dish on A pedestal

公元前7世纪
薄胎灰陶
高9.4、直径15.5厘米

7th century BCE
Bucchero
H. 9.4cm, D.15.5cm

陶盘
Plate

公元前7世纪
薄胎灰陶
高2.8、直径13.4厘米

7th century BCE
Bucchero
H.2.8cm, D.13.4cm

帕特拉陶碗
Patera

公元前7世纪
薄胎灰陶
高4.3、直径16厘米.

7th century BCE
Bucchero
H.4.3cm, D.16cm

陶碗
Bowl

公元前7世纪
薄胎灰陶
高8.3、直径19.8厘米

7th century BCE
Bucchero
H.8.3cm, D.19.8cm

陶圈足杯
Cup on A Pedestal

公元前7世纪
薄胎灰陶
高13.7、直径14.7厘米

7th century BCE
Bucchero
H.13.7cm, D.14.7cm

奥拉陶罐
Olla

公元前7世纪
薄胎灰陶
高9.7、直径8厘米

7th century BCE
Bucchero
H.9.7cm, D.8cm

奥拉陶罐
Olla

公元前7世纪
薄胎灰陶
高8.3、直径6.7厘米

7th century BCE
Bucchero
H. 8.3cm, D.6.7cm

欧帕陶壶
Olpe

公元前7世纪
薄胎灰陶
高16.6、直径7.8厘米

7th century BCE
Bucchero
H.16.6cm, D.7.8cm

凯特斯陶勺
Kyathos

公元前7世纪
薄胎灰陶
高9.3、直径6厘米

7th century BCE
Bucchero
H.9.3cm, D.6cm

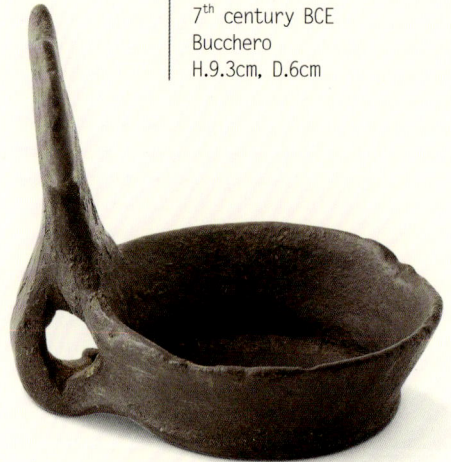

凯特斯陶勺
Kyathos

公元前7世纪
薄胎灰陶
高7.3、直径6.5厘米

7th century BCE
Bucchero
H.7.3cm, D.6.5cm

阿拉巴斯塔陶香水瓶
Alabastron

公元前7世纪
薄胎灰陶
高27.6、直径3.7厘米

7th century BCE
Bucchero
H.27.6cm, D.3.7cm

辛帕伦陶勺
Sympulum

公元前7世纪
薄胎灰陶
高13.8、直径6.5厘米

7th century BCE
Bucchero
H.13.8cm, D.6.5cm

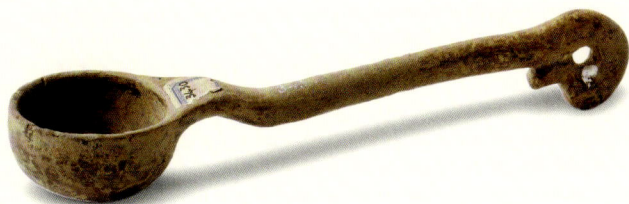

辛帕伦陶勺
Sympulum

公元前7世纪
薄胎灰陶
高11.6、直径5.3厘米

7th century BCE
Bucchero
H.11.6cm, D.5.3cm

小陶铲
Small Shovel

公元前7世纪
薄胎灰陶
高15.4、宽5.1厘米

7th century BCE
Bucchero
H.15.4cm, W.5.1cm

小陶铲
Small Shovel

公元前7世纪
薄胎灰陶
高16.4、宽2.5厘米

7th century BCE
Bucchero
H.16.4cm, W.2.5cm

陶盘
Tray

公元前7世纪
薄胎灰陶
高18.5、宽9.7厘米

7th century BCE
Bucchero
H.18.5cm, W.9.7cm

陶器盖
Cover

公元前7世纪
薄胎灰陶
高6、直径10.1厘米

7th century BCE
Bucchero
H.6cm, D.10.1cm

陶果盘
Fruit Bowl

公元前6世纪
薄胎灰陶
高20.5、直径37.5厘米

6th century BCE
Bucchero
H.20.5cm, D.37.5cm

来自丘西

这只果盘的环形把手顶部各装饰有一只小鸟，，口沿对称地装饰四只有女性面孔的椭圆形装饰。

From Chiusi
The bowl is decorated with four elliptical plates representing female faces in perspective on the board and plastic birds at the height of the loops.

陶酒杯
Glass

公元前6世纪
薄胎灰陶
高13.5、直径14厘米

6th century BCE
Bucchero
H.13.5cm, D.14cm

来自丘西

这件杯状器皿造型独特，杯身由高足和四片女子塑像支撑。女子掩映在层叠的腓尼基式棕叶饰间。

From Chiusi
The tank of this particular vessel drinking cup on a high foot is supported by four plates alternating a female figure shrouded in overlapping palmettes Phoenician.

黑陶杯
Glass

公元前6世纪
薄胎灰陶
高18.5、直径13.5厘米

6th century BCE
Bucchero
H.18.5cm, D.13.5cm

来自丘西

这是一只使用布凯罗黑陶工
艺制作的圆锥形高足杯，杯
身装饰着两只蜷伏的猫。

From Chiusi
Goblet of foot high conical bucchero
decorated manhole mold on bath
cats crouched.

镶头像黑陶杯
Glass With Applied Heads

公元前6世纪
薄胎灰陶
高15、直径17厘米

6th century BCE
Bucchero
H.15cm, D.17cm

来自丘西

这类黑陶高脚杯是丘西地区
出产的，杯缘装饰的女性头
像是使用铸模工艺制作的。

From Chiusi
Goblets of this type, made in area
Chiusine bucchero, show the female
heads realized in mold applied on
the edge of the vessel.

陶托架
Support

公元前6世纪
薄胎灰陶
高14、长13、宽13厘米

Bucchero
H.14cm, L.13cm, W.13cm

这件布凯罗黑陶工艺制作的
托架较大，托架上饰有精美
的装饰花纹，带有典型的丘
西特征。

The support of bucchero, over the
unusual shape, shows a refined
decoration traf gold. Typical of the
Chiusi.

奥伊洛克陶壶
Oinochoe With A Lid

公元前6世纪
薄胎灰陶
高29.7、直径17、盖高7.5厘米

6th century BCE
Bucchero
H.29.7cm, D.17cm, H.(lid) 7.5

来自丘西

这只黑陶酒壶颈部饰有一张
漂亮的女性面孔，造型别致
的壶盖顶上饰一只小鸟。

From Chiusi
The oinochoe bucchero neck
manhole cover has a beautiful female
mask designed to mold. The Curious
lid, on top of a bird.

凯特斯陶瓶
Kyathos

公元前6世纪
薄胎灰陶
通高19.04、直径16.5厘米

6th century BCE
Bucchero
H.(max)19.04cm, D.16.5cm

来自丘西

这只配有越过瓶身的环形把
手的陶瓶是酒会上饮酒器，
是典型的伊特鲁里亚器皿。

From Chiusi
Typically Etruscan vase, equipped
with large loop overhead, which is
used during the symposium to drink
wine. The exuberant decoration mold
on the tub see manhole environment.

安夫拉陶瓶
Amphora

公元前6世纪
薄胎灰陶
高43、最大直径28厘米

6th century BCE
Bucchero
H.43cm, Diam.(max)28cm

来自丘西

这只黑陶安夫拉陶瓶出产自
丘西地区。瓶身模仿金属器
皿饰一队骑士浮雕。

From Chiusi
Large amphora in bucchero
production Chiusi. The decoration
consists of a procession of horsemen
gradients on the body mimics the
ornate embossed metal vessels.

安夫拉黑陶瓶
Amphora

公元前6世纪
薄胎灰陶
高59、直径19厘米

6th century BCE
Bucchero
H.59cm, D.19cm

来自丘西

这只大型黑陶双耳瓶出产自
丘西。瓶身装饰精美，瓶口
边缘塑有几张女性面孔，瓶
身模仿金属器皿的浮雕，装
饰一队骑士形象。

From Chiusi
Large amphora in bucchero
production Chiusi. The decoration
consists of a series of female heads
applied to the brink and a procession
of horsemen gradients on the body
mimics the ornate embossed metal
vessels.

三叶形口缘奥伊洛克陶壶
Oinochoe With A Trilobate Rim

公元前6世纪
薄胎灰陶
高40、直径12厘米

6th century BCE
Bucchero
H.40cm, D.12cm

来自丘西

本件有着别致的三叶形壶
口，环形把手顶端的两侧则
各饰有一个圆轮。壶身图案
繁复精致，表现典型的布凯
罗黑陶装饰风格。

From Chiusi
Oinochoe trefoil mouth with circular
wheels on either side of the loop. The
body shows the typical decoration of
exuberant bucchero manhole.

黑彩陶器

在伊特鲁里亚文明的最后一个时期，这种风格被成批生产、甚至几乎工业化生产的黑彩器皿所替代。不过，有些黑彩陶器还是十分具有艺术价值的。这些陶器中，一部分是从希腊殖民地塔拉斯（Taras，今天阿普利亚区的塔兰托）进口的，剩下的则是伊特鲁里亚人模仿塔拉斯陶器制作的。

Black pottery

In the final period of the Etruscan civilization, this style was replaced by the serial, almost industrial, production of black painted vessels. Nonetheless, some of these were very artistic. These were, in part, imported from the Greek colony of Taras (modern- day Taranto in Apulia) and, for the rest, made by the Etruscans who imitated Taras potters.

斯图拉陶壶
Situla

公元前4-3世纪
黑陶
高24.7、直径21.7厘米

4-3th century BCE
Black Paint Ceramics
H.24.7cm, D.21.7cm

优雅的黑彩陶器的形式并展现了贵金属表面光泽。该类型是公元前四世纪初和三世纪晚期在沃特拉（Volterra）生产的。

The elegant black-glazed pottery vessel forms and reproduces the surface gloss of the most expensive metal prototypes. The model was produced in Volterra in the late third and early fourth century. B.C. E.

克拉特陶瓶
Crater

公元前4-3 世纪
黑陶
高22、直径20厘米

4-3th century BCE
Black Paint Ceramics
H.22cm、D.20cm

这件克拉特黑彩陶瓶形态优
雅、独特，肩部配有两只环
形把手，表现出典型的沃尔
泰拉陶器的特征。

Feature of this crater elegant black
paint are the two loops placed on
the shoulder of the vase-shaped
snake, typical of the best production
Volterra.

克拉特陶瓶
Large Crater

公元前4-3世纪
黑陶
高36、直径31厘米

4-3th century BCE
Black Paint Ceramics
H.36cm, D.31cm

这是一件用黑彩的大克拉特陶瓶，它是希腊和伊特鲁里亚仪式中最大的调酒器皿。

Large crater-shaped cup in black paint. The crater is the largest vessel in Greek and Etruscan ritual for the preparation of wine.

基里克斯陶杯
Kylix With Handles

公元前3-2世纪
黑陶
高4.8、直径14.8厘米

3-2th century BCE
Black Paint Ceramics
H.4.8cm, D.14.8cm

这件双耳杯造型优雅，运用黑彩式的内壁装饰有棕叶饰和莲花的浮雕装饰图案，表现出典型的希腊化时期风格。

The elegant cup black paint on the inside has a particular decoration embossed and engraved palmettes alternating with lotus flowers, typical of the Hellenistic period.

沃尔泰特拉的欧帕陶壶
Olpe From Volterra

公元前4-3世纪
黑陶
高20、最大直径15厘米

4-3th century BCE
Black Paint Ceramics
H.20cm, D.(max)15cm

这是典型的4世纪后期和3世纪早期由沃尔泰特拉出产的黑彩陶器。该瓶把手并底部饰有希腊森林之神西勒诺斯的头像。

Vases of this type are typical of the best production Volterra black paint of late fourth-early third century BCE At the base of the handle, the head of Silenus made a mold applied.

沃尔泰特拉的奥伊洛克陶壶
Oinochoe

公元前4-3世纪
黑陶
高30、最大直径19厘米

4-3th century BCE
Black Paint Ceramics
H.30cm, D.(max)19cm

来自沃尔泰拉

这是典型的4世纪后期和3世纪早期由沃尔泰拉出产的最好的黑彩陶器。该瓶把手底部饰有浇铸工艺制作的森林之神西勒诺斯的头像。

From Volterra
Vases of this type are typical of the best production Volterra black paint of late fourth-early third century BCE At the base of the handle, the head of Silenus made a mold applied.

斯加弗斯陶杯
Skyphos

公元前4-3世纪
黑陶
高16.7、直径17.5厘米

4-3th century BCE
Black Paint Ceramics
H.16.7cm, D.17.5cm

这只器皿采用了典型的双耳大饮杯造型，杯身从上到下逐渐变细，杯口的对称位置分布装有一只水平展开的把手。斯加弗斯是古希腊一种双耳在口沿的深腹杯。

Typical vessel potorio body with strongly tapered towards the bottom and two horizontal handles symmetrical edge.

陶盘
Dish

公元前2世纪
黑陶
高4.3、直径21厘米

2th century BCE
Black Paint Ceramics
H.4.3cm, D.21cm

这只大平底盘的内壁采用了黑彩工艺，盘中饰雕刻花纹，为典型的希腊化后期风格。

Large flat black paint decorated on the inside with impressed patterns and engraved typical of the late Hellenistic period.

帕特拉陶碗
Patera

公元前4-3世纪
黑陶
高4、直径19厘米

4-3th century BCE
Black Paint Ceramics
H.4cm, D.19cm

这件产自沃尔泰拉的黑彩仿金属器皿的陶碗风格独特，在碗内壁的圆凸和环线间刻有棕叶和莲花图案。

From Volterra.
Distinctive pottery vase in black paint which is inspired by metal prototypes. The decoration on the inside is composed of palmettes and lotus flowers etched between engraved circles.

奥伊洛克陶壶
Oinochoe

公元前4—3世纪
黑陶
高18、直径9厘米

4–3th century BCE
Black Paint Ceramics
H.18cm, D.9cm

本件是典型的公元前4世纪
后期和公元前3世纪早期沃
尔泰特拉出产的最好的黑彩
陶器。

**Vases of this type are typical of the
best production Volterra black paint
of late fourth-early third century
B.C.E.**

厨具

与这些餐具器皿和壁炉同时陪葬的，还包括生火所用的全套金属工具（火钳、拨火棍、炭架和烤肉叉），烹煮肉类的大锅炉，滤酒和倒酒用的工具（滤勺，长柄勺）及社交酒会大厅内使用的家具，例如枝状大烛台，这些均由青铜制作。

Cooking Utensils

In addition to the tableware and fire place objects, there were all the metal tools needed for the fire (tongs, pokers, firedogs and spits to roast meat), the large cauldrons for cooking meat, the tools to filter and pour wine (colum, simpulum) and the furniture for the symposium halls, such as candelabra, which were all made of bronze.

青铜匕
Knife

公元前7世纪
青铜
长18.3厘米

7th century BCE
Bronze
L.18.3cm

来自维图罗尼亚，塞克
洛·德格利·尤里瓦斯特

这把青铜餐刀是一种切肉用
的餐具，在伊特鲁里亚首领
们的厨房餐具中常见。

From Vetulonia, Circolo degli Ulivastri
The knife in bronze is very common
in instruments for cooking the meat
present in the kits of the Etruscan
princes.

铁斧
Axes

公元前7世纪
铁
长13-14、宽5.5-6.2厘米

7th century BCE
Iron
L.13-14cm,W.5.5-6.2cm

来自维图罗尼亚，塞克
洛·德格利·尤里瓦斯特

这两把铁斧的刀片呈梯形，
刀把底部可装入木柄。

From Vetulonia, Circolo degli Ulivastri
Two axes of iron with trapezoidal
blade provided at the base of a
handle intended to house a wooden
support.

青铜烤肉叉
Spits

公元前7世纪
青铜
长75.5-77厘米

7th century BCE
Bronze
L.75.5-77cm

来自维图罗尼亚
塞克洛·德·特图恩

这种烤肉叉在东方时期陪葬丰富的王公贵族的陵寝里十分普遍。叉身呈螺旋形，需与其他物品一起用来烤制肉类。

From Vetulonia, Circolo del Tritone
The skewers are widely spread in the rich princely grave of the Orientalizing period. Were involved, together with other objects of the service for cooking meat.

铁双翼炭架
Couple of Wing Fireplace

公元前7世纪
铁
高16、长33-36厘米

7th century BCE
Iron
H.16cm, L.33-36cm

来自奥维多

这是一对铁质炭架，可在铁架上烤制肉类。烧烤在古代社会不仅有着重大的祭祀意义，在社交和家庭生活中也有着重要意义。

From Orvieto
Pair of andirons in iron used to cook the meat on the grill. Cooking food takes in the ancient world significance not only sacred but also social and domestic.

青铜铲
Fire Shovel

公元前7世纪
青铜
长60厘米

7th century BCE
Bronze
L.60cm

来自维图罗尼亚
塞克洛·德·特图恩

本件在烹饪过程中使柴火聚拢，但本例的唯一作用是作为陪葬品。

From Vetulonia, Circolo del Tritone
Object used as the following to fix the focus during the cooking of meat. Had in this case a destination only funerary.

火钳
Fire Tongs

公元前7世纪
青铜
长50厘米

7th century BCE
Bronze
L.50cm

来自维图罗尼亚
塞克洛·德·特图恩

在烹饪过程中使柴火聚拢，但本例的唯一作用是作为陪葬品。

From Vetulonia, Circolo del Tritone

Object used as above to fix the focus during the cooking of meat. Had in this case a destination exclusively funerary.

陶炉
Stove

公元前7世纪
褐陶
高²¹、长45厘米

7th century BCE
Impasto
H.21cm, L.45cm

来自索瓦纳

本件采用了平行六面体造型，每个侧边均有三角形镂空作为装饰，顶部则配有一个漏斗状开口。这种火炉在索瓦纳和皮蒂利亚诺的陪葬品中非常常见，通常火盆一起使用。

From Sovana
The stove has a parallelepiped shape with triangular openings on the sides and a funnel-shaped orifice on the top. They are very popular among the grave goods of Sovana and Pitigliano, often associated with pallets of fire.

陶炉
Clay Stove

公元前6世纪
褐陶
高12.6、直径30.6厘米

6th century BCE
Impasto
H.12.6cm, D.30.6cm

来自波乔·布库
这是一只侧面由开口的圆形
烹饪器具，也是日常生活中
烹煮食物的物品。

From Poggio Buco
Cooker dough circular in shape with
openings at the sides also used in
everyday life for cooking food.

发现：塔拉莫纳奇奥神庙

在一座被称为"塔拉莫纳奇奥"的小山上，考古学家发现了"底比斯七英雄"神庙山墙装饰上的红陶碎片。这座小山坐落在第勒尼安海岸上的一个小海岬，位于奥尔贝泰洛（Orbetello）和格罗塞托（Grosseto）之间。这座小山的名字让人想起了曾经屹立在小山上，俯瞰着海湾的伊特鲁里亚城邦特拉蒙（特拉姆？）。1892年5月11日，在挖掘一座新要塞的地基时，一座古老的蓄水池重见天日，人们还在水池周围发现了许多山墙装饰的碎片，还有一些瓦檐饰和其他建筑红陶的残砖断瓦。这一离奇发现激起了人们极大的兴趣。后来的研究表明，这些碎片来自一座被大火夷为平地的神庙。

现在我们已经了解这座神庙的建筑布局，它屹立在塔拉莫纳奇奥城的东南方，地理位置稍低于小山的顶峰。神庙正门眺望着海岸线，当船只从南方驶来时，神庙就成了一处引人注目的地标，但从海湾北面向上观望时，神庙却隐而不见。从废墟中发现的残砖断瓦可证明，这是一座意大利—伊特鲁里亚式"tetrastylos sine postico"。神庙正面有四根圆柱，后面则是封闭的。神庙建于公元前4世纪下半叶，坐落在当时已被人废弃的一个地方，但在罗马征服当地之前这里还有人居住。这是一座奉献给两位神灵的伊特鲁里亚神庙，其中一位是提尼阿(Tinia)——伊特鲁里亚的至高无上之神，另一位则是常与提尼阿一起出现的女神。神庙山墙是公元前150年重建神庙时添加的，当时这座城市已在罗马统治之下。还有一种假设，认为山墙是在公元前225年罗马在塔拉莫纳奇奥攻克高卢人之后数年建造的。

挖掘过程中发现的火灾迹象"证明了公元前100年后不久，这座神庙就被大火夷为平地，而且再也没有重建。将神庙的毁灭和当时马里奥与新罗(Silla.)之间如火如荼的战事联系起来，或许有些意义。塔拉莫纳奇奥的市民有理由害怕新罗的报复，因为公元前87年马里奥从非洲返回途中在他们的港口登陆，并以塔拉莫纳奇奥为据点开始对新罗的夺权之战。当时，马里奥在50公里以外的萨图尼亚(Saturnia)击溃了新罗的舰队。但遗憾的是，没有留下任何证据，证明塔拉莫纳奇奥的大火与公元前82年马里奥的得胜存在联系。这场大会更有可能是一场"自然"灾害。塔拉莫纳奇奥神庙的山墙是目前我们所知的唯一一件伊特鲁里亚文化后期具有完整的雕塑和建筑装饰的山墙。

神话

　　《底比斯七英雄》是埃斯库罗斯所著悲剧三部曲中唯一保存至今的一部，其他两部《莱俄斯》和《俄狄浦斯》均已遗失，该三部剧曾帮助埃斯库罗斯获得公元前478年度悲剧大赛的头奖。它讲述了以Labdacean神话故事为题材的《底比斯史诗集》中的主要情节，即俄狄浦斯的两个儿子厄特俄克勒斯与波吕尼刻斯之间的战争的戏剧性结局。萨福克里斯也曾从这些故事中获得灵感，而写下剧作《安提戈涅》、《俄狄浦斯王》以及《俄狄浦斯在科勒罗斯》。在萨福克里斯之后，欧里庇得斯曾在公元前412年或409年左右首次出演《腓尼基妇女》。这是对这个悲剧的最后一次演绎，也是最接近塔拉莫纳奇奥神庙山墙上所述故事的演绎。

　　故事主要讲述了俄狄浦斯及其悲剧命运。他破解了怪物斯芬克斯的谜语，后误杀其父底比斯国王莱厄斯，娶其母乔卡斯塔为妻，并生下四个孩子厄特俄克勒斯、波吕尼刻斯、安提戈涅、伊斯墨涅。后来，作为对自己所犯罪行的惩罚，俄狄浦斯自刺双目，老后受到儿子的虐待，而他也对他们发下诅咒。

　　他说，将来有一天，他们两兄弟将会为争夺王位而决斗。为了避免这个厄运，两兄弟商议好，两人以一年为期，轮流统治国家，但厄特俄克勒斯任期结束后不愿交出统治权。

　　于是，波吕尼刻斯从岳父阿德拉斯托斯的国家阿戈斯发起复仇之战。他们组成远征队打算攻打底比斯，并夺回王位。七位英雄加入了这支远征队：阿戈斯国王阿德拉斯托斯、预言家安菲阿剌俄斯、国王之侄卡帕纽斯、堤丢斯、国王之兄弟希波迈冬和帕耳忒诺派俄斯，及波吕尼刻斯自己。

　　山墙上的浮雕描绘了战争的结果。画面中下方，目睹整个家族最终被毁灭的厄运，俄狄浦斯双膝跪地，双手伸向天空，面露绝望的神情。两旁则是在决斗中给予对方致命一击的两兄弟，一个倒在一个女人的怀里（安提戈涅或乔卡斯塔），另一个则倒在同伴怀中。画面上半部分，我们可以认出阿戈斯远征队中的其他两位英雄，其中一位是卡帕纽斯，他因为出言不逊而触怒宙斯，在他即将从梯子上跳下以为就要攻破底比斯的城墙时，被宙斯发出的闪电击毙。画面左边，则是远征队中唯一的幸存者阿德拉斯托斯，他正乘着战车从战场落荒而逃。右边则是预言家安菲阿剌俄斯，他早已预见了同伴和自己的死亡，此刻正要从宙斯在地上劈开的深渊中消失，这样，所有人中只有他可以活着进入地狱。拖着他的战车的四匹马此时正被代表死亡的半神猛烈地拉扯。

The discovery: the temple of Talamonaccio

The terracotta fragments which make up the pediment of the temple of "The Seven at Thebes» were found on a hill called Talamonaccio, a small headland on the Thyrrenian coast, between the towns of Orbetello and Grosseto. The name recalls the Etruscan city of Telamon (Tlamu?) which once rose on the hill, overlooking the bay. On May 11th 1892, while excavating the foundations for a new fort an old cistern was uncovered and around it were found many fragments of the decoration together with parts of the antefixes and other architectural terracottes. Such an extraordinary event caused great enthusiasm. Later it was discovered that the temple to which the fragments had belonged had been destroyed by fire.

The temple, of which today we know the plan, rose on the southeast side of Talamonaccio, slightly below the top of the hill. It's front looked towards the coastline and was a noticeable landmark for the ships coming in from the south, while it remained hidden from the underlying north side of the bay. From the ruins it has been possible to prove that it was an Italo-Etruscan "tetrastylos sine postico". It had four columns on the front while the back was closed. It was built in the latter half of the I V Century B. C. E.on a site which had been inhabited but at that moment, before the Roman conquest of this territory, had been abandoned. It was hence an Etruscan temple, dedicated to two deities. One of them was probably Tinia the supreme Etruscan god and the other a goddess commonly associated to him. The pediment was added only later on when the whole building was being restructured in 150 B. C. E. with the city already under the Roman influence. On the other hand a second hypothesis suggests that the pediment was built in the years immediately following the Roman victory over the Gauls which took place in 225 B. C. E.at Talamone.

Evidence of a fire was found during excavation "thus proving that shortly after 100 B. C. E.the temple was burnt to the ground and never rebuilt. It can be of interest to see a connection between the destruction of the temple and the civil war that raged at that time between Mario and Silla. The citizens of Talamone had reason to fear the vengeange of Silla as Mario returning from Africa had landed in their harbour in 87 B. C.E. and from their city had begun his fight for power against Silla.Unfortunately no proof remains to link the fire on the Talamonaccio hill to the victory in 82 B. C. E.to the Sillean troops at Saturnia a site 50 Km. away. The fire had probably more "natural" causes. The Talamone pediment is the only one of the late Etruscan period complete of sculptures and architectural decoration which we know of today.

The Myth

"Seven against Thebes" is the title of the only tragedy which has reached us of the trilogy, which includes "Laius" and "Oedipus", with which Aeschylus won the competition for tragedies in the year 468 B. C. E.It described one of the main episodes of the Thebeian Cycle which is made up of mythical Tales of the Labdaceans. It is the dramatic epilogue of the war between the two brothers Eteocles and Polynices. Sophocles was also inspired by these stories to represent "Antigones", "Oedipus Rex", "Oedipus Colonus". After him Euripedes around the years 412 or 409 B. C.E. gave his first performance of "The Phoenicians". This last interpretation of the myth is the one closest to the tale being represented on the temple 's pediment.

The main theme is Oedipus and his tragic destiny. He solved the Sphink's Enigma, and unknowingly killed his own father Laius king of Thebes, married his own mother Jacasta to give birth to four children Eteocles, Polynices, Antigones and Ismenes. As a punishment for his actions Oedipus blinded himself, then old and mistreated by his sons he threw a curse on them.

He said that one day they would have fought in battle one against the other for the kingdom. To avoid such fate the two brothers agreed to reign one year at a time, but when Eteocles ended his term he would not give up his rule.

Polynices then took refuge in Argos at his father's in law, Adrastos. Here they formed an army to fight against Thebes and win back the throne. Seven heroes took part in the expedition: Adrastos, Anphiaraos, Capaneus, Tdeus, Hippomedontes, Partenopeus and Polynices himself.

The relief represents the end of the fight. At lower centre Oedipus kneels with his arms to the sky in an expression of desperation while witnessing the final ruin of his family. At the sides the two brothers have mortally wounded each other in the fight and now fall, one in the arms of a woman (either Jocasta or Antigones), the other in those of a companion. Of the other heroes we can recognise in the upper part two warriors from Argos, Capaneus, killed by lightning sent by Zeus that he had angered with words of defiance, as he is about to fall from the ladder with which he had hoped to conquer the Tebeian walls. On the left, only survivor of the battle, Adrastos rides away from the battlefield on his fighting chariot. On the right the fortune-teller Anphiaraos, who had forseen the death of his companions and of himself is about to disappear in the abyss that Zeus has opened in the earth so that he alone of all the mortal beings can enter alive in the kingdom of Hell. The four horses drawing his chariot are being violently pulled by male and female demons of death.

塔拉莫奈陶三角楣饰
Pediment of Talamone

公元前2世纪
红陶
高147、长882厘米

2ᵗʰ century BCE
Terracotta
H.147cm, L.882cm

来自塔拉莫纳奇奥

这是一件漂亮的红陶三角楣饰，原本装饰在（托斯卡纳）塔拉莫奈的塔拉莫纳奇奥山顶上的神庙上。图像主题类似于"七雄攻忒拜"的传奇故事——这是希腊化时期的伊特鲁里亚广为流传的希腊神话。

From Talamone
The beautiful pediment made of terracotta decorated the pediment of the temple which stood on the hill of Talamonaccio at Talamone. The iconographic theme is reminiscent of the saga of the "Seven against Thebes," Greek myth which had a wide circulation in Etruria in the Hellenistic period.

俄狄浦斯与他的儿子
Oedipus and His Sons

安菲阿剌俄斯的被俘
The Kidnapping of Anphiaraos

俄狄浦斯与他的儿子

被旁人扶持着的俄狄浦斯双膝跪地，双手伸向天空，做出痛不欲生的姿势，仿佛在祈求神灵的怜悯。左边，一个女人（安提戈涅或乔卡斯塔）支撑着受了致命重伤的厄特俄克勒斯，右边，则是一位远征队同伴托着波吕尼刻斯的尸体。

OEDIPUS AND HIS SONS

Oedipus supported by a helper kneels lifting up his arms in an act of overwhelming pain as if to implore pity from the gods. To the left a woman (Jocasta or Antigones) sustains Eteocles mortally wounded, while a comrade, to the right, holds up the body of Polynices.

两位阿戈斯勇士中间的卡帕纽斯

卡帕纽斯攀上底比斯的城墙，他的两旁各站着一位浑身赤裸，摆出进攻姿势的勇士。在这三人与另一位勇士中间，还有一位长着翅膀、手举火把的女性形象，以及一位无名勇士的残躯。

CAPANEUS BETWEEN TWO ARGIVE WARRIORS

Capaneus climbs Thebes's walls, while on each side two naked warriors are pictured in an offensive stance. Between this group and the next one there is a winged female figure holding a torch and an anonymous varrior's torso.

阿德拉斯托斯与复仇女神

阿德拉斯托斯乘着战车离开战场，车上载有两位倒下的勇士，背对着我们的那位蜷着身子，躲在一匹马下面，并试图躲开马蹄的践踏。另一位则跪在地上，试图用盾牌保护自己。

身穿盔甲的英雄望着右边张开双翅拥抱着他身体的复仇女神。阿德拉斯托斯的战车与山墙边缘之间，还出现了三位战士的身影。

THE GROUP OF ADRASTOS AND THE FURY

Adrastos leaves the field of battle on his chariot charging over two fallen warriors, one turning his back to us is seen crouched under one of the horses trying to protect himself from the animal's hoof clutching its front leg. The other warrior on outstreched knees looks for safety behind his shield.

The hero in armour looks to the right where a Fury with open wings embraces his torso. Two or perhaps even three warriors filled the space between the chariot of Adrastos and the end of the pediment.

安菲阿剌俄斯的被俘

安菲阿剌俄斯正被自己的战车拖向地狱。一个年轻的半神正在三位复仇女神的帮助下将战车拉向深渊，安菲阿剌俄斯正要爬上战车，用大圆盾护着左边的身子，高举的右手仿佛表达恐惧之情。

THE KIDNAPPING OF ANPHIARAOS

Anphiaraos is drawn down into hell on his chariot. A young demon pulls the horses down the abyss helped by three winged Furies. Anphiaraos is about to climb his chariot, with the great round shield protecting the left side of his body, while the right arm was probably held up high in an act of fear.

建筑红陶：武尔奇，庞特·洛托的狄奥尼修斯神庙

　　远古时代的建筑是石头堆砌的，但上层部分（屋顶和门楣）是木头材质，外表覆盖有用钉子固定的各种彩绘红陶装饰元素。有些情况下，铁钉留下的痕迹仍然清晰可辨。在这座献给著名的希腊神祇狄奥尼修斯的小神庙里，装饰有模印浮雕的面板镶嵌在楣梁上和上方的三角形山墙上。伊特鲁里亚人通常在山墙上装饰高浮雕雕塑，正如塔拉莫纳奇奥神庙山墙所示。沿着屋檐（和今天一样，由红陶制作并涂成红色）则装饰着一排瓦檐饰——即瓦房屋檐外的一种直的饰物，用于遮掩瓦排的结合部。瓦檐饰是希腊和伊特鲁里亚建筑中一种常见的饰物，并有着各种不同的造型。女性头像是最普遍的造型——如本例所示——但美杜莎与西勒诺斯的头像也有发现。

Architectural Terracotta: Vulci, Temple of Dionysus at Ponte Rotto

In ancient times, buildings were made of stone, but the upper section (roof and architraves) was made of wood that was covered with various elements of painted terracotta that were nailed to the underlying wooden structure. The marks left by the iron nails are still visible in some cases. At this small temple dedicated to the famous Greek god Dionysus, the panels decorated with moulded reliefs were placed on the architrave and, higher up, on the borders of the triangular pediment. It was normal to position a high-relief sculpture on the pediment, as is the case for the Talamone temple. A series of antefixes - decorative elements that masked the semi-circular ends of the roof covering (also made of terracotta and painted red, like today) - were placed along the line of the eaves. Antefixes were common in Greek and Etruscan buildings and came in various shapes. A woman's head was common - and is the case here - but medusa or Silenus heads have also been found.

女性人头形陶瓦当
Female Head Shaped Antefix

公元前3 世纪
红陶
高21、宽25-32厘米

3th century BCE
Terracotta
H.21cm, W.25-32cm

来自武尔奇，庞特·洛托

这类红陶饰件是屋檐上的瓦
当，常有着各种造型，色彩
鲜亮。一般出现在希腊和伊
特鲁里亚时期的民间建筑和
神庙。

From Vulci, Ponte Rotto
The primary phases of terracotta
decorative elements were placed
at the ends of the rows of tiles of
the roof along the eaves. They were
variously shaped and painted in
bright colors. They are often found in
the sacred buildings and civil Greeks
and Etruscans.

刻有酒神与阿里阿德涅陶板
Architectonic Slab Representing Dionysus and Ariadne

公元前6世纪
红陶
高52、长53厘米

6th century BCE
Terracotta
H.52cm, L.53cm

来自武尔奇，庞特·洛托

本件是用红陶模制酒神与阿里阿德涅。

From Vulci, Ponte Rotto
Architectural terracotta mold depicting Dionysus and Ariadne seated.

陶建筑板
Architectural Plates

公元前6世纪
红陶
高21、长31厘米

6th century BCE
Terracotta
H.21cm, L.31cm

来自武尔奇，庞特·洛托

这类陶板是用来装饰在供奉酒神狄俄尼索的小神庙。有些这种陶板仍然保留着用于固定在孔眼里的钉子。

From Vulci, Ponte Rotto
Architectural slabs that decorated a small place of worship dedicated to Dionysus. Some of these still retain the nails for fixing housed in holes.

陶建筑板
Architectonic Slabs

公元前6世纪
陶
高21、长31厘米

6th century BCE
Berracotta
H.21cm, L.31cm

来自武尔奇, 庞特·洛托
这类运用浮雕工艺的条形红
陶建筑板材通常装饰在神庙
山形墙或屋顶侧面。

From Vulci, Ponte Rotto
These architectural terracottas (sime)
decorated in relief adorn the band
cgoldnamento the gable or side of
the roof of sacred buildings.

祭品

　　在圣殿，人们除举行常规的敬神仪式外，虔诚的教徒还会献上各种各样的供奉雕塑。这些雕塑通常由神庙附近的小作坊制作和售卖。供奉雕塑可分为多种不同的种类。例如，有代表供奉者的小型男女雕塑（例如布洛里奥[Brolio]的祭品），由青铜和红陶制作。大型雕塑甚至可以使用大理石雕塑，如本展中的女性雕像。许多情况下仅表现男性和女性的半身像，这也是一种古希腊兴起的一种较普遍的做法。

　　许多祭品被塑造成人体不同部位的造型，或用青铜制作，或用红陶制作。大多数情况下，这些祭品都与生育力有关，将其奉献给神灵是为了获得某些好处，或是作为康复后表示感谢的象征。此外，还有一些动物雕塑，例如公牛、小鹿、公猪、马匹等，都代表着献祭动物献给神祇。

Votive Offerings

In sanctuaries, in addition to the normal rituals for the deities, the faithful used to offer an array of votive statues. It was usual for these to be made and sold locally by small workshops near the temple. There are a number of different types. For example, there were small statues of either the man or woman presenting the offer (such as the Brolio votive offering), made of bronze and terracotta. Larger such statues could even be made of marble, such as the female statue. In many cases, only male and female busts were represented, keeping with a very common ancient-world practice that arose in Greece.

Many votive offerings were shaped like the different parts of the human body and made of bronze or terracotta. In most cases they had to do with fertility and were dedicated to a deity to obtain a benefit or as a token of gratitude for healing. In addition, there were also animal statues, like bulls, fawns, boars or horses that were the equivalent of a sacrifice to a god.

青铜膜拜者
Statue of A Worshipper

公元前3-2世纪
青铜
高15.2厘米

3-2th century BCE
Bronze
H.15.2cm

这位男性身披斗篷，头戴花冠，右手握着奠酒时用的帕特拉碗。这种类型的雕塑在公元前3世纪和公元前2世纪的伊特鲁里亚中北部极为普遍。

Male figure wearing a cloak with cgoldna on the head. He holds in his right hand a patera for libations. The type is widespread in central and northern Etruria in the third and second century. B.C. E.

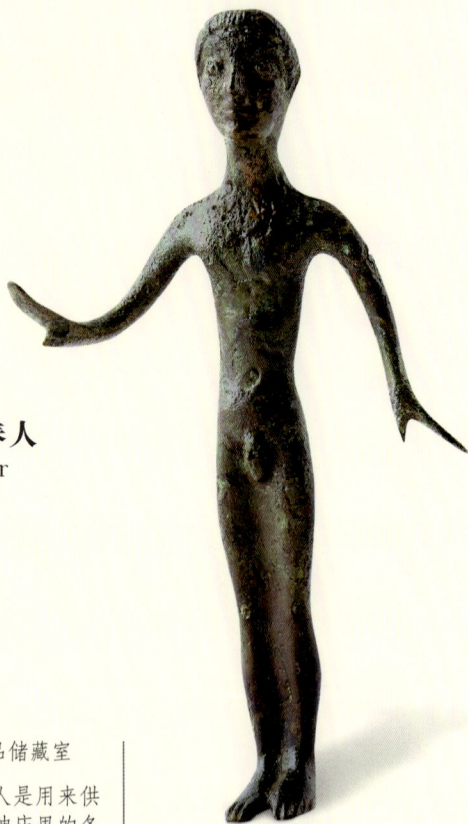

青铜男供养人
Male Offerer

公元前5世纪
青铜
高10.5厘米

5th century BCE
Bronze
H.10.5cm

来自布洛里奥祭品储藏室

这种青铜男供养人是用来供奉给伊特鲁里亚神庙里的各位神灵的。供养人有男有女，大多数来自布洛里奥的供奉殿，这些雕像体现了供养人的形象。

From Deposito votivo di Brolio
These small human figures made of bronze were given as gifts to various deities in the shrines Etruscans. All of these come from the votive deposit of Brolio and depict mostly male and female figures bidders.

青铜女供养人
Female Statue

公元前5世纪
青铜
高11.2厘米5 BCE

5th century BCE
Bronze
H.11.2cm

来自布洛里奥祭品储藏室

这种青铜男供养人是用来供奉给伊特鲁里亚神庙里的各位神灵的。供养人有男有女，大多数来自布洛里奥的供奉殿，这些雕像体现了供养人的形象。

From Deposito votivo di Brolio
These small human figures made of bronze were given as gifts to various deities in the shrines Etruscans. All of these come from the votive deposit of Brolio and depict mostly male and female figures bidders.

青铜女供养人
Female Statue

公元前6世纪
青铜
高8.2厘米

6th century BCE
Bronze
H.8.2cm

来自布洛里奥祭品储藏室

这尊雕塑展现了一位身披长袍，头戴高帽的女性形象。

From Deposito votivo di Brolio
The statue represents a female figure wrapped in a long robe with a tall hat on her Head.

青铜女子像
Female Statue

公元前4世纪
青铜
高7.1厘米

4th century BCE
Bronze
H.7.1cm

来自布洛里奥祭品储藏室

本件制作于公元前6世纪后期的伊特鲁里亚，描绘了一位伸展双臂的短发女性形象。

From Deposito votivo di Brolio
The statue was made in Etruria in the late sixth century BCE. It represents a female figure with arms outstretched and hair in a bob.

青铜女供养人
Female Statue

公元前6世纪
青铜
高7.1厘米

6th century BCE
Bronze
H.7.1cm

来自布洛里奥祭品储藏室

这种青铜男供养人是用来祭给伊特鲁里亚神庙里的各位神灵的。供养人有男有女，大多数来自布洛里奥的供奉殿，这些雕像体现了供养人的形象。

From Deposito votivo di Brolio
These small human figures made of bronze were given as gifts to various deities in the shrines Etruscans. All of these come from the votive deposit of Brolio and depict mostly male and female figures bidders.

青铜女供养人
Female Statue

公元前5世纪
青铜
高9.5厘米

5th century BCE
Bronze
B.9.5cm

来自布洛里奥祭品储藏室

这种青铜男供养人是用来供奉给伊特鲁里亚神庙里的各位神灵的。供养人有男有女，大多数来自布洛里奥的供奉殿，这些雕像体现了供养人的形象。

From Deposito votivo di Brolio
These small human figures made of bronze were given as gifts to various deities in the shrines Etruscans. All of these come from the votive deposit of Brolio and depict mostly male and female figures bidders.

青铜女供养人
Female Statue

公元前5世纪
青铜
高9.5厘米

5th century BCE
Bronze
H.9.5cm

来自布洛里奥祭品储藏室

这种青铜男供养人是用来供
奉给伊特鲁里亚神庙里的各
位神灵的。供养人有男有
女，大多数来自布洛里奥的
供奉殿，这些雕像体现了供
养人的形象。

From Deposito votivo di Brolio
These small human figures made of
bronze were given as gifts to various
deities in the shrines Etruscans. All of
these come from the votive deposit
of Brolio and depict mostly male and
female figures bidders.

青铜武士像
Statue of A Warrior

公元前6世纪
青铜
高23厘米

6th century BCE
Bronze
H.23cm

来自布洛里奥祭品储藏室

这尊武士雕塑来自伊特鲁里
亚南部最为著名的神殿，这
位武士表现出掷出长矛的动
作形象。他佩戴着护胫甲，
头戴一顶精致的科林斯式头
盔。

From Deposito votivo di Brolio
He warrior who comes from one of
the most prestigious votive deposits
in northern Etruria, is depicted in the
act of hurling a spear lost. He wears
leg greaves and a fine Corinthian
helmet.

青铜武士像
Statue of A Warrior

公元前6世纪
青铜
高24厘米

6th century BCE
Bronze
H.24cm

来自布洛里奥祭品储藏室

这尊武士雕塑来自伊特鲁里亚南部最为著名的神殿，这位武士右手掷出长矛，左手紧握盾牌。这是公元前6世纪末的希腊和伊特鲁里亚常见的雕塑形象。

From Deposito votivo di Brolio
The warrior who comes from one of the most prestigious votive deposits in northern Etruria, is depicted in the act of throwing a spear with his right hand while his left hand held a shield, according to a common pattern in Greece and Etruria at the end of the sixth sec. B.C. E.

大理石女子像
Statue of A Kore

公元前4世纪末
大理石
高68厘米

End 4th century BCE
Marble
H.68cm

这尊小雕像再现了一位身穿无袖束腰外衣的年轻女子，她右手提起裙摆，左手托着一只鸽子。

雕像头部的制作十分精细，但身体则似乎出自一位技术生疏的新手。这件雕塑可能原本是某一组女性殡葬雕塑中的一件。这类殡葬雕塑在沃尔泰拉地区十分普遍。

This statue represents a standing female figure wearing asleeveless chiton that is girdled beneathThe chest with a belt. With her right hand she raises the hemof her garment, while in her left hand she holds a dove.The head-notable for the hight quality of its modeling andfor its skillful details-does not belong to the body, wich appearsto have been executed by a less skillful and untrainedhand. The sculpture may be included amoung a group offemale funerary statues that functioned as *cippi* and werewidely distributed in the area of Volterra.

这种类似解剖学意义内脏造型的雕塑是圣图拉瑞最为普遍的一种祭品。这些内脏雕塑可由青铜或红陶制作，再现了人体的各种器官，这些雕塑具有很明确的健康或生殖力的意义，用来供奉给神灵以获取某种利益。

The anatomical devotional figures one of the most popular things in the temple. These are objects in terracotta, reproducing various parts of the human body, all clearly linked to the sphere of health and fertility, dedicated to the gods in order to obtain a benefit.

陶头颅
Head

公元前3世纪
红陶
高25、宽19厘米

3rd century BCE
Terracotta
H.25cm, W.19cm

陶肠
Intestine

公元前3-2世纪
红陶
高11、宽14厘米

3-2th century BCE
Terracotta
H.11cm, W.14cm

陶子宫
Uterus

公元前3-2世纪
红陶
长17、宽11厘米

3-2th century BCE
Terracotta
L.17cm, W.11cm

陶乳房
Breast

公元前3-2世纪
红陶
高6.5、直径8厘米

3-2th century BCE
Terracotta
H.6.5cm, D.8cm

陶肠
Bowels

公元前3-2世纪
红陶
高20、宽14厘米

3-2th century BCE
Terracotta
H.20cm, W.14cm

陶男性头颅
Male Head

公元前3世纪
红陶
高25、宽28厘米

3th century BCE
Terracotta
H.25cm, W.28cm

陶手
Hand

公元前3-2世纪
红陶
长19、宽8.5厘米

3-2th century BCE
Terracotta
L.19cm, W.8.5cm

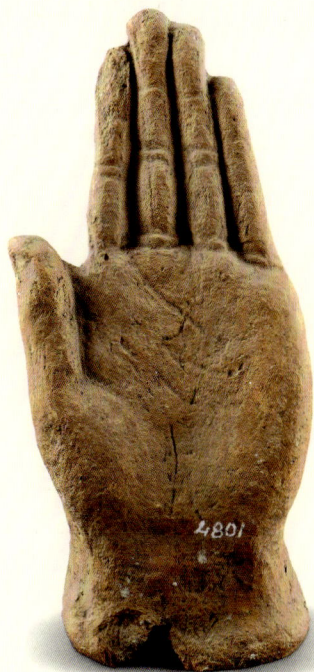

陶面具
Masque

公元前3-2世纪
红陶
高10、宽9.3厘米

3-2th century BCE
Terracotta
H.10cm, W.9.3cm

陶手指
Finger

公元前3-2世纪
红陶
长8、宽2.5厘米

3-2th century BCE
Terracotta
L.8cm, W.2.5cm

陶腿脚
Foot and Leg

公元前3-2世纪
红陶
高6.5厘米

3-2th century BCE
Terracotta
H.6.5cm

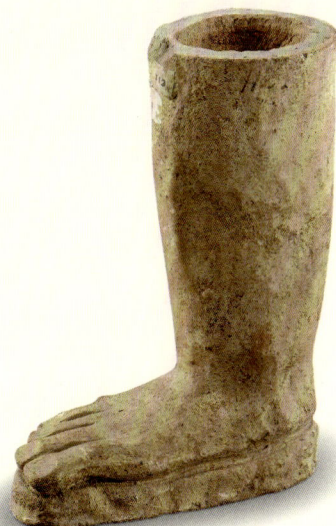

陶公牛
Bull

公元前3-2世纪
红陶
高13、长17厘米

3-2th century BCE
Terracotta
H.13cm, L.17cm

来自维欧（伊索拉·法尔奈斯）

在祭祀活动青铜或红陶雕塑的动物供品很常见，供奉其形象就相当于奉献了这种动物。

From Veio (Isola Farnese)
Votive animals in terracotta (or also bronze) are very common as the gift of a figurine of animal sacrifice was equivalent to making a real offering.

陶公牛
Bull

公元前3-2世纪
红陶
高11、长17厘米

3-2th century BCE
Terracotta
H.11cm, L.17cm

来自维欧（伊索拉·法尔奈斯）

在祭祀活动青铜或红陶雕塑的动物供品很常见，供奉其形象就相当于奉献了这种动物。

From Veio (Isola Farnese)
Votive animals in terracotta (or also bronze) are very common as the gift of a figurine of animal sacrifice was equivalent to making a real offering.

陶公猪
Boar

公元前3-2世纪
红陶
高8、长14厘米

3-2th century BCE
Terracotta
H.8cm, L.14cm

来自维欧（伊索拉·法尔奈斯）

在祭祀活动青铜或红陶雕塑的动物供品很常见，供奉其形象就相当于奉献了这种动物。

From Veio (Isola Farnese)
Votive animals in terracotta (or also bronze) are very common as the gift of a figurine of animal sacrifice was equivalent to making a real offering.

陶公猪
Boar

公元前3-2世纪
红陶
高8.3、长15.6厘米

3-2th century BCE
Terracotta
H.8.3cm, L.15.6cm

来自维欧（伊索拉·法尔奈斯）

在祭祀活动青铜或红陶雕塑的动物供品很常见，供奉其形象就相当于奉献了这种动物。

From Veio (Isola Farnese)
Votive animals in terracotta (or also bronze) are very common as the gift of a figurine of animal sacrifice was equivalent to making a real offering.

陶马
Horse

公元前3-2世纪
红陶
高15、长16厘米

3-2th century BCE
Terracotta
H.15cm, L.16cm

来自维欧（伊索拉·法尔奈斯）

在祭祀活动青铜或红陶雕塑的动物供品很常见，供奉其形象就相当于奉献了这种动物。

From Veio (Isola Farnese)
Votive animals in terracotta (or also bronze) are very common as the gift of a figurine of animal sacrifice was equivalent to making a real offering.

骨灰罐

　　这些人形器皿是一种用来盛放逝者骨灰的容器。这种物品在伊特鲁里亚城邦丘西十分普遍，生产于东方化时期和古风时期（公元前7–6世纪）。这种骨灰罐使用黏土制作，包括一个盛放火化后的骨灰的容器（瓶身）和一个人头形状的盖子。将骨灰瓮放置在王位上，则强调了逝者生前所取得的崇高社会地位。

Canopic Jars

These were anthropomorphic vessels used as containers for the ashes of the dead. They were typical of the Etruscan city of Chiusi and were produced in the Orientalizing and archaic ages (7-6 cent. BC). They are made of clay, with a container (the body) to hold the ashes of the cremated person. They had lids shaped like human heads. Placing the urn on the throne highlighted the high social status achieved by the deceased in life.

陶骨灰瓮
Canopus

公元前6世纪
褐陶
高44、最大直径31厘米

6th century BCE
Impasto
H. 44cm, L. (max)31cm

来自丘西

这种类型的骨灰瓮被认为是
较为晚期的物品。骨灰瓮肩
部的两只环形把手模仿了人
的两只胳膊，而瓮盖则为一
个圆雕人头。

From Chiusi
The cinerary urn is attributable
to the later production of these
characteristic vase.The two loops
on the shoulders of the container of
ashes simulate human arms, while
the cover is in this case composed of
a head in the round.

王座上的陶骨灰瓮
Canopus on A Throne

公元前7世纪
褐陶
高27.9厘米

7th century BCE
Impasto
H. 27.9cm

来自切托纳，城门，济罗墓 B

公元前7世纪至公元前6世纪丘西地区的骨灰瓮往往具有神、人同形同性的特性。本件为王座上放置盛有逝者骨灰的容器，容器带有人头形盖。骨灰瓮在王座上以体现了死者崇高的社会地位。

From Cetona, località Cancelli, tomba a ziro B
Cinerary anthropomorphic characteristic of Chiusi in the seventh and sixth century. B.C.E 'consists of a container in which were deposited the ashes of the cremated topped with a lid shaped like a human head. The location of the vessel on the throne emphasizes the high social status of the deceased.

王座上的女性陶骨灰瓮
Female Canopus on A Throne

公元前7-6世纪
红褐陶，棕彩
高36.2、宽33.8厘米

7-6th century BCE
Red Impasto, Brown Paint
H. 36.2cm, W. 33.8cm

来自丘西，济罗墓 A，1893
年购自Mignon

公元前7世纪至公元前6世纪
丘西地区的骨灰瓮往往具有
神、人同形同性的特性。本
件为王座上放置盛有逝者骨
灰的容器，容器带有人头形
盖。骨灰瓮在王座上以体现
了死者崇高的社会地位。

From Chiusi, tomba a ziro, acquisto
Mignoni 1893
Cinerary anthropomorphic
characteristic of Chiusi in the seventh
and sixth century. B.C.E 'consists of
a container in which were deposited
the ashes of the cremated topped
with a lid shaped like a human head.
The location of the vessel on the
throne emphasizes the high social
status of the deceased.

丧葬雕塑

使用当地石料制作的丧葬雕塑是伊特鲁里亚艺术中的一个最珍贵的种类。在伊特鲁里亚墓地中，大型墓穴入口通常放置神话动物或狮子之类猛兽的雕塑，以守卫入口。此外，还有标志着每个坟墓地点的石碑，毫无装饰的石碑下半部通常埋在地下。在大型墓穴中，例如托斯卡拉的维皮那那家族的墓地，则放置有长有翅膀的女性半神（万特）的雕塑，以守卫入口的安全。

Funerary Sculpture

Funerary sculpture, made using local stone, is one of the most precious elements of Etruscan art. Fantastic animals or fiery beasts, such as lions, were often positioned to guard the entrances to large monumental tombs in the Etruscan necropolises. By contrast, the steles marked each individual burial site, with the non-decorated lower part buried in the ground. In monumental tombs, such as the Vipinana's family tomb in Tuscania, a female winged demon (Vanth) was often placed at the entrance to guard it.

纪念碑
Monumental Slab

公元前7世纪
凝灰岩
高80、长115厘米

7th century BCE
Nenfro
H.80cm, L.115cm

来自塔尔奎尼亚

这类所谓的大型石碑在伊特鲁里亚纪念碑中组成了相当同质化的内容，毕竟伊特鲁里亚人号称来自塔尔奎尼亚（Tarquinia，属意大利拉齐奥大区的维泰博省）。这类石碑一般认为是置于在大型陵寝尽头。

fFrom Tarquinia
The so-called scale slabs constitute a class quite homogeneous among the monuments of the Etruscans, who all come from Tarquinia. It is widely recognized that they were placed at the input end of the monumental tombs.

费埃索式石碑
Fiesole Stele

公元前7世纪下半叶
石
高160厘米

Second half 7th century BCE
Stone
H.160cm

来自安特拉

费埃索式石碑之一种。矩形。
顶部方格中有宴会场景，下端
有两人对坐于桌旁。

From Antella (FI)
One of the numerous stelae of
Fiesole. It has a rectangular shape.
The top pane shows a banquet scene,
in the lower, two figures are seated at
a table.

石狮
Lion

公元前5世纪
石
高50、长65厘米

5th century BCE
Stone
H.50cm, L.65cm

来自蒙塔尔托·卡斯特罗

各种神兽或猛兽，如这个张口
的雄狮，通常置于伊特鲁里亚
的大型墓葬，把守入口。

From Montalto di Castro
Fantastic animals or wild beasts,
like this lion with gaping jaws,
often guarded the entrances of the great
Etruscan monumental tombs.

石狮
Funerary Lion

公元前6世纪
石
高7.7、长115厘米

6th century BCE
Nenfro
H.77cm, L.115cm

来自武尔奇

该神兽或猛兽，如张口的雄
狮，通常置于伊特鲁里亚的大
型墓葬，把守入口。

From Vulci
Fantastic animals or wild beasts,
as the lion with gaping jaws, were
often placed in Etruscan tombs
guarded the entrances of the
monumental tombs.

高浮雕万特女神
High Relief With Vanth

公元前4-3世纪
凝灰岩
高94厘米

4-3th century BCE
Nenfro
H.94cm

来自托斯卡纳

这尊珍贵的雕塑出自托斯卡纳地区的墓葬，描绘了生着双翼的死亡女神万特的形象。本件可能安放在墓葬以保卫入口。

From Tuscania
The prestigious statue that comes from the tomb of Vipinana Tuscania depicts the winged female demon Vanth. Probably the sculpture was placed at the tomb in order to maintain the input.

纳斯133号大墓中的随葬品

　　纳斯133号墓穴中的大量殉葬品体现了最富有的墓葬的所有特色元素。这些陪伴逝者走向来生的物品体现了逝者所属的阶级和崇高的社会地位，因为其中包括一些进口物品，例如从东方进口的陶器（小型爱奥尼亚式双耳酒罐和灰色布凯罗黑陶）和从阿提卡进口的陶器（绘有人物形象）。此外，还有一些典型的当地物品，例如布凯罗黑陶，特别是一些陶器、青铜工具和家具。所有这些物品按照大型希腊式社交酒会进行摆放，用于斟酒和饮酒的器皿摆放在双耳喷口杯（盛放葡萄酒的理想器皿）、餐具和厨房用具、混合和过滤葡萄酒的器具（滤勺和长柄勺），和枝形大烛台的周围。所有这些物品的摆放代表了逝者在来世举办的宴会。殉葬品中的织布机纺坠则清楚地表明，这些殉葬品的主人是一位女性，因为织布和纺纱均是女性专属的活动。

Grave Goods from Tomb 133 in Narce

　　The large number of grave goods from Tomb 133 in Narce show all the distinctive elements of the wealthiest burials. The objects that accompany the dead to the afterlife show the person's rank and high social status, since there are imported objects, such as the pottery from the East (small Ionic amphora and grey bucchero pottery) and from Attica (painted with figures). In addition, there also are typical local items, such as Bucchero pottery, but especially earthenware, bronze tools and furniture. All of this is laid out as a huge symposium, of Greek influence, where the vessels to pour and drink the wine are placed around the krater (the ideal wine container), tableware and kitchenware, utensils to mix and filter wine (simpulum and colum) and candelabra. All of this is arranged to represent the deceased's banquet in the afterlife. The loom weights clearly indicate that these grave goods were meant for a women, since spinning and weaving were exclusively a female activity.

莱凯特斯红绘陶瓶
Lekythos

公元前6-5世纪
红陶
高9.5、直径6.5厘米

6-5th century BCE
Red Figures Attic Ceramics
H.9.5cm, D.6.5cm

莱凯特斯是古希腊人的一种细颈涂油瓶。小瓶产于希腊，有一独特的圆锥形口，圆柱形短瓶颈连结着球形瓶身，下有宽圈足，带状手柄置于瓶颈和瓶肩处。

Small jar manufactured in Greece with distinct conical mouth, short and thin cylindrical neck connected to a globular body on wide ring foot. Ribbon handle set on the neck and shoulder.

克拉特红绘陶瓶
Crater

公元前6-5世纪
红陶
高35、直径35厘米

6-5th century BCE
Red Figures Attic Ceramics
H.35cm, D.35cm

克拉特陶瓶是宴席中最大的瓶子，用于混合酒水。精美的产品来自希腊的阿提卡（Attica），采用红绘式色图案技术。

The crater is the largest vessel in the service of the symposium. It was used for mixing fixed quantities of wine and water. The beautiful specimen was produced in Attica using the red figures technique.

斯泰莫斯红绘陶瓶
Stamnos

公元前6-5世纪
红陶
高37、最大直径38厘米

6-5th century BCE
Red Figures Attic Ceramics
H.37cm, D.(max)38cm

这种器皿的形式是两个手柄在瓶身最宽处。这种用红绘式技术装饰的时髦瓶子由希腊进口。

The form of the vessel appears to be characterized by the presence of two horizontal handles set on the maximum circumference of the body. It is a stylish container imported from Greece decorated in red figure technique.

257

安夫拉陶瓶
Amphora

公元前6-5世纪
陶
高11、最大直径7厘米

6-5th century BCE
Ceramics
H.11cm, D.(max)7cm

爱奥尼亚（小亚细亚）进口

该器皿是一个由东方进口精致的瓶子。瓶颈和瓶身上饰有略带红色平行线。

Ceramics imported from Ionia (now Asia Minore)
The vessel is a refined oriental import. It is decorated by a palmette on the neck and body by parallel horizontal bands in reddish paint.

斯加弗斯陶杯
Skyphos

公元前6-5世纪
陶
高10、直径18.5厘米

6-5th century BCE
Ceramics
H.10cm, D.18.5cm

锥形酒杯，两只平行的钮置于杯口下方。阿提卡制品。

Deep cone-shaped drinking cup equipped with two horizontal handles set just below the rim. Attica production.

伊奥洛克陶壶
Oinochoe

公元前6-5世纪
陶
高23.5、最大直径12厘米

6-5th century BCE
Ceramics
H.23.5cm, D.(max)12cm

本件用于宴会中倒酒，其陶土和彩绘具有阿提卡产品特征。

The function of this vessel was to pour wine during the symposium. The technical characteristics of the clay and paint relate to the production Attica.

伊奥洛克陶壶
Oinochoe

公元前6-5世纪
黑陶
高25、直径18厘米

6-5th century BCE
Black Bucchero
H.25cm, D.18cm

本件用于宴飨，向杯中到
酒，常在伊特鲁里亚的富人
墓中被发现。

Form that recurs frequently in
banquet services found in the rich
Etruscan tombs. Its function was to
pour the wine into the cups.

伊奥洛克陶壶
Oinochoe

公元前6-5世纪
黑陶
高21、直径16厘米

6-5th century BCE
Black Bucchero
H.21cm, D.16cm

本件用于宴飨，向杯中到
酒，常见于伊特鲁里亚的富
人墓中。

Form that recurs frequently in
banquet services found in the rich
Etruscan tombs. Its function was to
pour the wine into the cups.

坎达罗斯陶杯
Kantharos

公元前6-5世纪
黑陶
高12.5、宽17.5厘米

6-5th century BCE
Black Bucchero
H.12.5cm,W.17cm

本件为典型的伊特鲁里亚
杯，装有超出器身的大环
钮，在宴席中用来饮酒。

Typically Etruscan Vase, equipped
with large loops overhead, used
during the symposium to drink wine.

陶纺坠
Loom Weights

公元前6-5世纪
褐陶
高8.5、长6.5厘米

6-5th century BCE
Impasto
H.8.5cm, L.6.5cm

该工具上有一个圆孔，妇女在
纺织时以保证经线的张力。

This tool has a circular hole, and was
used by women during weaving to
keep tension in the warp threads.

凯特斯陶碗
Kyathos

公元前6-5世纪
薄胎灰陶
高21、最大直径19厘米

6-5th century BCE
Bucchero
H.21cm, D.(max)19cm

本件在宴席中用来从大腕中舀酒。器皿上带有一个造型优雅的超出器身的环柄，下部有高圈足。

Container used during the symposium to draw wine from a large bowl. It comes with an elegant loop overhead and a high flaring foot.

凯特斯陶碗
Kyathos

公元前6-5世纪
薄胎灰陶
高18、最大直径13厘米

6-5th century BCE
Bucchero
H.18cm, D.(max)13cm

本件在宴席中用来从大腕中舀酒。器皿上带有一个造型优雅的超出器身的环柄，下部有高圈足。

Container used during the symposium to draw wine from a large bowl. It comes with an elegant loop overhead and a high flaring foot.

欧帕陶壶
Olpe

公元前6-5世纪
薄胎灰陶
高15、宽12厘米

6-5th century BCE
Bucchero
H.15cm,W.12cm

本件侈口，束颈，溜肩，锥形腹，锥形圈足。

Receptacle with disc-shaped mouth, neck, conical, curved shoulder, belly and tapered ring foot.

安夫拉陶瓶
Amphora

公元前6-5世纪
薄胎灰陶
高20、最大直径13厘米

6-5th century BCE
Bucchero
H.20cm, D.(max)13cm

本件专用于储存酒水，两个曲柄上饰有优雅的图案。

The vessel is intended to contain liquids, shows two ribbon handles decorated with elegant motifs.

安夫拉陶瓶
Amphora

公元前6-5世纪
薄胎灰陶
高17、宽13.5厘米

6-5th century BCE
Bucchero
H.17cm, W.13.5cm

小瓶上有曲柄，并饰有精致的图案。

The small vessel shows a precious ribbon handle decorated with elaborate motifs.

伊奥洛克陶壶
Oinochoe

公元前6-5世纪
薄胎灰陶
高16、宽9厘米

6-5th century BCE
Bucchero
H.16cm, W.9cm

本件用于宴飨向杯中倒酒，常发现于伊特鲁里亚的富人墓中。

Form that recurs frequently in banquet services found in the rich Etruscan tombs. Its function was to pour wine into the cups.

奥拉陶罐
Olla

公元前6-5世纪
薄胎灰陶
高12.5、宽10厘米

6-5th century BCE
Bucchero
H.12.5cm,W.10cm

此类瓶子放在桌上用来盛放宴飨物品。

Vases of this type were used on the table to contain substances intended for the banquet.

矮圈足陶杯
Glass on A Pedestal

公元前6-5世纪
薄胎灰陶
高8、直径14厘米

6-5th century BCE
Bucchero
H.8cm, D.14cm

本件腹略深，矮圈足，杯身和足部阴刻弦纹。

With a rather deep bath and low flaring foot decorated with incised parallel lines and low flating foot.

布克凯洛陶碗
Bowl

公元前6-5世纪
薄胎灰陶
高5.5、直径17厘米

6-5th century BCE
Bucchero
H.5.5cm, D.17cm

布克凯洛是一种曲腹矮足圈
器皿。

Bucchero vase: low foot ring with
curvilinear walls.

陶碗
Bowl

公元前6-5世纪
薄胎灰陶
高10.5、直径13.5厘米

6-5th century BCE
Bucchero
H.10.5cm, D.13.5cm

布克凯洛是一种短身的矮圈
足器皿。

Bucchero vase with truncated walls
on low foot ring.

奥拉陶罐
Olla

公元前6-5世纪
褐陶
高5.2-7、直径6-8厘米

6-5th century BCE
Impasto
H.5.2-7cm, D.6-8cm

本件为圆口突出，卵形腹，平底的小心器皿。

Small container made of dough with distinct rim, ovoid body and flat bottom.

陶碗
Bowl

公元前6-5世纪
薄胎灰陶
高4、直径9厘米

6-5th century BCE
Grey Bucchero
H.4cm, D.9cm

该容器由浅腹附圈足构成。

Container consists of a low-walled tank fairing attached to a foot ring.

凯特伊陶勺
Miniature Kyathoi

公元前6-5世纪
薄胎灰陶
高5、最宽6.5厘米

6-5th century BCE
Grey Bucchero
H.5cm, W.(max)6.5cm

凯特伊是古希腊的一种环柄勺。这些小勺是类似的大勺的微缩件。

These small jars are miniature copies of similar-shaped but larger jars.

青铜盆
Basin

公元前6-5世纪
青铜
高5.7、直径19.5厘米

6-5th century BCE
Bronze
H.5.7cm, D.19.5cm

拥有垂直的边缘，浅盆和平底花托。此物常出现于典型的伊特鲁里亚富裕人家的墓葬中。

Receptacle with straight hem, low bath and flat bottom. They occur frequently with variants typical of rich Etruscan tombs.

宽边青铜盆
Basin With A Large Brim

公元前6-5世纪
青铜
高6、直径23.5厘米

6-5th century BCE
Bronze
H.6cm, D.23.5cm

此物不同于早期的宽平的轮缘，相对的在伊特鲁里亚常见到。

The object differs from the previous for the presence of a wide flat rim. Equally common in Etruria.

青铜盆
Basin

公元前6-5世纪
青铜
高7.5、直径23厘米

6-5th century BCE
Bronze
H.7.5cm, D.23cm

本件直壁，浅腹、平底，常见于伊特鲁里亚的典型富人墓葬。

Receptacle with straight hem, low bath and flat bottom. They occur frequently with variants typical of rich Etruscan tombs.

青铜叉
Meat Fork

公元前6-5世纪
青铜
长40、宽21厘米

6–5th century BCE
Bronze
L.40cm, W.21cm

青铜工具，用法不详。手柄
被设计成圆锥形以安装柄和
一个锋利的王冠形耙子。

Tools in bronze, of uncertain use with
truncated cone handles designed to
accommodate a wooden support
and a crown of sharp prongs.

青铜长柄过滤器
Colum

公元前6-5世纪
青铜
长28、直径14.5厘米

6–5th century BCE
Bronze
L.28cm, D.14.5cm

此类工具常在伊特鲁里亚随葬
品中发现，用于过滤葡萄酒。

Tool often found in Etruscan
funerary offerings because it was
used to filter wine.

青铜长柄勺
Simpulum

公元前6-5世纪
青铜
长17.5、直径7.2厘米

6–5th century BCE
Bronze
L.17.5cm, D.7.2cm

本件为舀取液体的工具，长
手柄端部饰有鸟头。

Simpulum needed to draw liquids
from containers. In this specimen
the long handle terminates in a head
with bird motifs.

青铜灯
Candelabrum

公元前6-5世纪
青铜
高101厘米

6-5th century BCE
Bronze
H.101cm

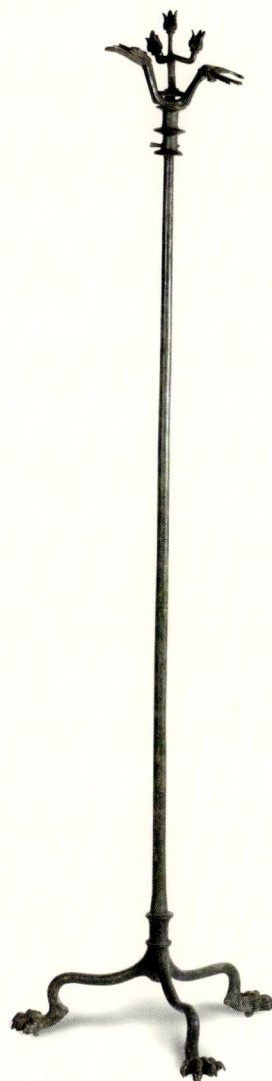

本件用于高级的宴会中照明。
它由一个三脚架，长圆柱灯杆
和齿状物以嵌入蜡烛。

This object intended to shed light
during the banquets of the characters
of high rank. It consists of a tripod, a
high cylindrical stem and prongs for
insertion of candles.

青铜壶
Jug

公元前6-5世纪
青铜
高10、最宽8厘米

6-5th century BCE
Bronze
H.10cm,W.(max)8cm

小型的卵形壶，用于舀酒。

The small container with ovoid body, was used to draw wine from a central bowl.

凯特斯青铜瓶
Kyathos

公元前6-5世纪
青铜
高6.5、宽7厘米

6-5th century BCE
Bronze
H.6.5cm, W.7cm

本件瓶身修长，用于从碗中取酒。

The container with elongated body was used to draw the wine from the central bowl.

青铜壶
Jug

公元前6–5世纪
青铜
高16、最宽12厘米

6–5th century BCE
Bronze
H.16cm,W.(max)12cm

墓葬出土。这样珍贵的青铜器皿与葡萄酒的消费有关。

Found in a tomb. These precious bronze vessels were linked to the consumption of wine.

欧帕青铜壶
Olpe

公元前6–5世纪
青铜
高22、最大直径18厘米

6–5th century BCE
Bronze
H.22cm, D.(max)18cm

造型优雅的铜瓶为球形壶身，它也有一些陶制制品。

Elegant bronze vase with globular body. Several replicas were made of ceramic.

索瓦纳墓中的随葬品

与纳斯墓中的殉葬品相比，索瓦纳墓中的殉葬品数量较少，说明逝者的社会地位较低一些。其中最重要的殉葬品是一件黑色的坎达罗斯双耳酒瓶（古希腊使用的一种最著名的双耳高脚瓶）。这类材料制作的最精美繁复的器皿（譬如本例所示，这件器皿由沃尔泰拉的专业作坊生产），清楚地体现了对金属器皿的模仿。随着时间的流逝，这种物品的生产变得越来越标准化，甚至接近工业化和批量化生产。

Grave Goods from the Sovana Tomb

The grave goods from the Sovana Tomb were smaller in number than those from Narce and this is indicative of the deceased's lower social status. It features a black kantharos (the Greek word for the most famous two-handled goblet in the ancient world). The most elaborate forms of this type of material showed (as in this case, where the vessel was produced by the specialized workshops of Volterra), the clear use of metal prototypes. Over time, this production would become more and more standardized, almost becoming industrial and serial.

青铜长柄过滤器
Colum

公元前3世纪
青铜
长28.5、直径12.7厘米

3th century BCE
Bronze
L.28.5cm, D.12.7cm

本件过滤器在宴飨时用于滤掉葡萄酒如玫瑰花瓣、水果、香料等中的杂质。

The sieve was used during the symposium to filter the Etruscan wine containing impurities such as rose petals, fruit, spices and other ingredients.

青铜单柄锅
Single Handle Baking-Pan

公元前3世纪
青铜
高4.3、直径26.5厘米

3th century BCE
Bronze
H.4.3cm, D.26.5cm

本件用来舀取和添加葡萄酒的器皿，常见于伊特鲁里亚中北部的随葬品。

Vessels of this type were used to contain the vessels used to draw and then add the wine. They are particularly common in funerary contexts of Etruria north-central.

线轴式凯特斯青铜勺
Spool Shaped Kyathos

公元前3世纪
青铜
高6.2-10、直径5-6.2、底径5.3-6.9厘米

3th century BCE
Bronze
H.6.2-10cm, D.5-6.2cm,D.(base)5.3-6.9cm

本件常见绕线轴样式，在伊特鲁里亚随葬品中常常一式五份，其主要功能是取酒，也有可能舀取其他的混合液体。

The characteristic kyathoi containers occur frequently, usually with five copies, in Etruscan grave goods. The primary function was to draw wine from containers but it is not impossible that they were units for mixing liquids.

伊奥洛克青铜壶
Oinochoe

公元前3世纪
青铜
高20.5、最大直径20厘米

3th century BCE
Bronze
H.20.5cm, D.(max)20cm

通常这种形式的伊奥洛克壶在公元前6世纪至公元前3世纪末在伊特鲁里亚，也在波河流域广为人知。

Form typically Etruscan oinochoe knew this widely known to the end of the VI and IV-III century. a. C. in Etruria, but also in the Po Valley.

斯泰莫斯式斯图拉罐
Stamnos Shaped Situla

公元前3世纪
青铜
高14.5、直径11.5、底径8.6厘米

3th century BCE
Bronze
H.14.5cm, D.11.5cm, D.(base)8.6cm

佩有活动环钮的各种尺寸的
容器常在宴会中盛装液体。

Containers of various sizes equipped
with loop mobile, often connected
to a chain suspension, which were
used during the symposium to
contain liquids.

坎达罗斯陶瓶
Kantharos

公元前3世纪
黑陶
高14、直径9.8、底径8厘米

3th century BCE
Black paint ceramics
H.14cm, D.9.8cm, D.(base)8cm

这件坎达罗斯陶瓶是沃尔泰
特拉最好的黑彩陶器，这种
受金属器皿影响的器皿，在
公元前四世纪晚期和二世纪
早期的伊特鲁里亚、意大利
北部广为传流行。

Produced by the best workshops of
Volterra black-painted pottery, the
kantharos with decorations inspired
by metal prototypes, were common
in Etruria and in northern Italy
between the late fourth and early
second century B.C.E..

石棺与骨灰瓮

　　伊特鲁里亚文化后期，墓葬从早期的墓冢（坟茔）演化成地下的多墓室墓穴，死者则安置在石棺或经火化后将骨灰保存在小骨灰瓮中。在这两种情况中，石棺或红陶棺上都装饰有华丽的高浮雕，并涂有油漆。装饰画面的主题多种多样，从神话故事中的场景（希腊神话和伊特鲁里亚神话）到对来世生活的描绘（例如，通往冥府的大门，旁边等待着来自地狱的魔鬼，它们标志着通往来世的道路，因而装饰在棺材中央）。棺盖则再现了逝者的形象，有时躺着，而更多情况下，是以宴会客人的姿态斜卧着身子。于是，这种以前就已经出现在各种殉葬器皿中的社交酒会仪式，又一次出现在了棺材上。这时，社交酒会的主题是通过男性和女性形象表现出来的，在社交酒会的庆典上，他们斜倚在堆满垫子的沙发上，通常手举高脚酒杯。

Sarcophaguses and Urns

In the late Etruscan civilization, the funerary monuments evolved from the early tumuli (burial mounds) to underground burial chambers with several rooms, where the dead were placed in sarcophaguses or cremated and the ashes preserved in small urns. In both cases, the stone or terracotta coffin was lavishly decorated with high-reliefs and painted. The iconography is very diverse, featuring anything from scenes tied to mythology (both Greek and Etruscan) to representations of the afterlife (such as the image of the door to Hades, with the demons from hell, which marks the passage to the afterlife and is located in the centre of the coffin). The lid represents the dead, either lying or, more frequently, partially reclined, in the position of a banquet guest. Thus, the idea of the symposium ritual, already known in previous ages through the vessels of the grave goods, is found again. In this period, it is conveyed through the figure, both male and female, reclining on a sofa full of cushions, during the celebration of a symposium, often holding wine goblets.

石棺
Sarcophagus

公元前2世纪
凝灰岩
长120、宽65、高70厘米

2th century BCE
Nenfro
L. 120cm, W. 65cm, H. 70cm

来自托斯卡纳，维皮那那墓

这具石棺出土自托斯卡纳最著名的墓葬，石棺的盖子上展现了一位斜倚着身子的男子形象，而矩形的棺身表面则雕刻有两位爱神丘比特共进盛宴的形象。

From Tuscania, tomba dei Vipinana
The sarcophagus, which comes from one of the most prestigious tombs of Tuscania, consists of a lid on which is represented a reclining male figure and a rectangular box that shows two cupids carved in feast.

石棺
Sarcophagus

公元前3世纪
石
高80厘米

3 BCE
Stone
H.80cm

这具石棺出土自托斯卡纳最著名的一座陵寝，石棺的盖子上展现了一位斜倚着身子的男子形象，而矩形的棺身表面则雕刻有一个神话故事的场景。

from Tuscania, tomba dei Vipinana
The sarcophagus, which comes from one of the most prestigious tombs of Tuscania, consists of a lid on which is represented a reclining male figure and a rectangular box carved with a scene that shows a mythological narrative.

女性造型雪花石膏骨灰盖瓮
Funerary Urn With Cover Shaped as A Female Figure

公元前3世纪
雪花石膏
通高110、长78、宽29厘米

3th century BCE
Alabaster
H.110cm, L.78cm,W.29cm

来自萨尔泰亚诺（SI）

这只骨灰瓮是用一整块取材自
当地的石灰石雕刻的。盖子
上是一位斜倚着身子的女性形
象，而瓮身则采用浮雕工艺雕
刻了一只咬长矛的狮子。

From Sarteano (SI)
The urn was entirely made from a
type of limestone stone retrieved
locally. On the cover is a veiled
female figure lying on the case while
it was carved in low relief a lion with
a spear through his teeth.

石灰华骨灰盖瓮
Funerary Urn With Cover

公元前2世纪
石灰华
罐：高22厘米，盖：高48厘米

2th century BCE
Travertine
coperchio: H.22cm, cassa: H.48cm

来自蒙泰隆(PG)

本件产自希腊化时期的佩鲁贾，这件骨灰瓮展示了一位骑着神话动物、全身武装的勇士。

From Monterone (PG)
The urn belongs to the prolific production of Perugia of the Hellenistic period. The case shows an armed warrior who rides a fantastic animal.

双人雪花石膏瓮
Double Urn

公元前2世纪
雪花石膏
高62、长83厘米

2th century BCE
Alabaster
H.62cm, L.83cm

来自蒙特里久尼，卡利斯那·赛普墓穴

这只雪花石膏雕刻的骨灰瓮造型独特，盖子上是一对披着斗篷的男女，覆盖头部是为了防止坟墓上方渗水带来的破坏。瓮身还刻有一长串伊特鲁里亚铭文。

From Monteriggioni, tomba dei Calisna Sepu
Urn made of alabaster. The cover shows a male and a female figure both wrapped in a cloak. The tile covering their heads was added later to protect them from water infiltration of the tomb. In the case there is a long inscription in Etruscan.

横卧人物雪花石膏骨灰瓮
Funeary Urn With Recumbent Figure

公元前2世纪
雪花石膏
高91

2th century BCE
Alabaster
H.91 cm

来自圣马提诺·埃科里（佛
罗伦萨）

骨灰瓮盖上横卧一休闲人物。

From San Martino ai Colli (Firenze)
Funerary urn with relaxed figure.

横卧人物雪花石膏骨灰盖瓮
Urn With Male Recumbent

公元前2世纪
雪花石膏
长56、宽23、高73厘米

2th century BCE
Alabaster
L. 56cm , W.23 cm, H.73cm

来自丘西

骨灰瓮上横卧一休闲人物。

From Chiusi
Funerary urn with relaxed figure.

丘西陶骨灰瓮
Urn From Chiusi

公元前2世纪
红陶
高32.8厘米

2th century BCE
Terracotta
H.32.8cm

来自丘西

希腊化时期的丘西地区大量生产这类红陶器。瓮盖上死者斜躺，头靠在枕头上。瓮身则描绘了临终永别的场景。

From Chiusi
Terracotta urns of this type were mass-produced in the territory of Chiusi in the Hellenistic period. On the cover, the deceased reclining resting on a large pillow, on the box farewell scene.

丘西陶骨灰瓮
Urn From Chiusi

公元前2世纪
陶
长33、宽19、高33厘米

2ᵗʰ century BCE
Terracotta
L. 33cm, W.19cm, H.33cm

来自丘西

希腊时期的丘西地区大量生产这类红陶器。瓮盖上死者斜躺，头靠在枕头上。瓮身上则描绘了"扶犁英雄"的形象。

From Chiusi
Terracotta urns of this type were mass-produced in the territory of Chiusi in the Hellenistic period. On the cover, the deceased reclining resting on a large pillow, on the box "hero with the plow."

沃尔泰拉式陶盖瓶
Kelebe From Volterra With A Lid

公元前4世纪
陶
高51、直径32厘米

4th century BCE
Etruscan red figures ceramics
H.51cm, D.32cm

来自蒙特鲁斯，佩鲁贾

本件是用红绘式工艺制作的伊特鲁里亚陶瓶，极富沃尔泰拉风格。公元前4世纪末期，这种陶瓶通常被用作盛放逝者骨灰的容器。

在伊特鲁里亚文明最后一个阶段，骨灰瓮的形状开始采取不同于维兰诺万时期（双锥形骨灰瓮）和古风时期骨灰瓮（藏尸罐）的形状。事实上，这些骨灰瓮的形状均表现出典型的社交酒会特征，同时也饰有人物形象——如本件，并配有盖子，形似真正的陶瓮。

From Monteluce, Perugia
These peculiar Etruscan vases decorated in the technique of red figures are characteristic of the Volterra where they were used as containers for the ashes of the dead at the end of the fourth century BCE. In this last phase of Etruscan civilization, the cinerary urns took on shapes that differed from those of the Villanovan period (biconical urns) and then the Archaic period (canopic jars). Infact, shapes that seem typical of symposium pottery, also decorated with figures, as in this case,equipped with lids, become real urns.

钟形陶奥拉罐
Bell Shaped Funerary Olla

公元前2世纪
陶
高22、最大直径23厘米

2th century BCE
Ceramics
H.22cm, D.(max)23cm

来自丘西

这类造型特别的骨灰瓮产自伊特鲁里亚城市丘西。瓮身塑造为钟状，并和古代的葬礼纪念碑、宗教纪念碑一样，饰有花彩饰物。

From Chiusi
This particular type of container was produced in the Etruscan town of Chiusi. It is bell-shaped and decorated with festoons of flowers and garlands, as the funeral and sacred monuments often were in ancient times.

托斯卡纳地区马特鲁里亚的葡萄地马利亚诺
Magliano

附　录
APPENDIX

伊特鲁里亚编年简史

公元前1000-公元前725年

维兰诺万时期：该时期得名于博洛尼亚附近的维兰诺万考古遗址，在这里首次确认了伊特鲁里亚人的石器时代早期的活动。大部分证据来自于独具特色的维兰诺万墓地——这实际上是散布着多个墓地的骨灰墓园，以火葬仪式、双锥形或棚屋形骨灰瓮，和标志着逝者地位的随葬品为特色。维兰诺万时期见证了手工作坊式生产的兴起，甚至可能见证了与腓尼基人的首次联系。维兰诺万时期大致与希腊的几何时期相对应，而事实上维兰诺万时期的物品的确饰有几何图案——尽管没有直接证据将这种风格与希腊联系起来。公元前750年，希腊在西部（那不勒斯湾）设立首个殖民地，其间，希腊人刚刚从腓尼基人那里借用了字母表，也由希腊的埃维厄人就此传入。

公元前725-公元前600年

东方化时期：从近东和地中海东部进口贵重物品标志着东方化时期的开始，同时也可能伴随着大批外国艺术家和工匠的涌入。与东方的联系带来具象艺术的"东方化"风格，同时，对欧洲最富有的一些矿藏的开发带来了财富的增长，结果便是出现了壮观的"王族"陵墓，陵墓通常规模庞大的土山——这可能是受到东方坟墓原型的启发，上面覆盖着古墓。社会分层与相伴相随的政治等级结构仍然存在，伊特鲁里亚人开始向南部（拉丁姆和坎帕尼亚）和北部（伊特鲁里亚-帕达那）进行扩张。

公元前600-公元前480年

古风时期：该术语来自希腊语。这一时期见证了伊特鲁里亚城邦国家权力的极度膨胀、社会结构的成长与所谓的城邦社会的发展。伊特鲁里亚文化保持着其强烈的地域特征，但总的来说，这段时期见证了规模更大的建筑、大型雕塑、墓室绘画和装饰的发展，以及希腊的爱奥尼亚式与阿提卡式的影响，包括大量阿提卡式黑绘陶器和红绘陶器的进口。来自希腊世界——尤其是希腊南部和沿海地区的强烈影响，成为古风时期的标志性特征。

公元前480-公元前300年

古典时期：这个术语同样借用自希腊语。这一时期，伊特鲁里亚人在库迈被锡拉库扎打败（公元前474年），伊特鲁里亚文明开始走向衰落。公元前5世纪被称为伊特鲁里亚人的危机时期，经济和物质文化生产走向低迷。公元前4世纪，伊特鲁里亚被高卢人驱逐回北部，罗马也开始向伊特鲁里亚南部进行扩张。

公元前300-公元前100年

伊特鲁里亚——罗马时期：大致与希腊和近东的希腊化时期相当，这段时期政治的动荡仍然持续。这段时期的大部分时间内，伊特鲁里亚被罗马控制，其物质文化呈现出工业化风格增强、个人化风格削弱的面貌，这使得一些学者提出"中产阶级"出现的可能。这段时期的标志性特征表现为南部意大利与西西里（大希腊）对伊特鲁里亚艺术的影响、大型公共建筑的出现，以及陶器与青铜器的大批量生产。公元前1世纪，伊特鲁里亚已经被完全并入罗马城邦，并于公元前90年接受罗马公民身份。

A BRIEF CHRONOLOGY OF THE ETRUSCANS

1000 BCE-725 BCE

THE VILLANOVAN PERIOD: named after the archaeological type site of Villanova, near Bologna, where the Early Iron Age manifestation of the Etruscans was first identified. Most of the evidence comes from the characteristic Villanovan cemeteries, virtual "urn fields" with single burials characterized by the rite of cremation, "biconical"or hut urns, and assemblages of tomb goods that mark the status of the individuals. The period saw the beginning of craFt production and possibly the first contact with the Phoenicians. The Villanovan period corresponds roughly to the Geometric period in Greece, and indeed Villanovan objects are adorned with geometric decoration, although there is no direct evidence linking this style to Greece. In 750 BCE, the first Greek colony was established in the West (in the bay of Naples), and at about this time the alphabet was borrowed from the Euboean Greeks who had just adopted it from the Phoenicians.

725 BCE-600 BCE

THE ORIENTALIZING PERIOD: marked by importation of prestige goods from the Near East and eastern Mediterranean, possibly with an influx of foreign artists and craftsmen as well. This contact resulted in an "Orientalizing" style of figural art, while increased wealth, Fueled by the exploitation of some of the richest mineral deposits in Europe, resulted in splendid, "Princely" family mausolea, often monumental and covered by tumuli, massive earth mountains that were probably inspired by eastern prototypes. Social stratification continues, with concomitant developments in political hierarchies, and the Etruscans begin their expansion to the south (Latium and Campania) and north (Etruria Padana).

600 BCE-480 BCE

THE ARCHAIC PERIOD: nomenclature derived from Greece. This period saw the greatest expansion of the power of the Etruscan city states, with the growth of social structures and the development of what has been called an urban society. Etruscan culture retains its strongly regional nature, but overall this period saw the development of larger buildings and monumental sculpture, painted or decorated chamber tombs, and Ionic and Attic Greek influence, including the importation of massive amounts of Attic Blackand Red-Figure ceramics. Strong influence from the Greek world, especially in the southern and coastal regions, characterizes the Archaic period.

480 BCE-300 BCE

THE CLASSICAL PERIOD: again the terminology is borrowed from Greece. This was a period of decline for the Etruscans; they were defeated by Syracuse at Cumae (474 BCE). The fifth century has been called a period of crisis for the Etruscans, with a downturn of commerce and in the production of material culture. The Fourth century saw the Etruscans pushed back in the north by the Gauls and the beginning of Roman expansion into the south of Etruria.

300 BCE-100 BCE

THE ETRUSCO ROMAN PERIOD: roughly contemporary to the Hellenistic period in Greece and the Near East, was a time of continued political instability. Etruria was controlled by Rome during most of this period, and material culture takes on a more industrial and less individualized look leading some scholars to suggest the appearance of a "middle class." The period is marked by the influence of southern Italy and Sicily (Magna Graecia) on Etruscan art, by large-scale public construction, and by mass production of ceramics, bronzes, etc. By the first century BCE the Etruscans had been Fully integrated into the Roman state, and in 90 BCE they received Roman citizenship.

希腊瓶式简图

VARIOUS SHAPES OF GREEK VASES

Exaleiptron

Early Aryballos

Red-figured Aryballos

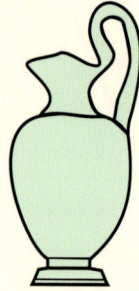
Oinochoe

Olpe

Pyxis Type A

Alabastron

Askos

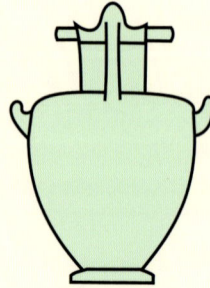
Hydrio

kalpis

Squat Lekythos

Shoulder Lekythos

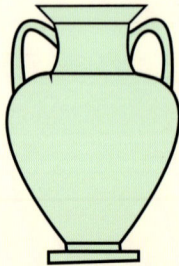
Neck Amphora

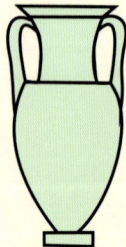
Nolan Amphora

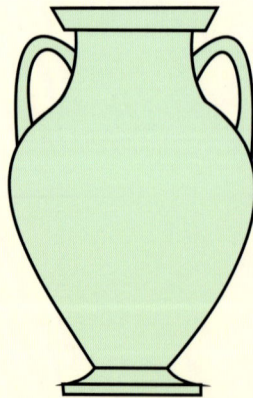
Amphora Typo A

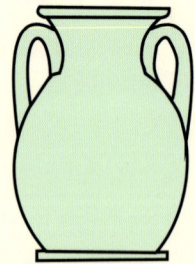
Pelike

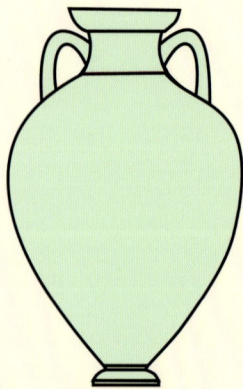
Panathenaic Amphora

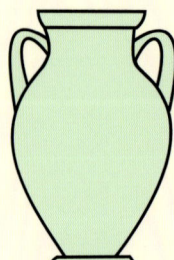
Amphora Type B

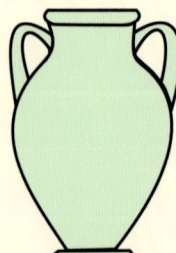
Amphora Type C

Loutrophoros

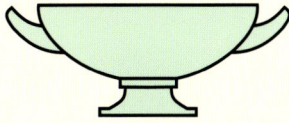

Kylix TypeA

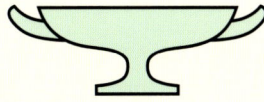

Kylix TypeB

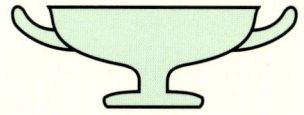

Kylix TypeC

Kantharos

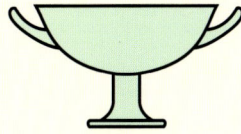

Lip-Cup

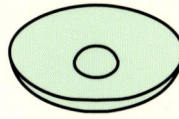

Phiute

Skyphos

Lekanis

Rnyton

Psyktor

Stamnos

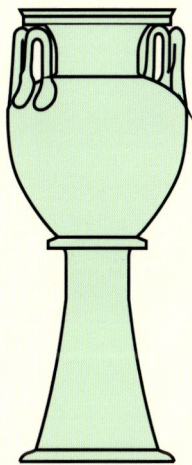

Lebes Gamikcs&Stand

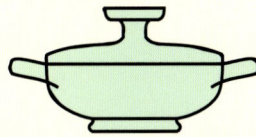

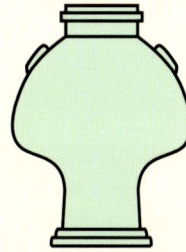

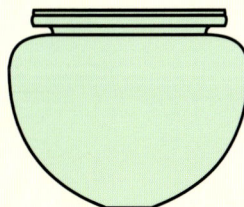

Dinos

Calyx-Krater

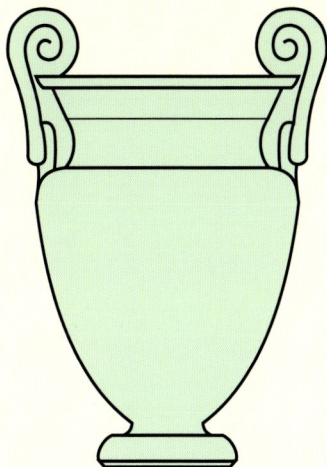

Volute-Krater

Column-Krater

Bell-Krater

词汇表　GLOSSARY

Acroteria

Statues or ornaments fastened to the end of a gable. Singular:

Acroterion

山墙饰

山墙一端的雕像或饰物

Alabastron

A small cylindrical vase with a round base used to hold ointments, perfumes or oils

阿拉巴斯塔香水瓶

一种柱状圜底装药膏、香水或精油的小瓶

Amphora

A two-handled vessel made to hold wine

安夫拉瓶

双耳酒器

Antefix

Plaques, sometimes ornately ornamented and painted, that were attached to the final cover tiles at the edge of a roof

瓦檐饰（瓦当）

遮盖屋檐瓦的华丽片状饰物

Apotropaic

Designed to protect or ward off evil

护身符

用于护身或避邪

Aryballs

Usually a small rounded vase used to hold perfumed oils bathing or adornment

阿利玻瓶（香油瓶）

装沐浴或修饰精油的圆形圜底小瓶

Askos

A vase in the form of an animal

阿斯克斯瓶

动物形器皿

Astragalus

A knucklebone or an imitation (bronze, clay, etc) of a knucklebone, sometimes used in a game that involved dice

骰子

距骨或（青铜、黏土等）仿制距骨，用做游戏中的骰子

Augur

An official who practiced divination through interpretation of natural phenomena, such as the flight of birds

占卜官

解释自然现象，如占卜鸟之飞行的官员

Biga

A chariot pulled by two horses

二轮战车

Bucchero

A characteristic type of Etruscan black pottery obtained by firing in a reducing atmosphere

布凯罗陶

在还原气氛下烧成的一种伊特鲁里亚薄胎黑陶

Bucchero pesante

Later (sixth-fifth century), heavier bucchero, often mold-made and mass produced

厚胎布凯罗

（公元前6-公元前5世纪）晚期，用模具大规模生产较厚的布凯罗陶器

Bucchero sottile

Early, thinner bucchero that often seems to reproduce metallic forms

薄胎布凯罗

早期稍薄的布凯罗陶器似仿金属的样式

Bulia

A circular bubble-shaped pendant able to hold a substance that would give it amuletic properties

护身符吊坠

一种具有护身符性质的可装东西的圆泡形吊坠

Caduceu

a winged stuff with two entwined snakes that is the characteristic attribute of Hermes/Mercury

手杖

翅膀相交的蛇是众神使者/水星的标志

Caere

The Latin name for the Great Etruscan city now called Cerveteri

卡西里

伊特鲁里亚城市现称切尔韦泰里的拉丁名

Canopic
An ancient Egyptian jar used to hold the organs of a mummified person. The term has erroneously applied to cinerary urns from the area around Chiusi
脏器罐
古埃及盛木乃伊脏器的罐子，该词误用为丘西地区的骨灰瓮

Cella。
The interior room(s) of a Classical temple. Plural: cellae
内殿
古典神庙的房间

Ceramics, black-figured
A Greek style of vase painting copied by the Etruscans used from the sixth to the fourth century B.C.E. onward where the background was painted and the figures are left "reserved" in the natural red color of the clay.
陶器，黑彩
公元前6到公元前4世纪，伊特鲁里亚复制希腊瓶画的一种风格，人物的背景"保留"黏土的天然红色。

Chimera
A fantastic composite monster: a combination of a lion, goat and snake
喀美拉
组合怪物：狮子、山羊和蛇的组合

Chiton
Female garment similar to a tunic
希顿古装
束腰女外套

Chthonian阴间
Having to do with underground or underworld divinities

Cippus
A pillar, column or other sculptural feature that served a funerary or commemorative nature
纪念碑
用于葬礼、纪念性的柱或雕塑

Dromos
The corridor that led to the inner chamber (s) of a tomb
墓道

Dinos
A rounded vessel with a wide mouth and no handles, sometimes placed on a matching stand. It was used to mix wine and water
迪诺斯瓶
圆形宽口无柄钵，在适当场合混合酒和水

Ex voto
An offering made with a vow
还愿品

Faience
Glazed ceramic material invented by the Egyptians, copied by Phoenicians and others, which was presumably an exotic item much admired and collected by the Etruscans from the Orientalizing period onward
费昂斯料器
埃及人发明、腓尼基人和他人模仿的釉陶，这大概是伊特鲁里亚人从东方化时期就开始收集的令他们羡艳的异国物品

Fibula(e)
An innovation of the Iron Age, a safety pin. Fibulae were functional and decorative: they were often made of precious metal and could be elaborately decorated
扣针
铁器时代的发明，一种安全性和装饰性的扣针，往往用贵金属制作并精心装饰

Foculus
A brazier
火盆

Gorgon
The mythological female monster beheaded by Perseus, whose gaze could turn people to stone. The Gorgon mask is called the Gorgoneion and has an apotropaic function
戈耳工
神话中的女妖，目光能把人变石头。戈耳工面具称Gorgoneion，有驱邪作用

Griffin
A fanstatic animal with a lion's body and a bird's head and wings
格里芬
一种狮身、鸟首、有翼的组合动物

Haruspex, Haruspices
An official who practiced the art of prophesying the future
占卜师
预测未来的专职人员

Himation
A m antle
希腊长袍

Hypogeum
An underground building : burial vault
地窖

Hydria
A three-handled vase made to hold water
提水罐
一种装水的三柄瓶

Impasto
Non-refined clay
混合陶
非精制的黏土

Kantharos
A footed vase with two upright handles that was often associated
with Dionysus
坎达罗斯杯
一种与酒神有关的带足双竖耳杯

Kline
A couch or bed
沙发床
一种沙发或床

Kotyle
A cup with two handles
双耳杯

Krater
A wide-mouthed vessel used to mix water and wine
克拉特瓶
一种用于混合水和酒的广口器皿

Kyathos
A cup with a single vertical handle
雅索司杯
一种单柄杯

Kylix
A footed cup with lateral handles
基里克斯陶杯
一种横柄带足杯

Lekythos
A cylindrical vase used for oils or perfumes. It had a single vertical
handle, narrow neck and small mouth
细颈瓶
一种装油或香水的单柄细颈瓶

Nenfro
The Italian name for a very porous type of stone
凝灰岩
意大利的一种多孔石材

Oinochoe
A pitcher
伊奥洛克壶
一种水罐

Olpe
A spoutless pitcher with a rounded lip
奥帕壶
一种圆唇无嘴的水壶

Palmette
A Classical ornamental motif that reproduces palm leaves in a
stylized way
棕叶饰
展现棕榈叶的经典装饰母题

Panathenaic
Connected to the Panathenaic games in Athens, held in honor of
Athena
泛雅典娜节
在雅典举行的一切与纪念雅典娜有关的活动

Patera
A shallow bowl similar to a phiale
帕特拉碗
一种类似盘的浅碗

Phiale
A shallow bowl without a foot
浅口碗
无足浅碗

Pileus

A pointed hat

尖帽

Pithos

A large ceramic storage container

大口坛

一种大型陶容器

Pronaos

An anteroom or antechamber to the inner room of a temple (the naos or cella)

门廊

神庙大厅或接待室（客厅或内殿）

Proto-Corinthian

Pottery produced in Corinth during the Orientalizing period

科林斯式陶器

东方化时期科林斯陶器制品

Pyxis

A lidded box

有盖盒

Quadriga

Two-wheeled chariot pulled by four horses

四马二轮战车

Scarab

An amulet in the form of the famous Egyptian dung beetle, a symbol of resurrection

圣甲虫

护身符，埃及的再生符号圣甲虫

Satyr, Silenos

Male followers of Dionysus

萨梯神

酒神的男仆

Sima

The gutter at the edge of a roof, usually made of terracotta in Etruria and often decorated in relief and painted

斯马

通常在伊特鲁里亚屋顶边缘挑口的浮雕和彩绘的红陶装饰

Simpulum

A ladle

长柄勺

Situla

A vessel shaped like a bucket

斯图拉瓶

一种桶状瓶

Skyphos

A drinking vessel in the form of a cup with two small horizontal handles

斯加弗斯杯

双柄饮杯

Stela

An upright slab, usually stone and often decorated or inscribed. Plural: stelae

石碑

一种树立的石板，通常有装饰或铭刻

Symposium

The after-dinner drinking party that was the provenance of males in ancient Greece. The term is often erroneously used as a synonym for the banquet of the Etruscans.

社交酒会

古希腊的男性晚餐后酒会，这个词常被误为伊特鲁里亚人的宴会。

Thymiaterion

A metal stand that could be used for burning scented substances, such as incense

香炉

一种带有金属支架的焚香器具

Tufa

A soft and usually very porous type of stone

石灰华

多孔的软石材

Tumulus

An artificial hill or mountain that covered a tomb chamber or group of chambers, characteristic of the Orientalizing and Archaic periods in Etruria

墓冢

东方化和古风时期伊特鲁里亚覆盖墓葬或墓室的封土

Unguentarium

a small vase, sometimes made of glass, that was used in antiquity to hold essences and perfumes

香水瓶

一种装精油和香水的玻璃小瓶

后　记
Postscript

　　《曙光时代——意大利的伊特鲁里亚文明》特展是继《辉煌时代——罗马帝国文物》特展之后的有关意大利古代文明的系列展。

　　展览缘起于2011年意大利特拉维索的卡萨雷兹博物馆馆长马达罗来武汉为引进楚国文物去意大利展出做准备，正好看到本馆在筹备《辉煌时代——罗马帝国文物》特展。马达罗馆长随即询问本馆是否有兴趣引进伊特鲁里亚文明展。

　　伊特鲁里亚文明是罗马文明之前的文化，是罗马文化的重要来源之一。罗马文明的许多重要因素如宗教仪式、神庙布局、城市规划、风俗习惯，艺术甚至文字都对罗马文化产生了深远影响。由于罗马帝国的兴起，伊特鲁里亚文化最终融入罗马，在中国——除了少数学者对该文化有所耳闻之外——遂鲜有人知。不过，只要提到母狼哺乳罗慕洛兄弟的铜雕和他们建立罗马的故事，大家都耳熟能详，而这些正是伊特鲁里亚人的创作，罗马立国之初的几代国王都是伊特鲁里亚人。

　　从文明的发展和融合来看，伊特鲁里亚人对罗马文明的贡献十分类似楚人在秦统一前为丰富华夏文明所做的贡献：这两个文化存在的时间相当（伊特鲁里亚人时间稍长一点），伊特鲁里亚人和楚人的确切来源学术界一直存在争论，都在两国局部地区发展壮大，最终都被其他文化统和，也都是近代以来才被关注。对已初步了解罗马文化的中国观众来说，引进反映伊特鲁里亚文明的展览，对进一步了解罗马文化的发展和观照中华文化的形成都有意义。

　　特别要指出的是，马达罗馆长所在的特拉维索卡萨雷兹博物馆，已连续十年承办由中国文物交流中心组织的"中华文明系列展"，并在意大利引起强烈反响。此次展览是他首次组织意大利多家博物馆的伊特鲁里亚文物来华展出，难度极大，原因是时间紧张，伊特鲁里亚文物又分散在意大利十多家博物馆，

如何逆向操作意大利文物来华展出，他尚无经验。但在意大利文化遗产部、托斯卡纳文物遗产监管局、特拉维索卡萨马卡基金会的支持下，困难逐一被克服，他也实现了中意两国文物展览双向交流的夙愿。

在本展览的筹备过程中，国家文物局始终予以关心，湖北、浙江、广东、陕西省的文化厅、文物局都予以大力支持。武汉及各地海关对展品的出入境也予以特别关照。文物出版社、中国对外翻译出版公司、汉森国际珍品运输公司等机构，以及马达罗馆长的长期合作伙伴陆辛先生都为展览的顺利举办付出了艰苦努力，我们在此一并致谢。

编者

2013年8月于武昌

责任印制：陈　杰

责任编辑：王　伟

图书在版编目（ＣＩＰ）数据

　　曙光时代 ：意大利的伊特鲁里亚文明 / 湖北省博物
馆编. -- 北京 ：文物出版社，2013.8
　　ISBN 978-7-5010-3829-9

　　Ⅰ．①曙… Ⅱ．①湖… Ⅲ．①伊特剌斯坎人－民族文
化②伊特剌斯坎人－文化遗址－考古发现 Ⅳ.
①K546.8②K885.468

　　中国版本图书馆CIP数据核字(2013)第222563号

曙光时代——意大利的伊特鲁里亚文明

编　　者	湖北省博物馆
出版发行	文物出版社
社　　址	北京市东直门内北小街2号楼
网　　址	www.wenwu.com
邮　　箱	web@wenwu.com
制版印刷	北京图文天地制版印刷有限公司
经　　销	新华书店
开　　本	889×1194　1/16
印　　张	18.75
版　　次	2013年9月第1版
印　　次	2013年9月第1次印刷
书　　号	ISBN 978-7-5010-3829-9
定　　价	320.00元